Poetry in Pedagogy

The essays compiled in *Poetry in Pedagogy: Intersections Across and Between the Disciplines* offer praxes of poetry that cultivate a community around students, language, and writing, while presenting opportunities to engage with new texts, new textual forms, and new forms of text-mediated learning. The volume considers, combines, and complements multiform poetry within and beyond existing Teaching & Learning paradigms as it traverses Asia, The Atlantic, and Virtual Space. By virtue of its mélange of intersecting trajectories, across and between oceans, genres, disciplines, and sympathies, *Poetry in Pedagogy* informs interdisciplinary educators and practitioners of creative writing & poetry involved in examining the multiform through international, cross-disciplinary contexts.

Dean A. F. Gui is an Instructor at The English Language Centre of Hong Kong Polytechnic University, Hong Kong. Dean A. F. Gui is a poet, an English teacher, and a doctoral student. His thesis, under the supervision of Dr. Jason S. Polley and Dr. Tammy Ho (HKBU), investigates the transformative potential of poetry in virtual environments.

Jason S. Polley is an Associate Professor at the Department of English Language & Literature of Hong Kong Baptist University, Hong Kong. Jason S. Polley teaches Indian English fiction, comics, literary journalism, and experimental criticism. He is co-editor of the 2018 volume *Cultural Conflict in Hong Kong*. He also has two creative nonfiction books: *Refrain* and *Cemetery Miss You*.

Poetry in Pedagogy

Intersections Across and Between
the Disciplines

**Edited by Dean A. F. Gui
and Jason S. Polley**

LONDON AND NEW YORK

First published 2021
by Routledge
2 Park Square, Milton Park, Abingdon, Oxon OX14 4RN

and by Routledge
52 Vanderbilt Avenue, New York, NY 10017

Routledge is an imprint of the Taylor & Francis Group, an informa business

© 2021 selection and editorial matter, Dean A. F. Gui and Jason S. Polley; individual chapters, the contributors

The right of Dean A. F. Gui and Jason S. Polley to be identified as the authors of the editorial material, and of the authors for their individual chapters, has been asserted in accordance with sections 77 and 78 of the Copyright, Designs and Patents Act 1988.

Trademark notice: Product or corporate names may be trademarks or registered trademarks, and are used only for identification and explanation without intent to infringe.

British Library Cataloguing-in-Publication Data

A catalogue record for this book is available from the British Library

Library of Congress Cataloging-in-Publication Data
A catalog record has been requested for this book

ISBN: 978-0-367-54451-5 (hbk)
ISBN: 978-0-367-54454-6 (pbk)
ISBN: 978-1-003-08937-7 (ebk)

Typeset in Galliard
by SPi Global, India

Contents

Figures

Tables

Contributors

Pauline Felicia Baird is an assistant professor at the Division of English and Applied Linguistics of the University of Guam. Pauline Felicia Baird has taught at all levels in various countries, including Trinidad, the USA, Palau, Guam, and Japan. Her research interests include interdisciplinary and community-based research and Caribbean women's studies.

Stephen Chapman is a postdoctoral researcher at the Centre National de Recherche Scientifique of Aix Marseille University, France. Stephen Chapman is a bioinformatician with expertise in mathematical modelling of metabolism and physiology. He also has experience in distance-learning tuition and has coordinated several online modules relating to biotechnology.

Dean A. F. Gui is an instructor at The English Language Centre of Hong Kong Polytechnic University, Hong Kong. Dean A. F. Gui is a poet, an English teacher, and a doctoral student. His thesis, under the supervision of Dr. Jason S. Polley and Dr. Tammy Ho (HKBU), investigates the transformative potential of poetry in virtual environments.

Stephanie Laine Hamilton is Proprietor of Zephyr Heritage Consulting, Canada. Stephanie Laine Hamilton is also a freelance academic living and working in the Canadian Rocky Mountains near Banff, Alberta. A classicist by training, her work and research increasingly focus on themes in western Canadian history.

Mary Jacob is a lecturer at the Learning and Teaching Enhancement Unit of Aberystwyth University. Mary Jacob is a poet, and she is also currently undertaking a practice-based PhD in poetry writing.

Jason E. H. Lee is a lecturer at the Department of English Language and Literature of Hong Kong Baptist University, Hong Kong. Jason Eng Hun Lee is a poet-scholar of postcolonial and diasporic Asian writing and Shakespeare. Lee's poetry collection, *Beds in the East*, was published in 2019. He also contributes regularly to the UK and Hong Kong poetry scenes.

Shirley Geok-lin Lim is Professor Emerita at the University of California, Santa Barbara, United States. Shirley Geok-lin Lim is an Asian/Ethnic/Transnational American Studies scholar who has served as Chair of Women's

Studies (UCSB) and Chair Professor of English (HKU). She is also a recipient of the Feminist Press Lifetime Achievement Award.

Jason S. Polley is an associate professor at the Department of English Language and Literature of Hong Kong Baptist University, Hong Kong. Jason S. Polley teaches Indian English fiction, comics, literary journalism, and experimental criticism. He is co-editor of the 2018 volume *Cultural Conflict in Hong Kong*. His two creative nonfiction books are *Refrain* and *Cemetery Miss You*.

James Shea is an associate professor at the Department of Humanities and Creative Writing of Hong Kong Baptist University, Hong Kong. James Shea is the associate director of the International Writers' Workshop at Hong Kong Baptist University. He is also the author of two collections of poems and recently received a fellowship from the National Endowment for the Arts.

W. Brian Whalley is Emeritus Professor, Queen's University Belfast, United Kingdom. W. Brian Whalley retired to Sheffield near the Pennines where he first became interested in geomorphology. Poetry came later. He also currently serves on the committee of the Norman Nicholson Society.

Preface

Figure P.1 'Intersections'.

The image opening this book about 'intersections' is an eponymous poem in the shape of a frangipani flower. 'Intersections' is one editor's humble (and humbling) attempt at navigating an online text manipulation generator, which required manually trackpad-drawing the desired mosaic. The poetic montage textually and visually showcases the cross-disciplinary and interdisciplinary praxes of poetry, pedagogy, and scholarship featured in this border-defying essay collection called *Poetry in Pedagogy: Intersections Across and Between the Disciplines* (Figure P.1).

Please grant us the opportunity to illustrate cross- and interdisciplinary praxes by way of a fragmented three-pronged keyword-modelled reading of the representative poem 'Intersections.'

Poetry

'Intersections' is a collaborative, interactive-machine generated, concrete-found poem. The poem proves collaborative because its textual content—its words—are contributed by the 10 authors collected in the volume *Poetry in Pedagogy*. This interactive-machine generation involved the following steps:

i)   extract one-sentence objectives from each respective essay abstract
ii) run the single-sentences through a word cloud machine,[1] filtered to remove 'stop words'—viz. he, the, have, and other more common tokens
iii) download the generated 'Word List' (which is sorted by usage frequency)
iv) run the 'Word List' through a 'Cut Up Machine'[2]
v)   interface the results with the 'Texter'[3] (Drawing with Words) generator
vi) bear in mind that manually drawn designs using trackpads/mice must be accomplished without error; designs move synchronously and chronologically and may require additional attempts.

'Intersections,' in fact, is a concrete-found poem, owing to the visual frangipani shape of the piece, the frangipani being always already a visual manifestation of intersections. The initial text of 'Intersections' was selected from abstracts belonging to earlier versions of the essays collected here. The recursive exercise of pasting, drawing, and whittling down the 'Word List' was repeated seemingly ad infinitum until the 'Word List' proved to be at once concise and representative. The final frangipani, after all was said and done, had to take into account each of the nine core essays in *Poetry in Pedagogy*.

Pedagogy

The collaborative, concrete-found poem 'Intersections' exists as an example of what Monica Prendergast theorizes as 'inquiry poetry' in the essay 'Inquiry and Poetry: Haiku on Audience and Performance in Education' (2004). Prendergast demonstrates how her coined 'inquiry haiku' can articulate the shape and significance of a topic while providing for reflections on immediate life experiences. The experiences she highlights integrate those of audience members, performers, and educators. We invite the reader to peruse the 'Intersections' poem once more, before considering the following classroom activity and assessment prompts (addressed in no particular order) illustrating the intersecting of poetry (specifically, 'Intersections') in pedagogy across a number of Disciplines:

i)   Select 50 of the most intriguing or beguiling words from your favourite book and transform these words or lines or 'pearls' into a concrete poem that visually says something about your selection. (Creative Writing)
ii) Gather original research abstracts and compare them to the final list of words appearing in the poem. Apply your knowledge of social semiotics to evidence drawn from the abstracts, and answer the following: Why are these words the ultimate inventory of words published by the author of this poem? (Sociology)
iii) Your term paper is an investigation into one of the following industries and its implementation of the frangipani: Biotechnology, Fashion and Cosmetics, Food & Drug Administration, Travel and Tourism, or Artisanry. (Final Year Project)

iv) Are the flaws noted in the poem—the bolded emphasis on certain words, and the seemingly favoured right side of the visual—instances of human error, computer error, or both? (Media Studies)

This intersecting across and between the disciplines engages learners while cultivating student-teacher communities of inquiry, ones that willingly problematize more traditional discipline-specific methodologies.

Scholarship

'Intersections' functions as a compressed example of the kinds of cross-disciplinary research the authors collected in *Poetry in Pedagogy* innovatively undertake, re-envision, and work to publish. As editors involved in this border-defying process, ironic in itself given that breaking borders (defying) first involves recognizing (reifying) their existence, we and our contributors have continued to experience the back-and-forth of critical pedagogical inquiry. We are therefore already involved in the revisionary scholarly practices that this collection aims to compel. We ask you, the reader, to critically examine this book in terms of its potential practicality in your evolving scholarly field. We ask you to collegially (re)consider the merits of teaching poetry, whatever your field or expertise. We also wish to engage you in wider deliberations about poetry's (potential) place in Teaching and Learning (T&L).

Again evoking Prendergast, we can engage with 'Intersections' by way of an adapted version of 'ekphrastic inquiry.' In her article 'Found Poetry as Literature Review: Research Poems on Audience and Performance' (2006), the 'aesthetic and intellectual choice,' she explains in first person, 'is drawn from my belief that the transitory, ephemeral, and affective nature of performance requires a similar form of writing.' This professed 'similar form of writing' is manifest as 'research poetry,' which is similar in approach to the traditional literature review. After all, the process includes sifting through significant material in search of relevant snippets, chunks of evidence, and indicative data. There are exceptions, however:

i) literary evaluation transforms into poetic transcription, whereby
ii) the poem that is laid down functions as a presentation of the self, as it results from a personal interaction with literature, which consequently
iii) establishes, for the reader (audience), a sense of the combined voices of the researcher and the research participant (subject).

As tertiary instructors, our occupation necessarily includes reflecting on our research as well as on our associated pedagogy. Several of the authors included in this book are English literature instructors who regularly write and publish poetry. Others included herein turn toward digital spaces and website development at once as researchers and as practitioners. This collection also includes instructors and researchers from the not-so-far-flung (it turns out) fields of science, history, and culture. Some contributors travel to glacial regions, others to tropical islands and villages over oceans and seas; others immerse themselves in their local countryside over hills and dales; while still others commune with the people of their (new) places, which includes pub and pub-patron life. All of these diverse and pedagogically fruitful experiences, and the assorted ways of contextualizing and reporting on these T&L praxes, offer unique ways in which to formally and informally integrate poetry into the academy.

The essays compiled in *Poetry in Pedagogy*, nevertheless, consider, combine, and complement 'poetry topics' not only from within but also from beyond existing T&L paradigms. This book assiduously presents and reflects on scholarly undertakings from and about regions including Asia (Hong Kong and Singapore), the Atlantic (The United Kingdom, The British Isles, New York City), the Caribbean, the West Coast (California, Southwest Alberta), as well as Virtual Space. We have authors from different disciplines at the same university who habitually communicate. We have authors from similar disciplines at different universities who communicate sporadically. We have a collaborative chapter from STEM scholars working at the same institution. We have authors whose relationship with former students extends beyond the classroom and across the years. We have contributors who really live to embody the poetry, pedagogy, and scholarship that they impart via regular visits home to reconnect with their local roots. Some of our contributors have improved the range and depth of their fields through innovative concepts and frameworks and green living practices. We like to refer to the latitudes encompassed in *Poetry in Pedagogy* as 'multiformalisms.' The manifold cross-disciplinary intersections of poetry, pedagogy, and scholarship championed by this book will, we trust, inform interdisciplinary educators and practitioners of creative writing and poetry, as well as seasoned and more junior scholars, from various backgrounds, interested in working beyond conventional disciplinary interpellation. Our readers, we like to Derrideanly think, will engage with multiformalisms beyond dualities, binaries, and dichotomies.

This project is the culmination of a (mostly, though not only, email) correspondence beginning in 2013 between two colleagues. One has an academic background in poetry. He is an English language teacher. The other's academic training is in contemporary literatures in Englishes. He's an undergraduate instructor and postgraduate supervisor in an English language and literature department. We personally hail from polar points on the globe. We professionally hail from different universities in Hong Kong. Our professional correspondence eventually evolved into professional mentoring: doctoral student and chief supervisor. The extended process of reining in this volume began with our combined aspiration to bring together educators from around the world in a bid to discuss poetry in the university classroom. We wanted to seriously address poetry—and not just use it as a top-down-directed, (almost) all-purpose institutional buzzword.

This volume arrives at an ideal time in the overhauling of contemporary education—a time when we must be evermore reminded of the limitless possibilities that poetry can provide for educators and for students. This book carves out cutting-edge creative pedagogical practices. These include increased emphases on the digital universes that evermore encourage far-flung intersections and associations. Perhaps this collection can serve as a launch-pad for further treatments of the commonalities of, in lieu of the divides between, academic disciplines. Finally, we hope that *Poetry in Pedagogy* offers a positive correction to the persistent paradox of cross- or inter-disciplinary studies: the building of walls only to climb over them. Here, some of the (artificial) boundaries between disciplines are coaxed into disappearing. And it is poetry in pedagogy, as assortment of 'multiformalist intersections,' that allows for disciplinary rapprochement.

Dean A. F. Gui
Jason S. Polley

Notes

1 Via WordClouds.com
2 Via LanguageIsAVirus.com
3 The Figure presented was completely generated using the "Texter" (Drawing with Words) app extension (and used with permission).

References

Prendergast, Monica. (2004). "Inquiry and Poetry: Haiku on audience and performance in education." *Language and Literacy*, 6.1.

Prendergast, Monica. (2006). "Found poetry as literature review: Research poems on audience and performance." *Qualitative Inquiry*, 12.2: 369–388.

Acknowledgements

The editors wish to acknowledge the numerous 'intersections' between individuals from our professional, our personal, our familial, and our poetic lives. Colleagues, friends—from online social and networking communities, both in and from Hong Kong, and beyond—who have supported, advised, and stepped up to a host of productive challenges over the process of planning and compiling the manuscript *Poetry in Pedagogy: Intersections Across and Between the Disciplines*. In particular, we would like to thank:

The Authors. It goes without saying, but we are grateful to this small but mighty team of authors who, throughout these many, many (and counting) months, have been patient yet keen, and kindly dedicated to the goals of this—our collective book.

The Reviewers. Each granted us invaluable time, insight, and expertise, thus vouching for the quality of every essay collected in this volume. In no order, the reviewers are Brian Lander, Dani Spinosa, Luisa A. Igloria, Michael O'Sullivan, Mike Ingham, Marshall Moore, Jason Lee, Liliana Vasques, and Eddie Tay (an additional show of gratitude to Joseph Tabbi for his counsel during the reviewing process).

The Contributors. The following is a list of individuals and corporations gracious enough to consent to the (re)publication of their work in the respective authors' chapters for our volume (Note: Within the relevant pages, credits have been replaced with the words, 'Used with permission' or referenced by Figure; for all other instances, acknowledgments have been made, directly, in text):

Preface	Figure P.1:	Tim Holman, https://tholman.com/texter/
Chapter 1	Figure 1.1:	Kevin de Groote, www.worditout.com
Chapter 2	'Form's what affirms':	'The Thousand and Second Night' from COLLECTED POEMS by James Merrill, copyright © 2001 by the Literary Estate of James Merrill at Washington University. Used by permission of Alfred A. Knopf, an imprint of the Knopf Doubleday Publishing Group, a division of Penguin Random House LLC. All rights reserved.

	(Stein, 1990: 11), (Stein, 1990: 60), & (Stein, 1990: 187):	Gertrude Stein (1990). *The autobiography of Alice B. Toklas.* Vintage. (Original work published 1933)
	(White, 1995: 193):	Heather White
	(Wong, 2015):	Pamela W. Y. Wong
	(Cheung, 2015):	Yoyo S. Y. Cheung
	James Merrill (2001: 673):	James Merrill (2001). Self-portrait in Tyvek™ windbreaker. In J. D. McClatchy & S. Yenser (Eds.), *Collected poems* (pp. 669–673), Alfred A. Knopf.
	(Yeung, 2015):	Eros K. S. E. Yeung
	(in Hinton, 1993: 58):	T'ao Ch'ien, excerpt from 'Wine Stop,' translated by David Hinton, from *The Selected Poems of T'ao Ch'ien.* Copyright © 1993 by David Hinton. Reprinted with the permission of The Permissions Company, LLC on behalf of Copper Canyon Press, www.coppercanyonpress. org .
	(in Choy, 2000: 243):	Elsie Choy (2000). *Leaves of prayer: The life and poetry of He Shuangqing, a farmwife in eighteenth-century China.* The Chinese University Press.
	(Chen, 2014):	Sienna Shimeng Chen
	(Eichhorn, 2009: 143):	Kate Eichhorn
Chapter 4	Table 4.1. 'The Singapore Grand Prix' (annotated poem):	Lam Fu Yuan, Kevin
	Figure 4.1: The Singapore Grand Prix	'SIA Singapore Grand Prix Light Up the Night' by Shade Fotoworks Automotive Photography is licensed under CC BY 2.0. To view a copy of this license, visit https://creativecommons.org/licenses/by/2.0/
	Figure 4.2: 'Die Die Cannot Finish Last!' (Singapore MRT)	'Rush hour' by Puss.In.The.Hood is licensed under CC BY 2.0. To view a copy of this license, visit https://creativecommons.org/licenses/by/2.0/
	Figure 4.3: 'Die Die Cannot Finish Last!' (Singapore Shoppers)	'2004_0710_095741AA' by Marufish is licensed under CC BY-SA 2.0. To view a copy of this license, visit https://creativecommons.org/licenses/by-sa/2.0/

	Figure 4.4: Braceros	'File:Bracero Workers.jpg' by Oregon State University is licensed under CC BY-SA 2.0. To view a copy of this license, visit https://creativecommons.org/licenses/by-sa/2.0
	'BLACK ICE' (poem), & Figure 4.5:	Pablo Robles
Chapter 5	(Polley, 2019):	Tammy Lai-Ming Ho
Chapter 6	Student comments ('Good poetry...,' and 'Overall I was...'):	Francesca Zaccagnino
	Student comments ('To me, I liked...,' 'I would recommend the use...,' and 'I would be open to...'):	Anna Suchy
	Figure 6.1:	David Greenslade
Chapter 7	(Mort, 2016: 27):	H. Mort
	Mark Goodwin's 'Forced Moment at El Torcal, Andalucia':	Mark Goodwin, Steps, Longbarrow Press, 2014
	(in Griffiths et al., 2017):	The extract from 'Elan Valley' by Hywel Griffiths first appeared in Hywel M. Griffiths, Gavin Goodwin, Tyler Keevil, Eurig Salisbury, Stephen Tooth & Dewi Roberts (2017), Searching for an Anthropo(s)cene in the Uplands of Mid Wales, *GeoHumanities*, 3:2, 567–579, DOI: 10.1080/2373566X.2017.1329631
	(Skelton, 2015: 26):	Extract from Behind the Fell Wall by Richard Skelton is used by kind permission of Little Toller Books
Chapter 8	Figure 8.1:	Eddie Tay
	(Ho, 2014):	Tammy Lai-Ming Ho
	(Chan, 2020):	Tom K. E. Chan
Chapter 9	Student comment:	Nicole Leon Guerrero

Our Indexer. Thank you, Margaret N.Y. Lam, for your conscientious work.

Our Publisher. We also enthusiastically thank Katie Peace (Senior Books Commissioning Editor for Routledge in Asia) and her dedicated team for their gracious help throughout this entire process.

... and finally, Dean would like to especially thank Jason S. Polley and Jason E. H. Lee for their unflinching guidance and direction (even during Dean's more 'difficult' moments) in shaping and bringing to fruition the vision for this volume. He is forever grateful.

1 A poetics of poetry in/and pedagogy
The multiform of tertiary education in Asia and the Atlantic

Dean A. F. Gui

Poetry: an aversion to definition?

The apparent challenges for a consensus in defining 'poetry' (see Figure 1.1)[1] are perhaps compounded by (i) the ever-shifting, complex applications and forms of poetry, (ii) the distinctive industries that adopt poetry (Mazza & Hayton 2013), and (iii) the pedagogical de-institutionalization of poetry in language classrooms around the world today (Early, Kendrick, & Potts 2015). Poetry, in fact, can deconstruct more traditional understandings of academic disciplines—and of academic disciplining. Though imperative to continued academic development, poetry cannot simply be instrumentalized. Thus, poetry's reach—writ large, poetry transcends simple top-down administrative pragmatics.

Given the relevance of poetry to this volume, which is a collection of essays working to destabilize time-honored positivist divides between (i) the creative and the critical, (ii) the humanities and the sciences, and (iii) L1 (first language) and L2 (second language) pedagogy, we have come to prize one understanding of poetry above all others. Perhaps contentious, perhaps antithetical to the classical spirit of poetry, we adopt Charles Bernstein's (1992) demarcation of poetry, to wit, 'Poetry is aversion of conformity' (1). Bernstein's tactful (and tactical) choice of words and semantics leaves open a wide range of possible interpretations of, and praxes for, poetry. Bernstein also clearly intimates what poetry is not: mere convention. Bernstein supplements his charged definition with an array of characteristics and illustrations. In the span of eight pages, he ends up likening the positive anarchism of poetry to

> the pursuit of new forms ... ; [the disruption of] literary business ... ; formal dissent ... ; [making] sounds possible to be heard that are not otherwise articulated ... ; the wrong way ... ; a poetics [of] multiple conflicting perspectives and types of languages and styles in the same poetic work or ... [the] same collection of essays ... that expresses the state of the art as it moves beyond the twentieth century ... ; [a platform] for the construction of social and imaginative facts and configurations avoided or overlooked ... ; [an invention] of new tools and forms that ... meet

Figure 1.1 Various Delineations of Poetry.

the challenges of the ever-changing present … ; an idealized multicultur-alism [of] poets from different communities reading each other's works … aware of developments … of the poetic spectrum; the introduction of multicultural curricula in the high schools and colleges … ; [outwardly directed] interests … to the unknown and the peripheral; [and] a [com-position of] content [created] through shapes, feelings, attitudes, and structures. (1–8)

This formal blurring and blending is found in the works of established and emerging poets from Gertrude Stein, Robert Hass, and Shirley Geok-lin Lim (whose research on e-poetry is featured in this book), to Caroline Bergvall, Gajanan Mishra, and Mona Attamimi, not to mention in the continuing *Best American Experimental Writing* anthology (*BAX*) series (Abramson, Damiani, & Kim, 2018). From foundational forms such as 'found poetry,' as conceived by Walter Benjamin (1999) in the early twentieth century, which proved unique insofar as it involved collecting existing lines (or pearls) from material production (verse, prose, and, later, film) in order to create new meaning, and William H. Burroughs and Brion Gysin's (1978) version of hybrid poetry in their famous cut-ups, to more recent forms like what Joel E. Jacobson (2009) dubs 'the almost-stories' of 'elliptical' poetry, as well as work in erasure poetry (cf. Leung 2017). Don Share (2008) blogged over a decade ago that this 'contemporary' poetry movement was 'a new mainstream,' one acting as 'a binary opposition' in the form of a progressive 'third way.'

Now that I have arrived at a suitable and practicable definition of poetry (in light, again, of this book and the pedagogic challenges poetry adduces), I will explain the naming of this book and justify (by way of comparative analysis) ascribing an identity to the 'intersections' of poetry and pedagogy, as a means to enlighten the reader to the complexities of poetry, pedagogy, and scholarship featured in this volume. I will also, near the end of this introduction, address the apparition of an unexpected poetics manifesting itself during the processes of collecting, editing, and reassembling these essays.

Intersections across and between: A naming

In attempting to frame the complex intersectional practices demonstrated in the chapters gathered herein, the term *multiform* was adopted. My argument concerning the distinction between 'Multiformalisms' and the 'Multiform' might *prima facie* appear complicated. But this is the position I take: aversion of conformity (as defined by Bernstein) is not an apposite indicator for a poetry that intersects across and between. Neither is an open poetics/form (as will be shown in Olsen momentarily). And, given my own understanding of how Finch and Schultz (2008) positioned 'multiformalisms' as an inclusion of all poetic forms (or formalisms), albeit an inclusion necessarily approached individually (i.e. one at a time), I shifted towards a 'multiform' praxis.

Multiform, as a subject/topic, is used in research, but I would say research that is more esoteric or abstract (as I show in the illustrations that follow). What bolsters the 'multiform' is the approach I understand the authors to have implemented in their respective *Poetry in Pedagogy* essay contributions. While re-reading these essays, I came to the realization that many of our authors do more than engage with hybrid or multi-mediated poetry—they also engage with the intersections of pedagogy, and those of scholarship. Some of our authors literally travel across oceans, over glaciers, and into the ocean to conduct their research. To me, these essay-engagements exemplify taking on many forms all at once, not one at a time *qua* multiformalisms. The essays also can be said to demonstrate a fusion of two forms to create one new form (this being a truer or purer form of hybridity). Of course, we can (and do) exhibit multiformalisms alongside hybridity in our praxes as well.

Hybrid and other contenders (Naming the book)

I initially proposed the term 'hybrid' as the germane visage to outlining an academic book dedicated to poetry in/and pedagogy.[2] We (including my co-editor and everyone else who contributed) initially engaged the term as ardently and receptively as Amy Moorman Robbins (2014), who speaks of hybridity as 'the' movement in 'blended aesthetics and generic exotics, [of] newness and fashionability, [of] progress and youth' (3–4). She, furthermore, specifically apprehends the hybrid poetic as *a neither-nor mixing* of all schools and forms. Several complications became evident, still, while this volume was being collected:

a) Certain literary and creative writing communities and nations globally have adopted the term 'hybrid' to operate as a political device to divide and oppose, with some dismissing it as a simple A+B formulation

(Robbins 2014: 8); while others, still, claim ownership over the term, inevitably omitting the poetics of muses[3] who forged hybrid figures, vocabularies, and genres of the English, African, Indian, and Caribbean postcolonial condition (Ramazani 2001).

b) The term 'hybrid' remains a term of binaries and dichotomies; it speaks to a fusion or coming together of two distinctive forms or opposites in order to form a third. And, even in the postcolonial hybridity theorized by Homi K. Bhabha, the hybrid form is burdened by new culture; it is formed from conflicting relationships between colonizer and colonized ('Other') (Bhabha 1995).

c) The 'new' movement mutes the history it shares in less-than-new traditions, including heroic narrative, biblical verse translation, lyric, riddle, allegory, gnomic verse, and book inscription (Maring 2017).

While many of the authors amalgamated here do engage with digital pedagogies and/or digital poetry, others do not, or they do so less acutely. James Shea engages his students with more traditional forms of Oulipo writing and sharing. Stephanie Laine Hamilton prefers the cento and cut-up modeled intertexuality of interpretive talk, archival research, student-oriented heritage tours, primary source research in pub crawl culture, and interaction and immersion with the communities and landscapes of the Canadian west. And Jason S. Polley (my co-editor) engrosses his students with performance poetry and collaborative poetry writing options vis-à-vis opening the fields of conventional letter writing.

By no means do I personally eschew the term 'hybrid': I used the term early in my research career (but perhaps too loosely) in a 2013 essay (see Gui 2013) on multiracial identity in the virtual world. Hybrid poetry places divergent forms and genres into conversation, positioning them within the current of contemporary poetry that now finds itself used in teaching and learning through, for instance, the multitude of lesson plans published online for primary and secondary schools (NCTE 2013; William Victor 2010). Nevertheless, the parameters of 'hybridity' do not quite converge on (or include) the complex intersections of pedagogy, learning, representations of the self, space, and poetry illustrated in the studies exhibited in this book.

Yet, this is not to say that the hybrid is entirely omitted from these works either—as this very apostrophe of 'hybridity' in the introduction to *Poetry in Pedagogy* evokes. Mary Jacob and Stephen Chapman, for example, work with the pure hybrid form of video poetry. Jason E. H. Lee, for his part, dually offers hybrid poetry. His primary and secondary students, by way of a Hong Kong-wide English poetry initiative run by English colleagues at Hong Kong Baptist University, were offered ekphrastic and dictionary poetry. And Pauline F. Baird, in her included essay, speaks of the hybrid and of hybridity while at the same time invoking poetic, pedagogic, and scholarly multiforms that threaten to burst the seams of the hybridity framework. Ultimately, the term 'Intersections'[4] formed the subtitle of *Poetry in Pedagogy*. A reconsideration of the breadth of disciplines, pedagogical approaches, global regions, and creative-critical media covered by the studies integrated here evidenced a collective crossing over and surpassing of the *duality* that the term 'hybridity' implies. My co-editor and I therefore wholeheartedly agreed to accommodate (and index) these expansions by way of replacing the term hybrid with the representative locution 'Intersections Across and Between' in our subtitle.

Multiform (Framing the intersections and a poetics)

In *Contemporary Poetry* (2011), Nerys Williams characterizes poetry for students through an extensive repository of ideas, movements, essays, and debates. This is performed as a means to bridge poetic form and philology through cultivating adaptive reading strategies while querying the plausibility of identifying the 'new' as 'contemporary.' Navigating through a series of possibilities and exemplars (not unlike our own deliberations as we assembled this volume), Williams ultimately reconciles himself to the term 'contemporary.' Still, Williams pauses in order to explicate Charles Olsen's 'composition by fields' in order to open poetics and its energies. He also speaks to Anne Finch and Susan M. Schultz's didactic, poetic formalism. Finch and Schultz's formalism results in a 'Postmodern Poetics,' so the subtitle of their book *Multiformalisms* (2008) intimates. Yet this openness to multifarious poetic (and theoretical) possibilities, as mentioned earlier, suggests an adherence to one (poetic) form at a time.

In a blog post reflecting on attention as experienced through virtual communities, David Palumbo-Liu (2010) notes (as a point of irony) Cathy Davidson's observation that 'our assumptions about how we connect have shifted, are varied, multiformal, each with its own rhythm, syntax, rhetoric' (para. 6). This 'shifting' is reproduced on a terrestrial level in W. Brian Whalley's chapter as the scientist postulates on poetry and the geomorphology of glacier ice. Conjuring, again, Bernstein's 'aversion of conformity' interlaced with Davidson's 'shifting,' Olsen's open poetics, and Finch and Schultz's didactic poetic formalism, I am able to discern a complication in the pragmatics of multiformalisms that finds reconciliation when adapted as 'multiform.' Consider: multiforms of poetry, multiforms of pedagogy, multiforms of scholarship. Consider many forms or appearances intersecting all at once—like the multiform of textual echoes,[5] the multiform of incarnations,[6] or even the multiform of clones.[7] The authors included in *Poetry in Pedagogy* do not settle on or favor any one form above or beyond any other. Rather, each displays an authoritative competence to endorse mutability across multiple forms. So I adopt the term *multiform*. It proves instrumental in framing our collected essays.

A poetics of poetry, pedagogy, and scholarship: ad hoc but feasible

I discovered an unexpectedly fortuitous template in the midst of composing this introduction. The template initially appeared as a series of words showing up consistently across the 11 chapters of this book. The following word series aligned to, and actually brought me back to, Aristotle's *Poetics*.[8] I thereby developed a very conceptual ideology for a multiform codex and/ of poetics:[9]

Legend: Words from the book title

Words from the original concordance list
WORD FAMILY

The scholars whose work comprises the volume *Poetry in Pedagogy: Intersections Across and Between the Disciplines* (*PiPID*) unitedly <u>intersect</u> in a <u>pedagogy</u> of **POETRY** that cultivates a community around **students**, **language**, and **writing**. The resulting **POEMS** crafted by the students (facilitated by the affordances of the **University**, and its various Literary and Poetic Canons) become potential opportunities to engage with **new** texts, new **textual** forms, and new **forms** of text-mediated **learning**. The <u>intersection</u> of teacher, learner, and poetic 'other' (and their resulting relationship) <u>across and between</u>, not only the traditional and familiar <u>Disciplines</u>, but also <u>across</u>, <u>between</u>, and interweaving through diverse spaces, including individual and collective mind-frames, cultural reception and influence, and (non-exhaustively) intercontinental/transnational institutional positioning of poetry, reveal, ever-so-fortuitously, a contemporary, multiform **POETICS** that distinguishes teacher and learner in a division of three ideations: **World** (**Practice**, **Experience**), **Academic** (**Knowledge**, **Life**), and **Reader** (**Cultural**, **Literary**).

The conceptual chart of the codex, which includes an embedded *Poetics*, serves as a guideline detailing the organizational and relational structures of this book. I adapt the names for my various codex structures from Johanna Drucker (1997).[10]

Aristotle's *Poetics* provides a relevant framework to the multiform infrastructure of poetry in/and pedagogy, as well as respective related scholarship. My resulting ideations—World, Academic, Reader—from the concordance list, and their corresponding qualities, find representation in literary theory focusing on tragedy, and in contemporary applications of this theory. *Mimesis*, for example, entails the imitation or representation of Nature and human nature. *Anagnorisis* involves recognition, a change from ignorance

Table 1.1 A Multiform Codex of Poetry and Pedagogy

Concepts	Audience Membership	Multiform	Productions	Scientific/Technical Processes
Poetry	Teachers	*Intersect* in a *pedagogy of poetry*	Unitedly cultivates a community of students, language, and writing as its precepts.	The essence of poetry, then, it can be argued, has been reincarnated by the practitioners of poetry featured in this book, through an implied (conscious or unconscious) shared consensus, that a guiding principle in their role as creative writing/poetry teachers and scholars is the cultivating of students, language, and writing.
Poems	Students	Potential opportunities to engage with new text, new textual forms, and new forms of text-mediated learning.	Crafted poems	*Universitas Scholarum*[a]
Poetics	Teacher, learner, and poetic 'other'	The intersecting *across and between*, not only the traditional and familiar *Disciplines*, but also across, between, and interweaving through the diverse spaces; the individual and collective mind-frames; cultural reception and influence; and (non-exhaustively) intercontinental/transnational institutional positioning of poetry	Distinguishes teacher and learner in a division of three ideations: • World (Practice, Experience) • Academic (Knowledge, Life) • Reader (Cultural, Literary)	Aristotle's *Poetics*: Mimesis Anagnorisis Catharsis Contemporary • explorers • storytellers • collaborators

a From an extrapolation of ways in which the 'modern university' has alienated its community members, Gadamer draws one redeeming characteristic that lessens the unease between student and teacher, through which mediation can transpire to freely—without judgement, prohibition, or Society's constraints and vicarious impositions—engage in a theoretical practice of life (or research): to function as a universitas scholarum (see Misgeld & Nicholson 1992). The aforementioned discord, however, resonates in the recent push in universities locally (in Asia) and internationally (in the West) to instrumentalize 'Creativity.' Academics are part and party to administrative drives to formally intertwine the creative and the vocational via new research and pedagogical practices, many of which merely pay lip service to 'Creativity,' thus reducing the term, and by extension poetry itself, to a professional buzzword.

to knowledge, a discovery of the self or the true nature of others. Finally, *Catharsis* is comprised of a purification or change in emotion, leading to renewal for learning, inference, and clarity in action. These theoretical elements resonate with my previously noted ideational qualities in that Practice and Experience ideally manifest as mimetic, Knowledge and Life ideally result in anagnorises, and Culture and Literature ideally engender catharsis. Using literal and figurative extensions, we can further uncover contemporary applications associated with theoretical elements that likewise resonate with my ideational divisions:

> Exploration (Tsekeris 2015) in *Mimesis* and World ('presentation of the self'): 'the self involves human beings' fruitful ability to understand and amend their mode of being, as well as the way in which they may differ from other people and the rest of the world' (1) by 'explor[ing] its ... possibilities' (11).
>
> Storytelling (Picucci 2014) in *Anagnorisis* and Academic ('realization'): In relation to gaming narratology and its foundations in Academia, '[t]he Pre-established type of narrative can be considered as the principal and most common storytelling architecture ... the constituents of a story go ... further back to Aristotle's definitions of *Hamartia* (fault), *Anagnorisis* (realization) and *Peripeteia* (reversal).'

Collaboration (Howell, Kelleher, Teehan, & Keating 2014) in *Catharsis* and Reader ('renewal for learning, inference'):

> the collaborative work of an interdisciplinary humanities and computer science team whereby traditional literary methodologies can be re-activated and regenerated rather than abandoned ... this may be particularly useful in teaching undergraduate students for whom developing a nuanced understanding of narrative technique is often a difficulty encountered in their initial years in literary studies ... to support 'generalist' readings, [and] to analyse how a novel may generate differing or shared 'specialist' responses.

Finally I also introduce Hans-Georg Gadamer's experience of interpretation as a means to organize my three 'Ideations' into logical, communicative flow in the process of learning. Gadamer (qtd in Misgeld & Nicholson 1992) implements a form of hermeneutics borrowed from the Rhetoricians. He evokes the three phases for the experience of interpretation (of the Word), emphasizing the importance of applying knowledge to action. As a parallel to the teaching and learning (or interpretation) of poetry, we can observe this approach as the underlying hermeneutical machine driving the poetics (codex) of the multiform as experienced by teacher and student (in their interpretations of multiform poetry). Multiform poetry in/and pedagogy has received negligible scholarly attention, confined mainly to concerns about contemporary poetry in terms of teaching and learning (Love 2012). This inattention—or lack or, even, aporia—proves especially apparent in universities across Asia.

This volume, then, provides a timely and foundational intervention to present-day initiatives in Asia (and around the world). We work seriously to address and assess creativity across the university—not just in arts and/ or humanities faculties. Moving from institutional buzzword to deliverable outcome, 'creativity' now finds itself modeled at the interface of interdisciplinary studies. Pace Gadamer, understanding or interpretation (of the text/language) is accomplished not only by understanding (*intelligentia*) and exegesis or exposition (*explicatio*), but also through responsibly and responsively living the values found in the text by example (*applicatio*). See Table 1.2, which parses our poetry in pedagogy poetics.

The studies compiled in in this book consider, combine, and supplement topics on multiform poetry within (and beyond) the Teaching and Learning (T&L) paradigm. This work was assiduously undertaken by scholars researching from and/or about Asia (Hong Kong and Singapore), the Atlantic (the United Kingdom, the British Isles, California and New York in the USA, and the Caribbean), and Virtual Space (no scholars, from this volume, identified this as a place of residence). The editors of *Poetry in Pedagogy* hope that this mélange of intersecting trajectories—oceans, genres, disciplines, sympathies—informs a readership of (i) interdisciplinary educators and practitioners of creative writing and poetry, who are (ii) either junior or wizened scholars interested in examining the multiform through international, cross-disciplinary contexts. We hope to have enabled our readers to:

- evaluate critically the usefulness of incorporating multiform poetry into the humanities classroom;
- create, perhaps with both proximal and far-flung colleagues, practical multiform usages for poetry in the classroom; and
- assess how poetry can be used and evaluated, generally, in teaching and learning.

I now turn to a brief digest of the essays gathered in *Poetry in Pedagogy: Intersections Across and Between the Disciplines.* But let me first note that several essays in this volume manifest the ideations of others—so this need not be the book's categorical lineup. This final order(ing), however, proved most practical in getting our oft-complex ideas across as clearly as possible.

Part I—*Anagnorisis*: storytelling as pedagogy

In this first set of chapters, we observe educators who engage with their students as storytellers in (more traditional) face-to-face settings. We see,

Table 1.2 A Multiform Poetics of Poetry in Pedagogy

Concepts	Audience Membership	Multi-formalisms	Productions	Scientific/Technical Processes	
Poetics	• teacher • learner • poetic 'other'	The intersecting *across and between*: • the traditional and familiar *Disciplines across, between, and interweaving through*: • the individual and collective mind-frames; • cultural reception and influence; and • (non-exhaustively) intercontinental/ transnational institutional positioning of poetry (space)	Distinguishes teacher and learner in a division of three ideations: • Academic/'intelligentia' (Knowledge, Life) • Reader/'explicatio' (Cultural, Literary) • World/'applicatio' (Practice, Experience)	(Scientific) Aristotle's *Poetics* (Learner): • Anagnorisis (Change: Ignorance, Knowledge) • Catharsis (Spectator: Mind, Body) • Mimesis (Creator of Texts/ Art: Reflect, Represent)	(Contemporary) Various movements/ practices respective to A's *Poetics* (Teacher): • Storytellers (https://en.wikipedia. org/wiki/Storytelling) • Collaborators (http:// digitalhumanities.org/dhq/ vol/14/1/000443/000443.html) • Explorers (Tsekeris 2015)

through Oulipo (Shea), cento and cut-up (Hamilton), and e-poetry (Lim), how learning results in 'realizations' attributed to *Anagnorisis*.

James Shea's 'Oulipo in Hong Kong: Welcoming unconventional forms in multilingual poetry workshops' (Chapter 2) posits the benefits of Oulipo poetry both as a novel instructional writing tool and as a hybrid pedagogy combining conventional and unconventional instruction, as informed by Shklovsky's (1965) work on defamiliarization. As a storyteller, Shea's teaching repertoire of unconventional poetic forms includes 'I Remember' poems in the manner of Joe Brainard as well as homophonic translations inspired by Celia and Louis Zukofsky—all with an emphasis on Oulipo (premised on the notion that one's writing cannot escape form, especially invisible, received rules) as a constraint-based writing method, but renewed (by way of Felski 2015) through a devising of one's own system and an amplifying of forms and rules in one's writing. Because Hong Kong is 'a city defined by constraints,' ones complemented by the territory's British colonial legacy, nontraditional forms of poetry (and pedagogy) can destabilize the British (colonial) canon. Consequently, ESL students embrace (through realization) enriched personal relationships to (even foreign) texts. This forgoes concerns about adhering to a/any Chinese poetic tradition. This tactic too enables L2 students to express themselves authentically in a second (or a foreign) language. As Hanauer proposes, this overall method, which creates spaces for experimentation, fosters a 'new way of seeing' (2014: 12) and, perhaps, being.

Stephanie Laine Hamilton likewise privileges storytelling. But she does this through Ancient formative examples. Her 'Trans-contemporary word culture: Late antique cento, twentieth century cut-up, and craft culture in the Canadian Rockies' (Chapter 3) integrates a comparative, post-structural analysis of twentieth-century cut-ups (Burroughs & Gysin 1978) and late Antique cento (McGill 2005). As a historian, Hamilton inquires into the interstitial natures of cento and cut-up, which are separated by over 15 centuries, to reveal how each subversive, hybrid poetic genre challenges the dominant literary culture of its time. The author additionally considers contemporary heritage industry practices in North America, and how the influence of contemporary applications of similar poetic methods can result in providing accessible heritage experiences, specifically, across the Canadian Rocky Mountains. Hamilton elucidates the extreme intertextuality of her historical pastiche. She characterizes cut-ups as physical source materials manipulated by a knife-blade, while cento(ne)s were constructed spontaneously, through memory. Both of these poetic formations influence broader twentieth-century literary composition and culture. Hamilton charts parallel connections to the composition and interplay of popular and hybrid histories. She gives talks and tours, does archival research, and spends time in built heritage spaces, including cemeteries, breweries, hotels, and residences. Her resulting heritage stories ultimately evolve into being audience-specific; she stitches together tailor-made, discrepant data depending on the interests and feedback from her in situ audience members. Hamilton's 'audience' is comprised of the 'thousands of students and heritage tourists' she addresses annually. The avowed 'realizations' of these students/tourists are made possible, in part, via the oral/written pendulum of stories Hamilton collects from tradesmen, scientists, exhibit designers, brewers/distillers, GIS and information specialists, trails specialists, and archaeologists that make up her primary sources.

Part I closes with 'Expanding genre and identities in digital poems: Generating ethos and pathos through code-switching and shifting multimedia platforms' (Chapter 4), wherein Shirley Geok-lin Lim queries changes in poetry as a genre as a result of the language text going through digitization. Lim notes the extent to which the electronic poetry of first-generation non-native English-speaking undergrads from Singapore and California revitalizes the pedagogical concerns of a growing subfield that recently emerged from an Aristotelian ethos and pathos that continues to mark poetry itself. Lim posits that technologies made available within the past two centuries (such as photography, video, and social media platforms) mediate the poet's reconstruction of poetic personae alongside social issues pertaining to ethos and pathos (e.g. the influence of Language Poetry on the development of the Tanka). Lim addresses a consequent proliferation of e-poetry. Her storytelling, as a creative writing teacher, is the pollination of reinterpreted print poems through student-directed (or bottom-up) linguistic strategies, such as code-switching, multilingual stylistics, and dialogic deployment of multiple vernacular registers (street and in-group slang). These techniques reshape student 'videos of digitised poems.' This reinforcement of Braj Kachru's (1976) World Englishes schema is reflected in, for example, e-poetry meditating on the meaning of books, on knowledge and truth, and on social inequality and injustice. Ethos and pathos are illustrated through a Singaporean student's traditional composition of a villanelle ('The Singapore Grand Prix'). Lim leaves us with additional (national and hegemonic) concerns to deliberate, all the while providing committed ruminations on the potential transformative effects of digitized poetry on the genre of poetry itself.

Part II—*Catharsis*: collaboration as pedagogy

In this second set of chapters, we observe educators who engage with their students as collaborators, through cross-genre, cross-agent, and cross-disciplinary commitments. Via collaborative poetry (Polley), video poetry (Jacob & Chapman), and elliptical poetry (Whalley), we observe how learning can educe 'renewal,' attributed to *Catharsis*.

Moving, initially at least, from dramatic and workshop spaces to the advanced criticism classroom, Jason S. Polley's 'Smuggling creativity into the classroom' (Chapter 5) combines Derrida's *différance* (1968) and Anne Frank's *Diary* (1990) to problematize the boundary between creativity and criticism. Polley deconstructs this imaginary binary in 'letter to a friend' seminar-room writing activities. In the case of the university classroom, Polley attempts to 'undo the artificial boundaries' between institutional directives and practical outcomes, in what Indigo Perry refers to as 'letting go of boundaries in our course design, teaching, and assessment' (Perry, qtd in Donnelly & Harper 2013: xxiv). As a collaborator, Polley educes Derridean 'Structure, Sign, and Play' in the form of a 'Letter to a friend' prompt that underpins classroom-specific activities, including: (i) an exit or entrance paper; (ii) a 10-minute entrance or exit in-class assignment; and (iii) a university classroom or college-level workshop on collaborative found-poems, as methods of reframing 'literary and critical writing as complementary practices' (Perry qtd in Donnelly & Harper 2013: Ibid). Polley also positions these creative-critical exercises as correctives to romanticized misconceptions about isolation, seclusion, and genius in authorship. Renewal through learning is witnessed in a workshop taken by Filipina foreign-domestic workers in Hong Kong, where participants first engage in intimate letter-writing, then highlight their favorite 'pearls' and disguise them by means of poetic translation, and finally collect these encoded or portmanteau pearls in group found poems. Workshop attendees, having experienced individual catharsis, poetic wordplay, and group collaboration, come to appreciate the (global) payoffs of proofreading as they redirected their attentions from self to audience, (perhaps) unknowingly embodying Hong Kong's trilingual and biliterate composition through interacting with different languages and by way of code-switching.

In 'Using video poetry to teach biotechnology' (Chapter 6) Mary Jacob and Stephen Chapman de- and re-territorialize boundaries between scientific and creative language in a distance-learning STEM module, thereby instantiating digital poetry as mediator for science, technology, engineering, and mathematics students in the UK. These explorations lead to what Deleuze and Guattari (1987) might call a rhizomatous creation, a scientific term the critical theorists borrow to connote the root-like possibility of unprecedented connections, directions, and dimensions without a traditional center. Jacob and Chapman's case study examines the affordances of incorporating video poems with STEM subjects, illustrated through distance-learning biotechnology modules, where students may initially lack a background in poetry. Collaboration is suggested through the first intervention, whereby poets are first invited to visit a biorefining farm, and then create video poems on biorefining technologies for students to review and respond to—this as means to leverage transmission-based teaching styles through the introduction of transactional and transformative teaching elements. Students proffer a sense of renewal in reports on aspects of video poetry most enjoyed from the first intervention. In the second intervention, students are invited to create their own video poems via a form of 'digital storytelling' based on two prompts: (i) 'tell the story of how we can improve the recycling rate of plastic packaging,' and, (ii) 'choose one type of bioplastic, be it biobased or biodegradable, and … explain the challenges facing the end of life options for your selected bioplastic type.' Student reactions to the second intervention evinced initial ambivalence, permeated by the appreciation that 'educating the public and informing policy makers' is invaluable to biotechnology. While student videos tended to exhibit 'storytelling' over 'poetry,' the application of principles disclosed unforeseen environmental contexts, such as one student's application of biotechnology principles to his professional fieldwork in Hong Kong.

W. Brian Whalley's 'An exploration of elliptic and hybrid poetry from a geomorphological viewpoint' (Chapter 7) concludes Part II by invoking the poetic landscapes of the British Isles to hybridize science with creativity and visualization. Whalley associates Schumm's (1956) seminal 'Badlands at Perth Amboy' with Hughes and Godwin's (1979) 'Remains of Elmet' to encourage student explication, rather than description, of particular landscapes as artworks. The collaborative element in Whalley's chapter emerges almost immediately, commencing with a definition. Geomorphology, so he explains, 'is the scientific study of landscapes, landforms, and their formative geological processes.' He proceeds by combining the 'scientific' with the 'literary,' as he considers how the 'ways of transmitting poetic information (spoken, written, visual),' verily integrate 'an area of developing interest in the arts via 'ecocriticism' (Clark 2015), contemporary 'nature poetry' (Gifford 1995), and 'eco-poetry' (Solnick 2016). He admits, however, that 'Geomorphologists are only just starting to grapple with this [idea].' Whalley's particular interest, though, seems to lean towards glacial ice from the Anthropocene period (an informal period of geological time dating from the commencement of significant human impact on Earth's geology and ecosystems). He notes the effects of glacial ice on landform evolution—floods, landslides, and coastal recession—as he seeks to identify scientific approaches to the Anthropocene through elliptical poetry (Hoagland 2006). Whalley makes use of three illustrations of 'anthropocene poetry.' He highlights landscape impressions and environmental change in Norman Nicholson's 'The Elm Decline' (Nicholson 1994), Simon Armitage's 'Stanza Stones' (Armitage et al. 2013), and his own poem (completed in 1990, and published for the first time here) 'BANDWIDTH.' The catharsis of his learners is inculcated through Whalley's personal appreciation of landscape science as a field of inquiry wherein the actual field/location of inquiry visibly alters over time. Readers, Whalley notes, may respond in particular ways to 'Location' (a geomorphological feature) in poetry, particularly after experiencing a location-altering event, like a flood.

Part III—*Mimesis*: exploration as pedagogy

In this third (and final) set of chapters, educators are explorers journeying with their learners through natural, cultural, and virtual spaces. As we see through ekphrastic poetry (Lee), ethno-poetry (Baird), and interstitial poetry (Gui), careful, directed teaching and learning can result in refined 'self-(re)presentation,' which we attribute to *Mimesis*.

We begin this final trilogy within a trilogy with Jason E. H. Lee's engagement of ekphrastic poetry and experimental performances in 'Found poetry and communal memory-making in the L2 classroom' (Chapter 8) and what Monica Prendergast et al. (2009) dub performative ethnography. Lee claims that found poetry, in general, functions not only as a useful prompt within the L2 creative-writing classroom, but also as a potential archival and memory-making tool that can bridge the creative disciplines with the rest of the humanities as well as the social sciences. Citing Henry Wei Leung's autoethnographic and sociohistorical hybrid poetry construction *Goddess of Democracy: An Occupy Lyric* (2017),[11] as a protest piece marking the 2014 Umbrella Movement in Hong Kong, he frames selected student activities around his perception of Hong Kong as an environment that has (i) cultivated varied and growing Anglophone poetic voices where (ii) English is spoken by the majority of its population as a second or third language yet persists as the designated medium of instruction in higher education; and (iii) whose communities fall prey to collective amnesia and are bereft of meaningful self-identification. Consequently, students are liberated from the pressures of conforming to the traditional diction of the Western poetic canon and encouraged to experiment with materials representative of their respective disciplinary backgrounds and varying language competencies.

Lee's explorative pedagogy excavates through exercises based on found poetry that implement image-text relations (ekphrastic poetry) as well as literary-language structures (dictionary poetry). Both can be adapted for cross-disciplinary purposes in the university classroom. These are illustrated through an experiential learning activity: selected finalists and awardees (upper primary to all secondary year levels) of the 2015–2016 Hong Kong Budding Poets Scheme were immersed in 'the rustic island' of Cheung Chau, and (with a photo-poem pamphlet produced from Eddie Tay's recent publication in hand) invited to wander along the island to find inspiration for composing personal found poems. The students' mimetic experience of the ekphrastic poetry activity materializes through the activity's learning outcomes: (i) rethinking your personal relationship with the immediate physical environment; (ii) raising awareness of social issues; and (iii) demonstrating agency in challenging (or reproducing) the views of the local bucolic community.

Moving from the islands of Hong Kong to those of the Caribbean, Pauline Felicia Baird explores the narratives of Buxton village women (residing in Guyana, the Bahamas, and New York) through ethno-poetry and cultural rhetorics methodologies, thereby adding another layer to hybridity in the classroom. In her chapter '(Re)orienting borders with hybrid poetry and tertiary pedagogy' (Chapter 9), which integrates de Certeau (1988), Mignolo (2011), and Riley-Mukavetz (2014), Baird considers how issues of voice, power, discourse, and identity in writing can exercise story as a de-colonial option. Baird's students enter one another's narratives, thus disrupting (and allegorically exposing) oft-overlooked, interpellative 'dominant discourses.' Engaging with the reader through a first-person, storytelling approach, the language in Baird's study is poetic and rhythmic. In defining hybridity, Baird denotes experimentation, by a composer, complete with mixing, blending, or creolizing (Hannerz 1997). Hybrid poetry results in a mix of old and new, of traditional and experimental approaches, to established poetic form (King et al. 2015).

Baird reminds us how she transcribed women's oral narratives to written prose (Baird 2016) before rearranging/repurposing them in verse. Baird's lived negotiations explore the self-representational. She notes spatial and pedagogical crossings. As an African-Guyanese US doctoral graduate, she journeys through oceanic spaces of the Atlantic (as a teacher) and the Caribbean Sea, towards her home island of Buxton Village in Guyana. The hybrid poetry she creates includes a consciousness of Caribbean ancestral knowledge: the telling of stories in other places, and from the places where we think and dwell. Baird's contributions to the classroom and the wider community celebrate women and their oral stories. During a curious moment of a possible 'absence of the self' (or the 'misplacement of the self'), Baird cannot find Buxton Village—her birthplace—on Google Maps. The rhetorical questioning that follows is evocative: if the search engines do not have it, does a place exist to others? How can I make women visible on landmasses that are themselves not always visible? Baird, tellingly, thus creates poetry from this discomfiting experience—and 'the self' is again reconstituted. When teachers involve students in the teaching process (such as imparting an understanding of hybrid poetry-as-methodology in cross-cultural pedagogy), so Baird exemplifies, hybrid poetry can transform into a rhetorical tool for cross- and inter-cultural conversation.

From the poetry of earth and oceans, we are teleported to a poetry of digital and in-between spaces, in this final chapter of our tri-trilogy. Dean A. F. Gui's conceptual study, 'Edifying and frangible creative artforms: A working definition for interstitial poetry and its conceptual framework for virtual environments' (Chapter 10), puts forth a working definition for *interstitial poetry* (IP) and a conceptual framework for aligning IP with virtual environments (VEs) as a means to study affordance and influence between IP, VEs, and respective interactive agents (digital and human). Invoking *interstitial literature*, as coined by H. I. Fenkl (2003), and *digital poetry*, suggested by C. T. Funkhouser (2012) to underpin a working definition of *interstitial poetry*, comparisons are made between the invoked highlighting parallels and deviations in attributes that inevitably manifest as five attributes for interstitial poetry. The resulting definition is a combination of shared and similar attributes from interstitial literature and digital poetry, which integrates distinctive features surmised from attributable deviations in each and is outlined as multimedia artform and art genre. In mapping IP with the *archive* metaphor, Gui suggests that poetry in VEs is more than 'just' esoteric instantiations of text and performance by users of the VE or any convenient gaming content added by developers. Instead, poetry in VEs additionally functions to store (as information) and disseminate (as knowledge) the experiences of individuals and distinct diasporas.

Another discovery, however, reveals the doubly unstable state of interstitial poetry when situated within virtual environments, marking two of IPs distinctive attributes. First, a tendency to be situated within spaces that are prone to internal and external disruptions, subjecting it to dependence on those spaces (to ensure preservation and survival). This dependence thereby has the consequence of marking its susceptibility to deletion, but not necessarily originating in a susceptible state (frangible). Upon adapting Kosari and Amoori's (2018) expressions of 'virtual space' to create a conceptual framework for interstitial poetry in VEs, in addition to incorporating Savin-Baden and Falconer (2016) as well as Klastrup and Tosca (2004) to help define the middle and center frames (or rings), Gui fashions a framework for the transformative potential of interstitial poetry through an illustration from the *World of Warcraft*® Quest: 'Alicia's Poem.' Gui further distinguishes interstitial poetry from transmediated, hybrid, and ekphrastic poetries. Learners, in this case, include researchers and academics whose 'self-presentation' occurs upon integrating the definition or conceptual framework into a Scholarship of Teaching and Learning. Learners also include the reader, the writer, and the student of poetry, all of whom re-examine other creative texts and other forms of poetry. An interweaving of narratives and imagery takes the reader on an exploratory journey of pedagogy and poetry that intends on providing a vocabulary to associate with IP, contributing to scholarship underway in creative writing and new media, and marking the unstable, paradoxical, and disruptive relationship between the interstice and poetry as IP's most potent and distinguishing characteristic.

The multiform world beyond poetics: *Universitas Scholarum* no more

In drawing a close to this introduction, and in order to mediate the continuing journey of our book, I wish to draw the reader's attention to the concluding chapter of *Poetry in Pedagogy* as I make some final, hopefully illuminating, observations. The last chapter of the volume, 'Intersectional poetry and techno cultural mobility: Reconstructing creativity, space, and pedagogy as global practice' (Chapter 11) is presented by Jason E. H. Lee in his reprisal not as the teacher of communal memory-making found poetry in the L2 classroom, but instead as a storyteller evoking an evening that ended in technological, mediated, and sensory onslaught. 'Sitting in my tiny Mongkok hotel room within earshot of yet another gathering protest against the local government' is not the opening to this chapter, but it does serve as an apropos visual for the state of Hong Kong—nay, the world—today: confinement to spaces (alone or not alone, ours or not ours), indoor media overload, outdoor human overload, all with, essentially, no real place to go to (or nowhere we want to go to).

Shaken from his hotel 'hallucinations,' Lee effectively connects 'the controversies and opportunities' (that the reader will note) in the chapters that follow to the irony and contradictions transpiring on a global level resulting, and compounded by, the COVID-19 global pestilence. Here we collectively recognize: the greater demands on internet bandwidth; the repurposing and resurfacing of online meeting spaces (like Google Meet), which compels an even greater demand for collaborative digital spaces; and the tendency for education institutes to duplicate or hurriedly launch watered-down and ineffectual versions of MOOCs (Massive Open Online Courses). In lamenting e-pedagogy lagging behind its technology, Lee also attempts to impress upon the reader poetry's own longevity and sway across and beyond the humanities and academia, not to mention industries like the news perceiving poets as creative beings who also perhaps naturally project a sense of hope and bold continuation. There is a certain melancholy, evocative of our cataclysmic times, meandering throughout Lee's concluding statements. However, it is this culminating introspection—'Perhaps ... we will realize just how far we have lost ourselves in this intersection between the material and digital world'—that proves simultaneously disheartening and humbling. Yet what I am made to be aware of here is that, while we celebrate and engage in the various multiforms and multimedia of our pedagogy, scholarship, and poetry in our classrooms, we must remember to stay vigilant and remain attentive to the world outside of our classrooms. We are all, as Lee reminds us, 'connected to these frenetic virtual moments.'

I know that my co-editor Jason S. Polley joins me in the assertion that this volume arrives at an ideal time in the overhauling of contemporary education—a time when we must be evermore reminded of the limitless possibilities poetry/creativity can provide. *Poetry in Pedagogy* sits on the cutting edge of new creative pedagogical practices, which include increased emphases on the digital universes increasingly encouraging far-flung intersections and collaborations. Herein, (artificial) boundaries between disciplines are made to disappear. And it is poetry that can allow for this rapprochement. As you navigate your way through the following chapters, consider reflecting upon this question (an adapted statement from the concluding chapter), even if it is a mere murmur drifting from your lips: If the imminent future of higher education (in a tentatively post-pandemic world) depends ever increasingly on learning with—or through—the digital, what experiences or knowledge will you (as teacher, scholar, poet) possess which prepares and qualifies you to engage with the new, future, intersecting, trans-technologies and academia that await you within the ironic walls of collaborative isolation?

Notes

1 The Word Cloud (Enideo, 2020, and used with permission) used for Figure 1.1 combines the following definitions of poetry:

- 'Poetry is what a bookstore puts in the section of that name' (Pinsky 1998: 126).
- 'To be a poem is to be a verbal object intended by its writer or discoverer for membership in the poetic tradition or, in other words, in the category "poetry"' (Ribeiro 2007: 190).

- '[P]oetry is more akin to philosophy and ... deals with general truths ... the kinds of things which a certain type of person would probably or inevitably do or say' (Aristotle, qtd in Yanal 1982: 499).
- '[T]hat feigning notable images of virtues, vices, or what else' (Phillip Sidney, qtd in Hyman 1970: 53).
- '[T]he acts of recognition (the paying of a certain kind of attention) through 'poetry-seeing eyes,' resulting in the emergence of poetic qualities [that we know] poems to possess' (Fish 1980: 326).
- '[T]he end of poetry is to please, and the name, we think, is strictly applicable to every metrical composition from which we derive pleasure without any laborious exercise of the understanding' (Lord Jeffrey, qtd in Biddle 1873: 61).
- '[T]he poem must be a work of art, that the poet is full of knowledge and understanding, and that he has the native endowment of inspiration; then poetry will be a thing to charm or to instruct or preferably both' (Horace, qtd in Frank 1935: 170).
- 'A poem is a linguistic type of which its creator intends that certain perceptible properties of its tokens be particularly emphasized in appreciation' (Sartwell 1991: 250).
- 'But why regret an eternal sun, if we are committed to the discovery of the divine light,—far from those who die with the seasons [poetry transcends death]' (Rimbaud, qtd in Oxenhandler 2009: 1616)
- 'Poetry (derived from the Greek *poiesis*, 'making') is a form of literature that uses aesthetic and often rhythmic qualities of language—such as phonaesthetics, sound symbolism, and metre—to evoke meanings in addition to, or in place of, the prosaic ostensible meaning' (Wikipedia contributors 2020).
- 'Poetry should surprise by a fine excess, and not by Singularity—it should strike the Reader as a wording of his own highest thoughts, and appear almost a Remembrance ... if [it] comes not as naturally as the Leaves to a tree it had better not come at all' (Keats 2009).
- '[T]he supreme fiction ... the single source of truth ... vital human experience ... a rhythmically shifting tension between self and world' (Stevens qtd in Riddel 1961: 22).

In addition, Dictionary.com (2020) includes these six (increasingly circular) definitions of the noun poetry: (i) 'the art of rhythmical composition, written or spoken, for exciting pleasure by beautiful, imaginative, or elevated thoughts'; (ii) 'literary work in metrical form; verse'; (iii) 'prose with poetic qualities'; (iv) 'poetic qualities however manifested: the poetry of simple acts and things'; (v) 'poetic spirit or feeling: The pianist played the prelude with poetry'; and (vi) 'something suggestive of or likened to poetry: the pure poetry of a beautiful view on a clear day.'

2 I precluded two other transitory contenders—namely, 'Contemporary' and 'Digital'—since associations of the former with terms including 'modern' and 'culture' are verily broad in spectrum, thus connoting a limited shelf life. The latter term, for its part, continues to exist in association with a form of culture and a medium that is specifically electronic (or technological) in nature.

3 Such as Louise Bennett, W. B. Yeats, Derek Walcott, A. K. Ramanujan, and Okot p'Bitek (according to Ramazani 2001).

4 As defined by the Merriam-Webster online dictionary: https://www.merriam-webster.com/dictionary/intersection. Accessed 1 July 2020.

5 In Heracles, Hylas, and the 'Homeric Hymn to Demeter' in Apollonius's *Argonautica* (2017), Barbara L. Clayton insinuates a 'multiform' of parallel structural elements between two stories.

6 The multiform (or the many faces) of Hinduism in Joseph McLelland's *This Wordly and Otherworldly: Hinduism and Buddhism* (2009).

7 In anime, the ability to multiply one's form or appear in various guises simultaneously is a popular property for magical and superpowered beings. In *Dragon Ball*, certain characters (like Tien Shinhan) can activate the Multi-Form power to clone tangible, equally powerful forms of themselves: https://dragonball.fandom.com/wiki/Multi-Form

8 Here's a concordance of words (generated through concordance tools offered by Berberich & Kleiber 2020 and Cobb 2020) appearing in all nine chapters of this book: literary, cultural, reader, life, knowledge, academic, experience, practice, century, world, poetic, learning, forms, text, new, university, poems, language, students, writing, and poetry.

9 I complemented the template mostly through deductive reasoning, but similarities in the steps I executed can be observed in 'exegetical procedure' (Torjesen 2011); reverse sequence reading (Ino et al. 2003; Casasanto & Bottini 2014); and distributed representation (Kawamoto 1988).

10 To view the full codex, see Table 1.1 (A Multiform Codex of Poetry and Pedagogy).

11 For a review of Leung's poetry collection see Polley's (2018) 'Eloquence, Anger, Sincerity: Henry Leung's *Goddess of Democracy*: an Occupy Lyric.' https://chajournal.blog/2018/02/10/goddess-of-democracy/

References

Abramson, S., Damiani, J., & Kim, M. M. (Eds.). (2018). *BAX 2018: Best American Experimental Writing*. Middletown, CT: Wesleyan University Press.

Andersen, O., & Haarberg, J. (2001). *Making Sense of Aristotle: Essays in Poetics*. London: Gerald Duckworth.

Armitage, S., Hall, P., & Lonsdale, T. (2013). *Stanza Stones*. London: Enitharmon Press.

Baird, P. F. (2016). *Towards a Cultural Rhetorics Approach to Caribbean Rhetoric: African Guyanese Women from the Village of Buxton Transforming Oral History* (doctoral dissertation). Retrieved from https://etd.ohiolink.edu/

Benjamin, W. (1999). *The Arcades Project*. Rolf Tiedermann (ed.), Howard Eiland and Kevin McLaughlin (trans.). Cambridge, MA: Harvard University Press. (Original work published in 1982).

Berberich, K., & Kleiber, I. (2020) Tools for corpus linguistics. *Impressum*. Accessed April 15 2020 at https://corpus-analysis.com/tag/concordancer#

Bernstein, C. (1992). *A Poetics*. Cambridge, MA: Harvard University Press.

Bhabha, H. (1995). Cultural diversity and cultural differences. In B. Ashcroft, G. Griffiths, & H. Tiffin (eds.), *The Post-Colonial Studies Reader*. New York: Routledge.

Biddle, H. (1873). *Prose Miscellany*. Cincinnati: R. Clarke. http://purl.dlib.indiana.edu/iudl/inauthors/VAB8226.

Brainard, J. (1970). *I Remember*. Lenox, MA: Angel Hair Books.

Burroughs, W. S., & Gysin, B. (1978). *The Third Mind*. New York: The Viking Press.

Casasanto, D., & Bottini, R. (2014). Mirror reading can reverse the flow of time. *Journal of Experimental Psychology: General*, 143(2), 473.

Certeau, M. D. (1988). *The Practice of Everyday Life*. Berkeley: University of California Press.

Clark, T. (2015). *Ecocriticism on the Edge: The Anthropocene as a Threshold Concept*. London: Bloomsbury Publishing.

Clayton, B. L. (2017). Heracles, Hylas, and the Homeric Hymn to Demeter in Apollonius's Argonautica. *Helios*, 44(2), 133–156.

Cobb, T. (2020) *Text Lex Compare v.4.3 [Lextutor]*. Accessed April 29 2020 at https://www.lextutor.ca/cgi-bin/tl_compare/index.pl?ups=3

Deleuze, G., & Guattari, F. (1987). *A Thousand Plateaus: Capitalism and Schizophrenia*. London, UK: Bloomsbury Academic.

Derrida, J. (1968). "Différance." In N. Badmington and J. Thomas (eds.), *The Routledge Critical and Cultural Theory Reader* (pp. 126–148). London: Routledge.

Dictionary.com (2020). "*Poetry.*" Dictionary.com Unabridged Based on *The Random House Unabridged Dictionary*, © Random House, Inc. 2020. https://www.dictionary.com/browse/poetry

Donnelly, D., & Harper, G. (2013). "Introduction: Key Issues and Global Perspectives in Creative Writing." In D. Donnelly and G. Harper (eds.), *Key Issues in Creative Writing* (pp. xiii–xxvi). Bristol: Multilingual Matters.

Drucker, J. (1997). The self-conscious codex: Artists' books and electronic media. *SubStance*, 26(1), 93–112.

Early, M., Kendrick, M., & Potts, D. (2015). Multimodality: Out from the margins of English language teaching. *TESOL Quarterly*, 49(3), 447–460.

Enideo. (2020). *WordItOut [jOuery]*. Accessed May 30 2020 at https://worditout.com

Felski, R. (2015). *The Limits of Critique*. Chicago: University of Chicago Press.

Fenkl, H. I. (2003). Towards a theory of the interstitial [Version 1.0]: The interstitial DMZ. *Interstitial Arts: Artists without Borders*. http://interstitial.dreamhosters.com/archive/why/the_interstitial_dmz_1.html

Finch, A., & Schultz, S. M. (eds). (2008). *Multiformalisms: Postmodern Poetics of Form*. Cincinnati, OH: Textos.

Fish, S. E. (1980). *Is There a Text in This Class? The Authority of Interpretive Communities*. Cambridge, MA: Harvard University Press.

Frank, A. (1990). *The Diary of a Young Girl*. B. M. Mooyart-Doubleday (trans.). New York: Doubleday. (First published 1947)

Frank, T. (1935). Horace's definition of poetry. *The Classical Journal*, 31(3), 167–174. Accessed May 28 2020 at www.jstor.org/stable/3291022

Funkhouser, C. T. (2012). *New Directions in Digital Poetry* (Vol. 1). London: A&C Black.

Gifford, T. (1995). *Green Voices: Understanding Contemporary Nature Poetry*. Manchester: Manchester University Press.

Gui, Dean A. F. (2013). Virtual hybridity: Multiracial identity in second life explored. In M. Childs & G. Withnail (eds.), *Experiential Learning in Virtual Worlds* (pp. 171–192). Oxford: InterDisciplinary Press.

Hanauer, D. (2014). Appreciating the beauty of second language poetry writing. In D. Disney (ed.), *Exploring Second Language Creative Writing: Beyond Babel* (pp. 11–22). John Benjamins.

Hannerz, U. (1997, 1 January). The world in creolization. In K. Barber & C. Young (Eds.), *Readings in African Popular Culture*. Bloomington, IN: Indiana University Press.

Hoagland, T. (2006). Fear of narrative and the skittery poem of our moment. *Poetry*, 87(6), 508–519.

Howell, S., Kelleher, M., Teehan, A., & Keating, J. (2014). A digital humanities approach to narrative voice in *The Secret Scripture*: Proposing a new research method. *Digital Humanities Quarterly*, 8(2).

Hughes, T., & Godwin, F. (1979). *Remains of Elmet: A Pennine Sequence*. London: Faber and Faber.

Hyman, V. R. (1970). Sidney's definition of poetry. *Studies in English Literature, 1500–1900*, 10(1), 49–62.

Ino, T., Asada, T., Hirose, S., Ito, J., & Fukuyama, H. (2003). Reverse sequencing syllables of spoken words activates primary visual cortex. *Neuroreport*, 14(15), 1895–1899. Retrieved from http://ovidsp.ovid.com/ovidweb.cgi?T=-JS&PAGE=reference&D=ovftf&NEWS=N&AN=00001756-200310270-00003

Jacobson, J. E. (2009). *Hybrid poetry: A poetic matter.* Accessed March 20 2014 at http://apoeticmatter.com/tag/hybrid-poetry/

Kachru, B. (1976). Models of English for the Third World: White man's linguistic burden or language pragmatics? *TESOL Quarterly*, 10, 221–239.

Kawamoto, A. H. (1988). Distributed representations of ambiguous words and their resolution in a connectionist network. In *Lexical Ambiguity Resolution* (pp. 195–228). San Mateo, CA: Morgan Kaufmann.

Keats, J. (2009). Selections from Keats's Letters (1817). *Poetry Foundation*, 13. Accessed April 10 2019 at https://www.poetryfoundation.org/articles/69384/selections-from-keatss-letters

King, L., Gubele, R., & Anderson, J. R. (2015). *Survivance, Sovereignty, and Story: Teaching American Indian Rhetorics.* Logan: Utah State University Press.

Klastrup, L., & Tosca, S. (2004, November). *Transmedial worlds-rethinking cyberworld design.* In *2004 International Conference on Cyberworlds* (pp. 409–416). Tokyo: IEEE. doi: 10.1109/CW.2004.67

Kosari, M., & Amoori, A. (2018). Thirdspace: The trialectics of the real, virtual and blended spaces. *Journal of Cyberspace Studies*, 2(2), 163–185.

Leung, H. W. (2017). *Goddess of Democracy: An Occupy Lyric.* Oakland, CA: Omnidawn Press.

Love, C. T. (2012). Dialing into a circle of trust: A "medium" tech experiment and poetic evaluation. Teaching and learning from the inside out: Revitalizing ourselves and our institutions.

Maring, H. (ed.) (2017). Hybrid poetics in Old English verse. In *Signs That Sing: Hybrid Poetics in Old English Verse* (pp. 8–33). Gainesville: University Press of Florida. doi:10.2307/j.ctvx072nh.6

Mazza, N. F., & Hayton, C. J. (2013). Poetry therapy: An investigation of a multidimensional clinical model. *The Arts in Psychotherapy*, 40(1), 53–60.

McGill, S. (2005). *Virgil Recomposed: The Mythological and Secular Centos in Antiquity.* Oxford: Oxford University Press.

McLelland, J. (2009). Thiswordly and otherworldly: Hinduism and Buddhism. *The Free Library.* Accessed February 1 2019 at https://www.thefreelibrary.com/Thiswordly+and+otherworldly%3a+Hinduism+and+Buddhism.-a0212686298

Mignolo, D. W. (2011). *The Darker Side of Western Modernity: Global Futures, Decolonial Options.* Durham, NC: Duke University Press.

Misgeld, D., & Nicholson, G. (Eds.). (1992). *Hans-Georg Gadamer on Education, Poetry, and History: Applied Hermeneutics.* Albany: SUNY Press.

NCTE. (2013). *Found Poems/Parallel Poems.* ReadWriteThink.org. Accessed November 15 2013 at http://www.readwritethink.org/classroom-resources/lesson-plans/found-poems-parallel-poems-33.html

Nicholson, N. (1994). *Collected Poems.* London: Faber and Faber.

Oxenhandler, N. (2009). *Rimbaud: The Cost of Genius.* Columbus: Ohio State University Press. doi:10.2307/j.ctv1725r9k

Palumbo-Liu, D. (2010). Attention, poetics, media, collaboration. *Arcade: Literature, the Humanities, & the World*. Blog. https://arcade.stanford.edu/blogs/attention-poetics-media-collaboration

Picucci, M. A. (2014). When Video Games Tell Stories: A Model of Video Game Narrative Architectures. *Caracteres: Estudios Culturales y Críticos de la Esfera Digital*, 3, 99–117.

Pinsky, R. (1998). *The Sounds of Poetry: A Brief Guide* (p. 126). New York: Farrar, Strauss and Giroux.

Polley, J. S. (2018). *Eloquence, anger, sincerity: Henry Leung's Goddess of Democracy: An occupy lyric. Cha* (April), n.p. https://chajournal.blog/2018/02/10/goddess-of-democracy/

Polley, J. S., Ho, T. L. M., & Lee, J. E. H. (eds.) (2017). *Words Are Worlds: The Magic of Hong Kong's Local. Hong Kong Budding Poet's English Award 2015–16 Anthology*. Hong Kong: Government Logistics Dept.

Prendergast, M., Leggo, C., & Sameshima, P. (Eds.). (2009). *Poetic Inquiry: Vibrant Voices in the Social Sciences*. Rotterdam: Sense Publishers.

Ramazani, J. (2001). *The Hybrid Muse: Postcolonial Poetry in English*. Chicago: University of Chicago Press.

Ribeiro, A. C. (2007). Intending to repeat: A definition of poetry. *Journal of Aesthetics and Art Criticism*, 65(2), 189–201.

Riddel, J. (1961). Wallace Stevens' "Notes toward a Supreme Fiction". *Wisconsin Studies in Contemporary Literature*, 2(2), 20–42.

Riley-Mukavetz, A. M. (2014). Towards a cultural rhetorics methodology: Making research matter with multi-generational women from the Little Traverse Bay Band. *Rhetoric, Professional Communication and Globalization*, 5(1), 108–124.

Robbins, A. M. (2014). *American Hybrid Poetics: Gender, Mass Culture, and Form*. New Brunswick, NJ: Rutgers University Press.

Sartwell, C. (1991). Substance and significance: A theory of poetry. *Philosophy and Literature*, 15, 246–259.

Savin-Baden, M., & Falconer, L. (2016). Learning at the interstices: Locating practical philosophies for understanding physical/virtual inter-spaces. *Interactive Learning Environments*, 24(5), 991–1003.

Schumm, S. A. (1956). Evolution of drainage systems and slopes in badlands at Perth Amboy, New Jersey. *Geological Society of America Bulletin*, 67(5), 597–646.

Share, D. (2008). The hybrid-way or the highway. *Harriet: A Poetry Blog*. The Poetry Foundation. Accessed September 29 2014 at http://www.poetryfoundation.org/harriet/2008/10/the-hybrid-way-or-the-highway/?woo

Shklovsky, V. (1965). Art as technique. In L. T. Lemon & M. J. Reis (eds. & trans.), *Russian Formalist Criticism: Four Essays*, 2nd edition (pp. 3–24). Lincoln: University of Nebraska Press. (Original work published 1917)

Solnick, S. (2016). *Poetry and the Anthropocene: Ecology, Biology and Technology in Contemporary British and Irish Poetry*. London: Routledge.

Torjesen, K. J. (2011). *Hermeneutical Procedure and Theological Method in Origen's Exegesis* (Vol. 28). Berlin: Walter de Gruyter.

Tsekeris, C. (2015). Contextualising the self in contemporary social science. *Contemporary Social Science*, 10(1), 1–14.

Wikipedia contributors. (2020, May 28). Poetry. *Wikipedia, The Free Encyclopedia*. Accessed May 28 2020 at https://en.wikipedia.org/w/index.php?title=Poetry&oldid=959438522

Williams, N. (2011). *Contemporary Poetry*. Edinburgh: Edinburgh University Press.

William Victor, S. L. (2010). How to write found poetry. *Creative Writing Now*. Accessed November 15 2013 at http://www.creative-writing-now.com/found-poetry.html

Yanal, R. J. (1982). Aristotle's definition of poetry. *Nous*, 16(4), 499–525.

Part I

Anagnorisis: Storytelling as pedagogy

2 Oulipo in Hong Kong

Welcoming unconventional forms in poetry writing workshops

James Shea

Form's what affirms.

—James Merrill, 'The Thousand and Second Night'
(Used with permission.)

Preface

My first encounter with the intersection of imitation and affect in the classroom took place in a literature survey course at a liberal arts university in Nebraska where my students and I discussed Gertrude Stein's *The Autobiography of Alice B. Toklas* (1933/1990). I asked students to name all of the characteristics of Stein's prose style. We came up with this list:

1. First person from an intimate's point of view;
2. Using the protagonist's full name, e.g. 'Gertrude Stein who has an explosive temper ...' (Stein 1933/1990: 11) (Used with permission);
3. Run-on sentences;
4. Short (monosyllabic) words in an energetic, frenetic voice;
5. Not very emotional, but blunt;
6. Something novel occurring often, such as always meeting someone new;
7. Specific details describing minor things;
8. No capitalization for some proper nouns, e.g. '... few frenchmen did in those days' (Stein 1933/1990: 60) (Used with permission);
9. No quotation marks for quotes;
10. No question marks for questions.

I then invited students to write a long paragraph describing their real life from the previous few weeks in the voice of their roommate (or sibling or parent, if they lived at home). The students wrote their paragraphs in class and read some aloud. This exchange of 'flash memoirs' in Stein's unorthodox style was a welcome break from our normal discussions, and it gave students a sense of not only what Stein was saying, but how she was saying it: how her form and style suited the content and drove her narrative.

The exercise also set up a discussion about a key passage, arguably the climax of her memoir, in a late chapter titled 'The War.' On her way by car to the frontlines in Alsace, she's had an accident and damaged her mudguard. After getting it replaced, she approached the 'battle-fields.' The implication is that new mudguards may be necessary to protect her car from blood as much as from mud (Stein 1933/1990):

> Soon we came to the battle-fields and the lines of trenches of both sides. To any one who did not see it as it was then it is impossible to imagine it. It was not terrifying it was strange. We were used to ruined houses and even ruined towns but this was different. It was a landscape. And it belonged to no country. (187)
>
> (Used with permission.)

It is not clear if she has come upon the dead bodies of soldiers in the trenches, but Stein, for the first time in the book, is at a loss for words: 'it is impossible to imagine it.' In a book rich with descriptions, here she refrains from describing—rather, she becomes vague and abstract, the language slows down, the sentences become comparatively normalized, the narrator shifts from the playful 'Gertrude Stein' to the collective pronoun 'we,' and the narration moves on quickly to another subject in the next paragraph. The passage is powerful, but it is even more powerful when students experience her style by way of their own words—her frenetic, head-long prose suddenly becoming halting and hesitant. Detecting this shift can be enhanced by imitation, one of the hallmarks of creative writing pedagogy and a technique that lends itself to the literature classroom as a way to delay analysis and to allow an opening for a deeper, affective response in the reader.

Constraint-based writing

As of 2013, I have been teaching creative writing to multilingual[1] students in the Department of Humanities and Creative Writing at Hong Kong Baptist University, which offers Hong Kong's first and only bilingual BA degree in creative and professional writing. Founded in 2012, this undergraduate program requires students to take an equal number of courses in English and Chinese that include both creative and professional writing classes. In my course 'Poetry Writing Workshop,' I employ both traditional and unconventional poetic forms by way of imitation exercises, and this pedagogical approach offers insights into teaching hybrid poetry writing that points a way forward for instructors to apply a 'hybrid pedagogy' to both the creative writing classroom and the literature classroom. Given that comparatively little scholarship on teaching English-language poetry in Hong Kong's tertiary institutions exists, this essay contextualizes my use of constraint-based writing methods by way of Rita Felski's recent arguments about renewing literary studies. Just as hybrid poetry that combines traditional and experimental lineages can offer novel approaches for poetry writing instruction, a hybrid pedagogy in one's own teaching—that includes both conventional and unconventional forms in the creative writing classroom, and imitation exercises alongside literary analysis in the literature classroom—can allow students to see a fuller range of what a literary text can be. Imitation, in particular, fosters an affective engagement that enriches a student's relationship to a text.

Form in poetry typically refers to traditional structures, like the sonnet and the sestina, that employ patterns of rhyme and meter. In the case of meter, for example, stressed and unstressed syllables are the DNA of English—you cannot write English without engaging, usually subconsciously, its inherent rhythms. Some would argue that casual speech in English has a natural iambic cadence, so even free verse that eschews meter often possesses the ghost of iambic rhythms (Finch 1993). There are other examples of formal devices in English-language poetry, such as alliteration (*Beowulf*), anaphora (*Jubilate Agno*), and prose poems (*Tender Buttons*). In the twenty-first century, however, when free verse is the norm and students can compose and save poems on their cellphones without the need for mnemonic devices, the unconventional forms of 'hybrid poetry,' such as constraint-based writing, that do not require rhyme and meter can take hold: they provide the pleasures of form without needing to find original rhymes and to master meter, especially in the case of students in an English as a second language (ESL) classroom.

'Constraint-based writing' refers to a broad spectrum of literature that encompasses mainly the Oulipo tradition and its offshoots, but includes any work based on a form devised at the outset of writing. In *Many Subtle Channels: In Praise of Potential Literature*, Daniel Levin Becker (2012) quotes from Gilbert Sorrentino's syllabus at Stanford to define 'constrained writing': '"Generative devices" are consciously selected, preconceived structures, forms, limitations, constraints, developed by the writer before the act of writing. The writing is then made according to the 'laws' set in place by the chosen constraint' (13). Sorrentino's (1999) novel *Gold Fools*, for example, is written entirely in interrogative sentences.

The past decade has seen a rise in scholarship on the value of poetry writing in the ESL classroom: Fang-Yu Liao (2016); Dan Disney (2014); David Hanauer (2010, 2011, 2014); Rebecca Todd Garvin (2013); and Lara Marie Hauer (2017). A lead proponent is Hanauer, whose claim about the beauty of second-language poetry resonates with my own experience. Here are Hanauer's (2014) own words:

> second language writing is beautiful, aesthetically pleasing, innovative and designed to surprise. In fact, as a second language writing instructor for the last twenty years, I can testify that one of the nicest aspects of my work has been those moments at which I saw a phrase written by a second language learner that would have sounded unusual coming from a first language writer. (12)

Speaking more broadly of writing courses, Hanauer (2014) argues that a typical pedagogical approach encourages students to 'produce a series of cloned texts which all manifest the same set of linguistic features' (12).

According to Hanauer (2014), 'A basic outcome of this pedagogical process is that the individuality of a second language learner is completely erased and marginalized' (12). He advocates using poetry writing in ESL courses to foster creativity, and by poetry writing, he appears to mean imagistic free verse, given his cited examples. Although he does not distinguish between the form of a business letter and poetic forms, I differ from Hanauer's implication that 'cloned texts' necessarily lead to an erasure of a student's individuality, because although the use of poetic forms entails a kind of 'cloning,' in practice, students are empowered to create original works within a formal framework, in the same way that a game's rules permit playfulness.

I view my students as writing poems, not exercises or assignments, even if we may use those terms on occasion. When any student believes, rightly, that she or he is expected to write real poems and those poems are being read and critiqued as real poems, then strange things begin to happen: the student approaches writing with greater enjoyment, and with more confidence that the work is being read seriously, and students begin to critique each other's writing with greater engagement. The class feels less like school and more like a conversation between writers. This welcoming space for treating their work as poetry is reinforced by the assurance that their poems will be read as works-in-progress that likely require revision. I do not grade their weekly submissions, but I do provide written feedback, so they can revise their work for their Final Portfolios, which I do grade. This was also the case when I taught poetry writing workshops in the United States: I never assigned a letter grade to an individual poem, but rather waited until the Final Portfolio to assign a holistic grade, based partly on how seriously students tried to revise their work, as well as the overall quality of the work.

To foster poetry writing among my students in Hong Kong, many of whom are writing poetry in English for the first time, I tend to use looser poetic forms, forms that employ the touch of form. Some unconventional forms that I teach include: (i) N+7 ('replacing each noun (N) with the seventh following it in a dictionary' (Queneau, cited in Matthews & Brotchie 1998: 198) as a revision exercise for one of their own poems; (ii) 'I Remember' poems in the manner of Joe Brainard; (iii) homophonic translations inspired by Celia and Louis Zukofsky; (iv) erasure poems; (v) poems about a punctuation mark modeled after Eugène Guillevic's book *Geometries* (2010) in which each poem is in response to a different geometric shape; (vi) 'object poems' that must use all 20 nouns that I provide; and (vii) a writing prompt from the poet Graham Foust (2010), i.e. poems that use the same pronoun as the first word of each line in the style of John Ashbery's early poem 'He.'

Many of these forms rely on imitation, a practice that can be traced back to antiquity: encouraged by all the major classical Greek and Roman rhetoricians, imitation of model texts was a fundamental mode of instruction in ancient Rome and Athens as well as during the Renaissance period—it included imitating forms with new content, and imitating content with new forms. As Raffaella Cribiore notes in *Gymnastics of the Mind* (2001): 'Imitation of literary models was at the core of a program in rhetoric: through close reading of the texts, it became possible to assimilate vocabulary, style, and organization of the elements of discourse' (225). In the classical Chinese poetic tradition, imitation poems were also common, often anthologized together, and constituted a 'kind of literary criticism by presenting various models of literary history' (Williams 2015: 3). Widespread in creative writing workshops, imitation exercises have slowly found their way into literature courses as well. Bartholomew Brinkman (2010), for instance, describes his practice of using imitation in the 'critical classroom,' such as when students rewrite Wallace Stevens's 'The Snow Man' with the 'dialect-heavy style of Langston Hughes' (160). Brinkman requires both a creative work and a piece of critical reflection, the latter of which is graded.

I do not reject traditional forms in the classroom entirely. However, I tend to prefer unconventional forms for a few reasons. First, nontraditional forms can destabilize the Anglo-Saxon canon, especially given Britain's colonial legacy in Hong Kong. Most of my students, when asked to write a poem, will compose a poem in rhyme, because they assume that's what English poems should do, based on what they have read in secondary school and in most university courses. Unconventional forms broaden what an English poem can sound like for students. They also permit students to forgo concerns about adhering to the Chinese poetic tradition, which can feel equally overwhelming for young students, by creating a space for experimentation. Writing a poem can become game-like, and students, accustomed to executing tasks for class, find that writing in a given form allows them a manageable approach to express themselves in a second language. Such Oulipian writing methods permit students to encounter poetry writing in a foreign language less as a monumental effort and more as approachable play.

Second, these poetic forms avoid favoring international students who may be more familiar with traditional forms and have stronger overall writing skills than their ESL classmates. Such forms equalize the experience of writing poetry for all students, because although their abilities in English may vary, they must all engage with the same unconventional forms. It invites gentle competition as well as solidarity, in that they all have the same form with which to contend. And when they workshop each other's poems, there's a second layer of interest, because the students want to see how their classmates have handled the challenge.

Third, unconventional poetic forms are generally more accessible than traditional forms, because they do not rely on successful original rhymes or meter, which can be difficult to manage, even in the most experienced poet's hands. These kinds of forms open the writing process to serendipitous discoveries by estranging the actual experience of writing a poem. Students stop worrying about their language ability and start thinking about the form, which allows them to write something they otherwise never would have imagined writing. James Merrill described this phenomenon in an interview, saying, 'For the poet, it is vital that formal demands be made upon him (or her); attending to them leaves the subconscious free to infiltrate the poem' (White 1995: 193) (Used with permission.).

One concern with using such forms extensively is the potential reduction of writing poems to a frivolous exercise. However, we address this viewpoint openly as a gateway into discussing the myriad ways of composing poetry, and I always ask students to write a 'free' poem without prescribed formal requirements—this way they discover a *sui generis* form along the way. I invite them to begin with a blank page from a notebook, in the spirit of William Stafford's essay 'A Way of Writing' (1970/1982), and to follow their train of thought on the page. It is important for students to wrestle with silence as they write, and I don't want them to rely exclusively on assigned forms. Yet given that my class may be the only chance they have to write poems, as my students must study creative writing in English in other genres, creative writing in Chinese, and professional writing in English and Chinese, I want to provide the scaffolding for them to start writing immediately. Generally, constraint-based writing exercises engender an experimental atmosphere in which students feel less burdened by adhering to a received tradition in favor of exploring new ways of writing. I also found this to be true when I taught poetry writing workshops in the United States, where my students struggled with meter and traditional forms and appreciated learning unconventional forms as an entryway into writing poems. Returning to Hanauer (2014) for a moment, I find that his praise of unorthodox language found in poems written by ESL students is worth noting:

> These are moments at which a language learner working with all her/his language resources (both first and second languages) constructs an utterance that is truly unique to her/his linguistic knowledge and historical, cultural exposure. For me, it is the unusualness and strangeness of the writing that makes it so enjoyable to read. (12)

Having taught English for many years, I've enjoyed many lovely 'mistakes' in both native English speakers and ESL students. Hanauer implies, but does not address clearly, that ESL students are aware of the poetic quality of their unorthodox language; but I'm not so sure. The instructor should explain when a student's language is not clear or 'correct,' but at the same time allow the student to retain the idiosyncrasy, after realizing it may be beautiful or effective. Another way of putting this is to say that although I value the discourse of 'World Englishes' (Bolton 2013), I find that my students want to learn what is functionally standard English—even, or perhaps especially, if they decide eventually to break the rules.

In the same essay, Hanauer refers to a 'new way of seeing' that ESL students can discover, which evokes the Russian formalist Viktor Shklovsky's theory of art as estrangement or defamiliarization. Shklovsky (1917/1965) wrote memorably that 'art exists that one may recover the sensation of life; it exists to make one feel things, to make the stone stony' (1917/1965: 12). He believed that art helps us to feel our way back into the world. Often overlooked is the purpose behind Shklovsky's thesis that art should make the world strange: the goal is to wake up the reader to the reality of the world, and in particular, to the suffering of others. In 'Art as Technique,' he provides an example of estrangement by quoting from a story by Tolstoy in which a horse is the narrator (Ibid: 13–15). Tolstoy startles the reader into becoming more conscious of the practice of owning animals, drawing attention to their misery. The implication for creative writing students is that new ways of seeing the world through literary creation may allow them to cultivate empathy for others.

Oulipo in Hong Kong

The use of unconventional forms in my poetry writing courses is inspired largely by Oulipo[2] writers whose basic idea was that one's writing cannot escape form, especially invisible, received rules, which often remain unacknowledged; so why not devise one's own system and at least have some say over the rules one is following—why not amplify the forms and rules in our writing? Founded in 1960 by François Le Lionnais (1901–1984) and Raymond Queneau (1903–1976), the Oulipo movement arose partly out of a rejection of surrealism, especially its generative method of automatic writing and reliance on the writer's unconsciousness as the wellspring of expression. A former surrealist himself, Raymond Queneau said famously that his fellow writers were 'rats who must build the labyrinth from which they propose to escape' (in Lescure 1998: 37). Oulipo practioners invented elaborate constraints that were inspired, in part, by the sciences and mathematical formulas. One of the earliest examples of Oulipian writing is Queneau's 1961 volume *Hundred Thousand Billion Poems* (*Cent mille milliards de poèmes*), a thin book of ten sonnets in which each line may be replaced with a corresponding line from the other sonnets, resulting in the potential for 100 trillion different poems, i.e. 'more sonnets than all the sonnets ever written, or, for that matter more text than had ever been written by all humans at that time' (Poucel 2012: 987). Another classic example is Georges Perec's 1969 novel *A Void* (*La disparition*), a lipogram that omits the letter 'e' (Perec 1969/2008). The Oulipo movement in France today remains small but active, and its approach to writing serves as inspiration for digital poets who work with computational writing, algorithms, and machine-generated poetry.[3]

Despite Oulipo's skepticism toward surrealism, one of my constraint-based poetry writing exercises is an imitation of André Breton's 'L'Union libre' (or 'Free Union' in David Antin's translation). I ask students to write a poem in the style of Breton's 'list poem' or literary blazon, i.e. a catalog of physical attributes describing one's beloved; but I tell them to write about any person who comes to mind. My student Pamela transformed Breton's poem into a surreal celebration of her brother:

My Brother
an imitation of André Breton's *Free Union*

He whose eyes are the chestnuts in the dream of a squirrel;
Whose cheek is the evening sky with glowing clouds and sunset;

Whose nose is the bud of a white rose;
Whose ear is a conch that delivers the tidal orchestra from the sea;
Whose lips are the candy canes hidden in a Christmas sock;
Whose fist is the bunny's tail;
Whose toes are grapes freshly picked in a basket;
Whose wrist is a boomerang;
Whose elbow is a blown orange bubble gum;
Whose eyebrows are the strokes drawn on the sand,
drawn by a seagull with a branch in its mouth;
Whose teeth are ceramic tiles in a new cottage;
Whose voice is the cracking, burning woods in the stove in winter;
Whose dream is the clownfish who dances with the sea anemone
and swings with the waves of the ocean;
Whose heart is a strawberry candy stuffed with mustard.

(Wong 2015) (Used with permission.)

Highly inventive ('Whose toes are grapes freshly picked in a basket') with a sly music ('stuffed with mustard'), the student rewrote a love poem about Breton's wife as a poem about sibling love with all the dazzle and surprise of the surrealist original.

I also invite students to write their own version of John Ashbery's poem 'He' by selecting any pronoun, such as 'She,' 'It,' 'We,' 'They,' or 'He' and beginning each line with this word. I encourage them to follow Ashbery's approach: write 12 quatrains (48 lines), change the tone of the poem from line to line, mix enjambment and end-stopped lines to create formal tension, and consider using dialogue to generate variation. Here are the opening, middle, and final stanzas of 'In the Darkness,' a 12-stanza poem by my student Yoyo:

He was born from the blood,
his parent's blood,
in an alley.
There was no one who
clapped for his birth.

He was raised by bats.
They fed him by fear,
and let him rely on it.
That's why he had no fear anymore.

...

His voice is husky,
as metal scratches on the glass.
He has no accent,
from anywhere.
He speaks his own English.

...

He is a monster
in the darkness.
And shouts to the man
who invaded his territory.

(Cheung 2015) (Used with permission.)

These lines capture the same ominous, dream-like atmosphere of Ashbery's poem, but the gothic imagery suggests a student steeped in the popular culture of vampire stories. The closing images of a man who 'speaks his own English' and 'shouts to the man / who invaded his territory' evokes a colonial discourse and invites a reflection on the geopolitics of Hong Kong today.

A common exercise in writing courses is to imitate Joe Brainard's *I Remember* (1970) as a starting point for students to write poems with concrete images and to draw upon their life experiences. It's an ideal exercise, especially for second language learners as they can grasp the premise quickly. The challenge, and what I emphasize repeatedly when doing imitations of forms, is to generate surprise and variation within the poem's rigid framework, or, to borrow an image from James Merrill (2001), 'To keep the blue wave dancing in its prison' (673) (Used with permission). Here is the second half of my student Eros's poem 'I Remember':

> I remember the bitter white bubbles on top of my father's cup of beer to be my first taste of alcohol.
> I remember the first ever Chinese New Year that I spent alone as the punishment for bad academic results in secondary school.
> I remember ballet lessons.
> I remember lucid dreams.
> I remember drinking bubble milk tea in the café in front of the school gate.
> I remember running on the streets of Hong Kong Island in a city hunt.
> I remember watching the whole series of Cardcaptor Sakura before final examinations.
> I remember baking banana cake in a wrong scale.

(Yeung 2015) (Used with permission.)

This poem echoes Brainard's references to popular culture ('Cardcaptor Sakura'), family members ('my father'), and embarrassing revelations ('bad academic results'). It ends on an image ('baking banana bread in a wrong scale') that can be taken as a metaphor for the awkward missteps of childhood, which is also found in Brainard.

My final example is from the Chinese literary tradition, which I try to incorporate into my writing courses in Hong Kong whenever possible, in order to draw connections between the Western poetic tradition and my students' heritage. Classical Chinese poetry is well known for its various rules in terms of rhyme schemes and tonal patterns,[4] but Jin dynasty poet Tao Qian (356–427) wrote a poem called 'Wine Stop' that resembles the playfulness of Oulipo: it uses the word 'stop' in every line, such as these opening lines: 'I've stopped. Here in town, where idleness/coming of itself stopped my far wandering,/I've stopped sitting anywhere but deep shade/and stopped going out my brambleweave gate' (in Hinton 1993: 58) (Used with permission). Tao Qian's repeated use of 'stop' resonates from a spiritual perspective in terms of pausing or resting in the Daoist sense of 'non-action' (Williams 2019).

Another example from the Chinese tradition is the poem 'Bringing Lunch to the Field' by He Shuangqing, a poet from the Qing dynasty. Her poem repeats the word 'spring' in every line, as in the opening: 'The purple path is alive with spring,/I cover my forehead with a light spring scarf,/Set out to bring lunch to the spring planting./The small plum is spring-thin in blossoms;/The fine grass is spring-radiant;' (in Choy 2000: 243) (Used with permission). Just as Tao Qian and He Shuangqing broke from convention and wrote in unorthodox forms, so too can my students value experimentation in the Chinese poetic tradition and find an approach to write poems that do not align with received forms in English or Chinese. I instruct students to select a single word and write a poem in which each line uses that word or its variation, such as Christine's version 'Weaver and Weave':

> Woven into the Hong Kong threads, my future was.
> You were weaving with blurry presbyopic glasses,
> with weaved back.
>
> You would send me a weave, you said.
> Before I began weaving my destiny,
> in another territory.
>
> You regarded a natural weave as unbridled life,
> the flesh pink as weavers' blood.
> Weaving my dream was your dream
> that had never come true
> that you were weaving.
>
> Using flesh pink threads and natural weaves,
> you wove a flesh pink sweater,
> even though I wouldn't need this kind of weave
> in such a hot basket city.
>
> However, my weaver
> what you were weaving
> was a woven encumbrance to me
> rather than a courage to weave.
>
> (Chen 2014)(Used with permission.)

The speaker feels a frustration with whom I take to be a parental figure—and we can detect a growing emotional distance between them. The poem expresses a coming of age in the speaker and exhibits an emerging sense of independence common in students like Christine, who relocated to Hong Kong from mainland China for their university studies.

Hong Kong as constraint-based

Some critics, such as Juliana Spahr and Stephanie Young in *The /n/oulipian Analects* (2007), argue that the original Oulipo writers were generally unengaged with political questions, uninterested in larger power structures or, worse, reinforced the patriarchal system in France. According to these critics, the Oulipo movement consisted mainly of men and exhibited a persistent chauvinism: 'Lots of men doing crosswords,' in the words of an anonymous woman writer quoted by Lauren Elkin and Veronica Scott Esposito in *The End of Oulipo? An Attempt at Exhausting a Movement* (2013: 78). As Louis Bury observes, however, 'Just because Oulipo's writing practices are artistically avant-garde does not mean that their politics must be loud and progressive as well.' Bury locates the anxiety about the leftist politics of the writers in the fact that they 'never explicitly link their artistic practices to their political beliefs and actions' (2015: 43). Notably, Bury offers tantalizing readings of the latent politics in the work of contemporary writers in the Oulipo tradition, such as Christian Bök and Harryette Mullen, whom Bury sees as contending with 'cultural excess' through constraint: 'constraint, rather than being an unpleasant form of coercion, becomes a helpful mechanism for navigating quantitative overload—becomes, paradoxically, liberating' (2015: 18). He links a resurgence of Oulipian writings in the twenty-first century to 'anxieties about freedom and choice in our current historical moment, in the same way that the advent of Oulipo in 1960 can be seen as a subconscious response to French Existential thought of the 1940s and 1950s' (Ibid). Referring to Doug Nufer's novel *Never Again* (2004), a work that does not use the same word twice, Bury suggests that the entire project is 'an allegory for, or an enactment of, the unchecked usage of natural resources'— although Bury also considers that the writing itself exemplifies excess in its odd, rhetorical flights that strain grammatical sense (Ibid).

What, then, can we make of the cultural context in Hong Kong for constraint-based writing by students? Hong Kong is a city defined by constraints—economic, geographic, and political. The year 2017 marked the highest Gini coefficient in Hong Kong in 45 years (Yiu & McIntyre 2017); some 200,000 people live in extremely small quarters called 'coffin homes' (Taylor 2017); and university graduates can no longer afford to buy a home, even with a full-time job (Ye 2016). Geographically, Hong Kong is 427 square miles (Saiidi 2017) with the fourth-highest population density in the world (Porter 2018). And politically, Hong Kong's Basic Law, often called a 'mini-constitution,' is constrained by the Standing Committee of the National People's Congress in Beijing, which can make a final ruling on any Hong Kong court's decision. In 2018, for instance, said Standing Committee declared that legislators could be disqualified from running for office if they support an independent Hong Kong (Cheung, Cheung, & Ng 2018).

To be an artist within a larger structure of constraints and to discover ways to challenge norms is a demanding task, but one that can be explored in the classroom. By experimenting with both traditional and unconventional poetic forms, my students gain the attendant insight that there is 'freedom through discipline,' that is, a new structure is always needed to escape one's present confines. Art-making in Hong Kong can be an active choice to put oneself in control of certain constraints and to reflect upon the larger rules that govern society. Games, in particular, can serve as sites of transformation wherein the goal is not to 'win,' but rather to discover alternate ways of seeing the world. Scholar and video-game designer Ian Bogost, citing Johan Huizinga's concept of play as entering a 'magic circle,' suggests that 'there is a gap in the magic circle through which players carry subjectivity in and out of the game space' (Bogost 2008: 135). Play is not an isolated experience outside of real life; rather, it can be a means to 'expose and explore complicated human conditions, rather than offering mere interruption and diversion' (Ibid: 136). New media art forms, especially in the realm of video games and play, shed light on how play can be self-reflective and serve as a critique of society.

Implicit in constraint-based poetry is the possibility of freedom, or at a minimum, an understanding of one's constraints. One example of a text that interrogates the relationship between constraint and freedom is M. NourbeSe Philip's 200-page poem *Zong!* that uses only language from the 500-word court decision *Gregson v. Gilbert* that provided a legal framework for slave traders to collect insurance after they threw slaves overboard during the Zong Massacre in 1781. Philip's book-length poem led her to an insight about the relationship between constraint and freedom:

> One of our founding cultural myths in the West is that of freedom—we can do or say anything (within certain constraints, of course); we are free to go out and find our constraints, poach on other cultures and so on. What I began to understand is that even when we think we are freest, if we lift—I want to say that veil of freedom—underneath will be found many unspoken constraints.
>
> (Eichhorn 2009: 143)

Constraint-based writing in the classroom allows students, whether they are in Hong Kong or elsewhere, to engender not so much an escape from the labyrinth, but insights into the labyrinth in which they live.

Toward affective engagement: imitation as method

In a review of Bury's *Exercises in Criticism: The Theory and Practice of Literary Constraint* (2015), Adam Katz (2015) recognizes the pedagogical potential for Oulipian writing methods and the practice of imitation exercises as a means to understand a text:

> The playful nature of constraint-based writing is evident, and an important point in its favor. Teachers are currently being urged to draw upon the pedagogical potentialities of video games, and we certainly should

exploit the cognitive dimensions of such activities—but there may be more to gain by engaging students in the pedagogical potentialities in the very first game space: human language, with its vast array of sound shapes, shades of meaning, and forms of articulation. (3)

An imitation exercise can help students to see a text as a source for new knowledge, and it can defamiliarize a text by giving students an affective experience of the work through a close reading. A poem can become a 'game space' for play, experimentation, and discovery.

Marjorie Perloff (2006) once framed the rise of creative writing in oppositional terms to literary studies, stating: 'in our moment, creative writing is perhaps best understood as the revenge of literature on the increasingly sociological, political, and anthropological emphasis of English studies' (4). More recently, Marilynne Robinson (2017), the American novelist and professor of creative writing at the Iowa Writers' Workshop, made a similar point, but with a call for a 'conceptual language' that can 'recover the animating spirit of the humanities' (33). Robinson (2017) also shared the following detail: 'I have had students tell me that they had never heard the word 'beautiful' applied to a piece of prose until they came to us at the workshop' (Ibid). Rita Felski's work (2008, 2015) provides the beginnings of a 'conceptual language' that can bridge literary studies and creative writing, as it admits the complexity of aesthetic and emotional reactions to literature ('the thickness of aesthetic experience,' as Felski puts it). Creative writing practices—whether they are imitations of poems or stories in a literature course, or imitations of unconventional poetic forms in a creative writing workshop—can be a means by which to enlarge what we mean by literary studies.

Felski's aim is a critique of critique that reimagines a new approach to interpretation (2015: 9–10). Writing against the 'hermeneutics of suspicion' (Paul Ricœur) found in literary criticism, she seeks 'to de-essentialize the practice of suspicious reading by disinvesting it of presumptions of inherent rigor or intrinsic radicalism—thereby freeing up literary studies to embrace a wider range of affective styles and modes of argument' (Felski 2015: 3). She calls for critics 'to experiment with modes of argument less tightly bound to exposure, demystification, and the lure of the negative' (Ibid: 120). Felski does not advocate a single way forward in terms of literary studies, but in addition to naming actor-network theory (Bruno Latour) and post-historicist criticism (Marielle Macé) as viable critical frameworks, she cites 'affective hermeneutics' (Yves Citton) as a model. On the importance of affect, Felski writes:

> Emotions are not mere icing on the cake—at best a pleasurable distraction, at worst a mystifying spell to be broken so that the work of hard-nosed analysis can begin. Rather, affective engagement is the very means by which literary works are able to reach, reorient, and even reconfigure their readers.
>
> (Ibid: 177)

Emotional engagement is never far from the creative writing classroom, where an exercise may entail asking students to write about a powerful childhood memory, or where students may respond to a fellow student's work by saying, 'I liked this … ' and 'I was moved by …'

The practice of imitation is a primary example of a pedagogical approach that invites affective engagement, in that students are encouraged to inhabit a writer's style and to remain open to its emotional registers. In an imitation exercise, which entails doing a close reading of a text to articulate its features and then emulating the text, students must encounter the text's form and content in an intimate, personal way, because they must place themselves at the center of the style. Imitation entails a phenomenological experience with a literary text because the necessary attention to the text's surface is a way of looking at, rather than seeing through, a text. Imitation becomes a strategy to unlock an affective response to a text by focusing attention on its particularities or idiosyncrasies, which Felski privileges (Ibid: 167). Favoring description over interpretation (Ibid: 190), she argues for the possibility of the critic to be 'touched by the genuine strangeness and otherness of the work of art' (Ibid: 39). In contrast to contextualization as a method of analysis, imitation requires description—being able to describe the features of the text, so that those features can be imitated. Felski points to Bruno Latour quoting the architect Rem Koolhaas on the problem with contexualization: 'It's a way of stopping the description when you are too tired or lazy to go on' (Ibid: 152).

Teaching unconventional poetic forms, such as constraint-based writing, alongside traditional forms invites a hybrid pedagogy in the creative writing classroom. Constraint-based writing, especially in the Hong Kong context, is a valuable method of teaching poetry writing and expanding students' perceptions of what a poem can be. The use of imitation, which lies at the heart of such activities, entails an affective response in students that opens the possibility for its deployment in the literature classroom. This twin application of imitation promises to renew students' emotional engagement with literary studies, as they encounter a text not only as something to analyze, but as a work that can transform them.

Notes

1 By 'multilingual,' I mean students who are mainly native speakers of Cantonese, but who also speak English and Mandarin; some students who are native speakers of Mandarin and also speak English and Cantonese; and some international students who speak their native language and English.
2 'Oulipo' is an abbreviation of *Ouvroir de littérature potentielle*, or 'workshop of potential literature.'
3 See *The New Media Reader* (Wardrip-Fruin & Montfort 2003) for evidence of Oulipo's importance in the development of new media theory and practice.
4 See Cai (2007) for an accessible primer on the rich formal complexity of classical Chinese poetry.

References

Bogost, I. (2008). *Unit operations: An approach to videogame criticism.* Cambridge, MA: MIT Press.

Bolton, K. (2013). World Englishes, globalisation, and language worlds. In N.-L. Johannesson, G. Melchers, & B. Björkman (Eds.), *Of butterflies and birds, of dialects and genres: Essays in honour of Philip Shaw* (pp. 227–251). Stockholm: Acta Universitatis Stockholmiensis.

Brainard, J. (1970). *I remember.* Lenox, MA: Angel Hair Books.

Brinkman, B. (2010). Imitations, manipulations and interpretations: Creative writing in the critical classroom. *Iowa Journal of Cultural Studies, 12*(1), 158–163.

Bury, L. (2015). *Exercises in criticism: The theory and practice of literary constraint.* Champaign, IL: Dalkey Archive Press.

Cai, Z.-Q. (Ed.). (2007). *How to read Chinese poetry: A guided anthology.* New York: Columbia University Press.

Chen, S. (2014). Weaver and weave. Retrieved from HKBU Heritage: http://heritage.lib.hkbu.edu.hk/view.php?id=10990

Cheung, G., Cheung, T., & Ng, J. (2018, July 20). China's top body lays down law on Hong Kong oath-taking. *South China Morning Post.* Retrieved from https://www.scmp.com/

Cheung, Y. (2015). In the darkness. Retrieved from HKBU Heritage: http://heritage.lib.hkbu.edu.hk/view.php?id=11074

Choy, E. (2000). *Leaves of prayer: The life and poetry of He Shuangqing, a farmwife in eighteenth-century China.* Hong Kong: The Chinese University Press.

Cribiore, R. (2001). *Gymnastics of the mind: Greek education in Hellenistic and Roman Egypt.* Princeton, NJ: Princeton University Press.

Disney, D. (Ed.) (2014). *Exploring second language creative writing: Beyond Babel.* Amsterdam: John Benjamins.

Eichhorn, K. (2009). An interview with M. N. Philip. In K. Eichhorn & H. Milne (Eds.), *Prismatic publics: Innovative Canadian women's poetry and poetics* (p. 143). Toronto: Coach House Books.

Elkin, L., & Esposito, V. S. (2013). *The end of Oulipo? An attempt to exhaust a movement.* Winchester, UK: Zero Books.

Felski, R. (2008). *Uses of literature.* Malden, MA: Wiley-Blackwell.

Felski, R. (2015). *The limits of critique.* Chicago: University of Chicago Press.

Finch, A. (1993). *The ghost of meter: Culture and prosody in American free verse.* Ann Arbor: University of Michigan Press.

Foust, G. (2010). Teaching John Ashbery. In J. M. Wilkinson (Ed.), *Poets on teaching: A sourcebook* (pp. 102–104). Iowa City: University of Iowa Press.

Garvin, R. T. (2013). Researching Chinese history and culture through poetry writing in an EFL composition class. *L2 Journal, 5*(1), 76–94.

Guillevic, E. (2010). *Geometries.* (R. Sieburth, Trans.). Brooklyn, NY: Ugly Duckling Presse.

Hanauer, D. (2010). *Poetry as research: Exploring second language poetry writing.* Amsterdam: John Benjamins.

Hanauer, D. (2011). Meaningful literacy: Writing poetry in the language classroom. *Language Teaching, 45*(1), 105–115.

Hanauer, D. (2014). Appreciating the beauty of second language poetry writing. In D. Disney (Ed.), *Exploring second language creative writing: Beyond Babel* (pp. 11–22). Amsterdam: John Benjamins.

Hauer, L. M. (2017). Evaluating second language student poetry: A study of instructors. *Journal of Literature in Language Teaching*, 6(1), 7–20.

Hinton, D. (Trans.). (1993). *Selected poems of T'ao Ch'ien*. Port Townsend, WA: Copper Canyon Press.

Katz, A. (2015). *Exercises in criticism: The theory and practice of literary constraint. Louis Bury* [Book Review]. *Double Helix*, 3, 1–3.

Lescure, J. (1998) Brief History of the Oulipo. In Motte, W. F. (Trans. and Ed.). *Oulipo: A primer of potential literature* (pp. 32–39). Normal, IL: Dalkey Archive Press.

Levin Becker, D. (2012). *Many subtle channels: In praise of potential literature*. Cambridge, MA: Harvard University Press.

Liao, F. Y. (2016). Identities in an ESL poetry book: A case study of one Chinese student. *Journal of Literature in Language Teaching*, 5(1), 46–61.

Matthews, H., & Brotchie, A. (Eds.). (1998). *Oulipo compendium*. London: Atlas Press.

Merrill, J. (2001). Self-portrait in Tyvek™ windbreaker. In J.D. McClatchy & S. Yenser (Eds.), *Collected Poems* (pp. 669–673). New York: Alfred A. Knopf.

Nufer, D. (2004). *Never Again*. New York: Black Square Editions.

Perec, G. (1969/2008). *Void*. New York: Vintage. (Original work published 1969)

Perloff, M. (2006, Spring). "Creative writing" among the disciplines. *MLA Newsletter* (President's Column), 38(1), 3–4.

Porter, L. (2018, 11 July). Mapped: The world's most—and least—crowded countries. *The Telegraph*. Retrieved from https://www.telegraph.co.uk/travel/maps-and-graphics/The-worlds-least-densely-populated-countries/

Poucel, J. (2012). Oulipo. In R. Green, S. Cushman, & C. Cavanagh (Eds.), *The Princeton encyclopedia of poetry and poetics* (4th ed., pp. 987–988). Princeton, NJ: Princeton University Press. Retrieved from https://login.lib-ezproxy.hkbu.edu.hk/login?qurl=https%3A%2F%2Fsearch.credoreference.com%2Fcontent%2Fentry%2Fprpoetry%2Foulipo%2F0%3FinstitutionId%3D6521

Robinson, M. (2017, 9 November). What are we doing here? *The New York Review of Books*. Retrieved January 5 2018, from http://www.nybooks.com/articles/2017/11/09/what-are-we-doing-here/

Saiidi, U (2017, 9 April). Here's why Hong Kong housing is so expensive. *CNBC*. Retrieved from https://www.cnbc.com/2017/04/09/heres-why-hong-kong-housing-is-so-expensive.html

Shklovsky, V. (1917/1965). Art as technique. In L. T. Lemon & M. J. Reis (Eds. & Trans.), *Russian formalist criticism: Four essays, second edition* (pp. 3–24). Lincoln: University of Nebraska Press. (Original work published 1917)

Sorrentino, G. (1999). *Gold fools*. Los Angeles: Green Integer.

Spahr, J. & Young, S. (2007). "& and" and foulipo. In C. Wertheim & M. Viegener (Eds.), *The /n/oulipian analects* (no page). Los Angeles, CA: Les Figues Press.

Stafford, W. (1970/1982). *A way of writing*. In D. Hall (Ed.), *Claims for poetry*. Ann Arbor: University of Michigan Press. (Original work publishd in 1970).

Stein, G. (1993/1990). *The autobiography of Alice B. Toklas*. New York: Vintage. (Original work published 1933)

Taylor, A. (2017, May 16). The "Coffin Homes" of Hong Kong. *The Atlantic*. Retrieved from https://www.theatlantic.com/photo/2017/05/the-coffin-homes-of-hong-kong/526881/

Wardrip-Fruin, N., & Montfort, N. (Eds.). (2003). *The new media reader*. Cambridge: MIT Press.

White, H. (1995). An interview with James Merrill. *Ploughshares*, 21(4), 190–195. Retrieved from http://www.jstor.org/stable/40354686

Williams, N. (2015). *Imitations of the self: Jiang Yan and Chinese poetics*. London: Brill.

Williams, N. (2019). Personal communication, 11 March.

Wong, W. Y. (2015). *My brother: An imitation of André Breton's Free Union*. Retrieved from HKBU Heritage: http://heritage.lib.hkbu.edu.hk/view.php?id=11075

Ye, J. (2016, 15 November). Dream of owning a home is over for most young Hong Kong people. *South China Morning Post*. Retrieved from https://www.scmp.com/

Yeung, K. S. E. (2015). *I remember*. Retrieved from HKBU Heritage: http://heritage.lib.hkbu.edu.hk/view.php?id=11073

Yiu, P., & McIntyre, S. (2017, 27 June). Hong Kong wealth gap at its widest in decades as handover anniversary nears. *Reuters*. Retrieved from https://www.reuters.com/

3 Trans-contemporary word culture

Late antique cento, twentieth century cut-up, and craft culture in the Canadian rockies

Stephanie Laine Hamilton

Introduction

Cut-up and *cento* are temporally distinct genres of pastiche literature that were traditionally dismissed as 'unintelligible' or as 'mere amusements' (Lydenberg 1987: 55; Smolak 1979: 29–49).[1] Several recent academic works focusing on the philological, structural, and (more so in the case of cut-up) poststructural aspects of these two genres offer hybrid interpretations. Due to similarities between these genres in method and form, synthesizing existing theoretical and cultural frameworks across disciplines allows for further understanding of Late Antique cento.[2] Respective contemporary cultures inform the author, the audience, and the work/text they create and share in common. History basks in the unknowable infiniteness omnipresent in contemporary literary theory, especially when the evidence is limited, as it often is when considering the ancient world. History can only be *an* interpretation—indefinite particle. So, the goal here is entirely viable: to gain *an* interpretation of uncertain aspects of ancient literary culture based on the comparative analyses of method, authorship, and reception of distinct (but surprisingly similar) types of hybrid poetry—Late Antique cento and mid-twentieth-century cut-up.

How is the study of hybrid poetry useful to classical studies? Hybrid poetic examples from the past prove to deconstruct more traditional understandings of academic disciplines (like classics) through comparative and poststructural approaches—work with and within these hybrid genres related to the classical world affects broader scholarship trends. Note that this was not at all the case when I started collecting the resources that would become this article almost a decade ago. In my work as an analytic autoethnographer in North America's heritage industry, found poems are created from the tidbits collected in the archives and from the contributions of tour-participants, creating a feedback loop that results in a variety of cogent hybrid heritage narratives. Cento and cut-up disrupted understood literary systems in their respective periods. Today, redefined hybrid historical praxes can function to represent dynamic and active voices from both the past and the present, resulting in hybrid, heritage-forward experiential forms that affect an audience.

This chapter serves as the perfect example of hybrid pedagogy in practice, as demonstrated by the pastiche way this piece came together over the better part of ten years. Here we will consider the comparative affect pastiche hybrid genres have on audiences across a wide time frame—considered here are cento, cut-up, and more general hybrid historical praxes today. The influence of hybrid poetic methodology is pervasive—it extends from the ancient world to the present day, reaching beyond poststructural comparative analysis of past forms to daily heritage tourist experiences in Canadian national parks and historic sites. The types of work I predominantly engage with interweaves all source materials together—not just the people, but also the words and the objects that remain from the past. Ignored historic artifacts become the found pearls around which hybrid poetic narratives are built. What was *once known* becomes *unknown* only to be reconfigured into a *new known*. Method, authorship, and reception of the two past hybrid poetic forms (cento and cut-up) will be examined before considering how contemporary applications of similar hybrid poetic methods can result in accessible heritage experiences in the Canadian Rocky Mountains today.

Parallel method

Pastiche literary forms are characterized by extreme intertextuality. Cut-up and cento are no exception. The cut-up method is exemplified perhaps most famously by William S. Burroughs's literary work through the 1960s and 1970s. Pages of physical source-works (largely linear narrative texts including newspaper articles, creative works, known works, unknown works, political speeches, and, later, other aural media) are literally cut up into sections with razor blades or scissors. The sections are rearranged and retyped resulting in an alternate physical text. Cut-up technique is deliberate in its method, but ultimately, and perhaps unavoidably, aleatory as a result. The cut-up method was accidently discovered by visual artist Brion Gysin at the Beat Hotel in Paris in 1959. Gysin shared the method with his roommate William S. Burroughs. The latter explains, 'Take a page. ... Cut down the middle and cross the middle. ... Rearrange the sections. ... You have a new page. Sometimes it says much the same thing. Sometimes something quite different' (Burroughs & Gysin 1978: 2). The method applied in the creation of cento by various authors through the Imperial and Late Antique periods of Roman Antiquity (first to sixth centuries CE) functions along lines that are surprisingly similar to those of twentieth-century cut-ups.

Cento derives from the Latin for 'patchwork' (*cento, -onis*, m.). Cento is a poetic sequence made up of recognizable shorter sections from one or more existing poems. Long-established and well-known Latin and Greek source-works (predominantly Virgil and Homer) were cut line by line down the middle (*caesura*), recomposed, and retransmitted—as alternate 'texts' expressing alternative themes. Cento was less random in method and intent than cut-up, especially since the results tended to be specifically guided by topic (McGill 2005: 119–153). The themes explored in surviving cento include 'mythological inquiry' (i.e. Mavortius's *Iudicum Paradis*), 'parody of what's trivial' (i.e. *de Alea*, author unknown), and 'what's wittily obscene' (i.e. Luxorius's *Epithalaminium Fridi*). As in the comparatively belated case of Burroughs, we have several examples of cento authors describing the process in their prefatory notes. Ausonius of Bordeaux tells us, 'The game is to harmonize different meanings, to make pieces arbitrarily connected seem naturally related, to prevent the widely disparate from proclaiming the violence by which they were joined together' (*Cento Nuptialis*, XVII; Ausonius 1919). Despite similarities, centonian method is more deliberate than that of cut-up. Where cut-up celebrates in obvious juxtapositions contained within the crammed lines, cento focuses on projection of seamless synthesis between disparate poetic units.

There is a further distinction between these methodologically similar hybrid poetic genres. Cut-up makes use of physical source materials manipulated in a physical sense by blade. With cento, however, source materials were not physical: they were for the most part constructed of works committed to memory. Cento was consistently mnemonic, and often spontaneous, in its composition. Early on, cento was a source of impromptu aural performance practiced at dinner parties and other elite social events. Cento is (at least partially) an aspect of residual orality, part of a performance tradition meant to be heard, not read. Low overall literacy rates in Roman antiquity would have contributed to a very oral and visual culture in the greater Roman world. Usher (1998: 157) cites Ong's work in consideration of residual orality having a pronounced impact on composition of cento (Ong 1982: 31–77). It just so happens, nevertheless, that some examples of cento were preserved for posterity in print. As one expects when considering the cultural spaces of the ancient world, we have a limited amount of physical source materials to consider in the literary case of cento: approximately two thousand lines. Cut-ups, by contrast, fall into a more physical, literary tradition that is meant to be read, and we still have accessible copies of the full works. Regardless of these differences, I consider both genres and their significations specifically in their final/static written forms.[3]

Parallel authorship

In the case of both cut-up and cento, known authorship is dominated by educated individuals of relatively well-known and/or socially mobile statuses. The most well-known popularizer of the cut-up method is William S. Burroughs, an iconoclastic icon who demands little in the way of formal introduction (Baker 2010; Miles 2015; Murphy 1997; Sobieszek 1996). Descended from a prominent Missouri family, Burroughs obtained his BA in English literature from Harvard in 1936. He subsequently pursued sporadic formal graduate work in medicine (Vienna, 1936–1937), psychology (Columbia and Harvard, both 1938), and Mayan archaeology (Harvard, 1938–1940).[4] A lifelong student, Burroughs traveled a great deal, and he conducted many detailed and informal studies in areas including anthropology, religion, semiotics, drug culture, and other subcultural groups that prob-lematized established hegemonic systems of control. The Burroughs cut-up period is classified in variable ways. Yet it is endemic of the bulk of his work through the 1960s and 1970s—*Naked Lunch* (1959/1992), *The Soft Machine* (1961/1992), *The Ticket That Exploded* (1962/1992), *Nova Express* (1964/1992s), *Minutes to Go* (1968), *Exterminator!* (1966/1973), and *The Third Mind* (1978).[5]

Alternatively, unknowsn authorship characterizes many partial examples of cento from Late Antiquity. However, there are several complete cento of known authorship that were penned by learned Romans.[6] Two complete, Christian-topic cento have been studied more intensively than the others, one Latin (Proba's *Cento Probae*, ca. 320–380 CE) and one Greek (Eudo-cia's *Homerocentra*, post-439 CE). Both were authored by prominent Late Antique women, which in and of itself is unique to ancient literary survival trends. Proba was the wife of a prominent Roman statesman in the era of Julian the Apostate (ca. mid-300s CE). Eudocia was a fifth-century Byz-antine empress. Due to the station and background of these women, it is expected that both were highly educated. Cento of known and educated authorship also includes Ausonius of Bordeaux (grammarian, statesman, and advisor to emperors Valentian I and Gratian, ca. fourth century CE) and Hosidius Geta (student of grammarian and rhetorician, Quintillian, ca. third century CE). Although prefatory (and periphatory) remarks were far less numerous than in the case of Burroughs, the ancient remarks made by known and unknown authors of cento act much like readily available Bur-roughs interviews and correspondence on cut-up. They provide clues as to method and purpose, regardless of whether the works they composed were sanctioned by those who received them.

Parallel reception

Hybrid literary forms ranged widely in their perceived quality and were often cast aside as hard to read or straight-up ridiculous by contemporary *and* future audiences, not to mention by those composing them. Upon the accidental discovery of cut-ups in Paris, Gysin and Burroughs were struck by the amusing results of these literary experiments. Fifteen hundred years prior, slightly southwest of what is now Paris, Ausonius of Bordeaux relates a notion similar to Gysin's in the preface to *A Nuptial Cento*, where he states that the composition of cento is 'a slight work, trifling and worthless' (XVII; Ausonius 1919). The overall whimsy seen early with each genre, however, shifts: we have the formulaic application of the cut-up method by Burroughs; we have that of cento by early Christian writers, like Proba. The results of these early experiments are implemented with a rigor seldom rec-ognized by near-contemporaries of these selfsame authors. Christian cento, regardless of perceived quality, enjoyed a fair degree of popularity in their socially immediate milieus (Usher 1998).[7] As Christian doctrine and prac-tices were increasingly standardized over the fifth and sixth centuries CE, positive reception to cento declined exponentially. Christian cento penned by the likes of Proba were ultimately dismissed by later Christian hegemons and influential historical chroniclers—such as Jerome (ca. fourth century CE), Pope Gelasius (ca. fifth century CE), and Isiodorus (ca. sixth century CE). Viewed as little more than experimental forms of literary amusement, there was no serious academic scrutiny of either hybrid poetic genre until the 1980s.

The last thirty-five years has seen a dramatic increase in academic interest in cut-up and cento. In 1987, Robin Lydenberg set out to restore Burroughs's cut-up experiments to their central role within the icon's literary canon. Since Lydenberg (1987) demonstrated how 'these narratives which many critics have dismissed as unreadable offer new ways of reading and thinking' (55), increased attention continues to be paid to the role of the hybrid literary genre of cut-ups in broader twentieth-century literary composition and culture. Similarly, the long-standing prejudices that dominated 'traditional' classical studies through most of the modern and postmodern eras affect perceptions of cento. Examples of cento are traditionally 'treated at best with amused tolerance, and at worst with angry distain' in academic scholarship (Green 1995: 551). Each form was simply considered 'low' from the get-go and consequently dismissed.[8] Burroughs's most prolific cut-up period sees his experimental works systematically attacked by American censors and feminist critics alike. Many second-wave feminists dismissed Burroughs as a misogynist, where the same feminisms simultaneously fueled a serious and renewed interest in studying Late Antique cento, resulting in translation, critical apparatus, and analysis of specific cento appearing through the 1980s and 1990s (Clark & Hatch 1981; Usher 1998; Wilson-Kastner 1981). This relation is due to instances of known female authorship of Christian cento. Much of that academic work stems from pluralistic second-wave feminist foci on the rediscovery of women in the past, the politics of female authorship, and literary representations of women. These aspects influence the current treatise, but here we are concerned more with third-wave feminist thrusts accentuating deconstructions of power relations beyond authorship to the text's cultural stimuli and to language itself. Studies focus primarily on formal aspects of the genre and historical authorship of cento, and these aspects inform broader implications in terms of Roman literary culture—particularly how the early church understood and employed non-Christian literature in Christian texts. Certainly, cento has been identified as a manifestation of the interplay between ancient Christianity and classical culture. But what resonates from the texts themselves within their respective ancient contexts?

Due to the obvious gap in temporal proximity, no one-to-one ratio can be assumed in the linking of these genres. The relationship between the execution of these experimental hybrid poetic forms and the dissemination of these forms within dominant cultural and semiotic systems merits further consideration. Due to a recent rash of academic literature on both cut-up and cento, the time is ripe to consider what the application of method and form can tell us about the cultural and literary contexts within which each hybrid form counterculturally functions. This exploration is not necessarily concerned with any formalist, close reading of the specific works, as much work has been done on formal close reading for themes, authorship, and philology (Ehrling 2011; Green 1997; McGill 2005; Sivan 1993; Usher, 1998). This exploration is concerned with the overall implementation of the methods themselves and what the results convey more broadly about cultural literary spaces and hybrid poetic reception in the past.

Method revisited

Central to the method of both cut-up and cento is the deliberate and systematic dismantling of existing source materials to re-compose alternative narratives. Burroughs has called himself a literary plagiarist; however, cut-ups were not the only twentieth-century literary or artistic experiments that transgressed broadly held copyright conventions. In light of cut-up's method, how could this be anything otherwise, especially since Burroughs himself states that 'A writer does not own words any more than a painter owns colors. So let's dispense of this originality fetish ... look, listen, transcribe and forget about being original' (Lydenberg 1987: 49). Cento as a practice established in Late Antiquity cannot really be subjected to copyright legalities, at least not as we've understood them since the late 1800s (McCutcheon 2012: 71). Regardless, any concept of 'plagiarism' was definitely unknown to Roman thought. In fact, Roman literary culture is rife with heavy-handed borrowing from existing works and texts, or what contemporary academic sensibility might consider 'copyrighted material.'[9] That said, we must consider what is being reproduced alongside the methods of reproduction in order to consider what they represent to the authors and their respective audiences.

According to Barthes's definition in "From Work to Text," the canonical works of the ancient world simultaneously functioned as texts. If the *work* is concrete, what is held in the hand (or in the book), then the *text* (better thought of as a methodological field) can be held only through active discourse. It is through *text* that interpretations and understandings proliferate (Barthes 1971/1979: 1:2 & 3:1; cf. Eco 1967/1989: 73). The source materials used in the production of cento are works *and* texts simultaneously. These are thereby perpetually available for reinterpretation. The texts of Virgil and Homer are part of the 'literary' canon in which every elite Roman man, woman, and child was well-versed via years of formal education. A part of formal education focused on the deliberate manipulation of these canonical texts toward variable rhetorical and didactic ends (Kaster 1988). For example, these texts were used to develop the oratory tools to draft political speeches and develop legal reasoning. These associational blocks, spawned by recognized word groupings from the 'textual' canon, were (and still are) extremely powerful when viably manipulated. Recognized word groupings delivered an easily identifiable charge by way of associational thinking. Canonical texts were widely and freely utilized, manipulated, and disseminated—cento's manipulation of associational blocks being one example of 'how.' This contributed to the continuous transmission and ultimate survival of these works as preserved in communal memory *and* in written form.

Some of Burroughs's source materials for cut-ups could also be considered canonical in nature. Burroughs tells us he makes use of Rimbaud, Shakespeare, Joyce, Kafka, Eliot, Conrad, Greene, Genet, Kerouac, and 'someone named Jack Sterne' in *Nova Express* (Knickerbocker 1965: 27–29). The result of cut-up and cento 'could be interpreted as being somewhat sacrilegious in its total disregard for the literary canon' (Robinson 2006: 75). We might too take into account how these attendant texts expressed revelations on topics ranging from the simple and/or mundane to the uncomfortable and/or erotic. Regardless of perceived quality, it is the 'diversity of subjects [that] fostered the notion that the original source material had a universal character.'[10] This is an important point of connection over both genres.

The general reception of Virgil and other canonical source materials in Late Antiquity has been one of the questions central to classical studies of cento. It's become best practice to consider the source materials of cento, and Virgil in particular, as types of 'open work' that represent a literal 'field of possibilities' in active reception by an audience intimately acquainted with the traditional words and agendas of Virgil—Augustan or otherwise (Ehrling 2011; McGill 2005; Pelttari 2015). This is not unlike Barthes's conception of the nature of texts. In the centonian context, Virgil's work, McGill explains, becomes a sort of 'master poem' containing seeds of an infinite number of other poems (2005). Concerning cut-up, Burroughs himself tells us, 'Any narrative passage or any passage, say, of poetic images is subject to any number of variations, all of which may be interesting and valid in their own right' (Miles 2002: 115).

This idea extends to cento, in that canonical texts contain and reveal alternative interpretations as systems themselves, as well as aspects of composition that are distinctive features resonating through broader Roman Late Antique literary culture (McGill 2002: 128; Pelttari 2015: 8, 108).

The manipulation of source texts via the cut-up and cento method has the capacity, through fragmented reproduction, to reveal a (perhaps) diminished but (undeniably) reactivated 'aura' stemming from originary works/texts. According to Benjamin, 'One might generalize by saying the technique of reproduction detaches the reproduced object from the domain of tradition. Making reproductions substitutes a plurality of copies for a unique existence.' These processes lead to a tremendous shattering of tradition which is the obverse of the contemporary crisis and renewal of mankind (Benjamin 1936/2006: 3). Pelttari (2015) suggests the extent of the interconnection within hybrid poetic works in Late Antiquity was not only manipulated by the author but also variably (re)interpreted by the audience/reader. Consider the traditional, philological focus on exactly this in standard treatments of cento. For a long time, Classicists were obsessed with what came from where (read: what was 'copied' from whom), especially as it relates the 'copying' nature of Roman from Greek originals. This trend is not unique to obviously hybrid forms like cento, but it extends to most forms of ancient literature (cf. Barthes 1971/1979; Benjamin 1936/2006; Bloom 1973). The overall idea pertaining to cut-up *and* cento is that radical literary experiments can push the notions identified from understood language systems beyond their recognized limits of representation, consequently opening the texts and their embedded control systems and associational truths to radical reconfigurations (Usher 1998: 57–77; Land 2005: 450; Pelttari 2015: 160).

All texts are intertextual by nature. All language and literary systems function to communicate through continual deconstruction and reconstruction of established segments and pieces. Extreme methods of intertextuality are synonymous with the avant-garde, typically noted from the Dadaist and surrealist movements of the 1920s and 1930s to present twenty-first-century clashes between print and digital media. Burroughs's cut-up method has been labeled 'one of the most radical techniques of the twentieth century' (Robinson 2006: 76; Land 2005: 450). A sentiment pertaining equally to cento, which has been called a 'radical form of segmentation' and 'an extreme case of intertextuality' (Albu 2011: para. 12). Cento, most specifically due to its application in method, was a Late Antique reification of avant-garde or experimental literature. As such, it was not mainstream. Cento functioned within the liminal space it created by virtue of its existence—these were marginalized opinions and realities from outside the mainstream being broadcasted (back) toward the center. Burroughs tells us that 'cut-ups are for everyone,' but as Punday asks, 'is the point of such 'intermedia' works to challenge categories, or to escape them?' In this case, regarding production as well as consumption, it is relevant either way (Burroughs & Gysin 1978: 31; Punday 2007: 14). The 'word as virus' claim is central to Burroughs's theory of language and control systems. The idea is that reality was and is controlled by hidden and intrinsic systems. According to the (in)famous iconoclast, the aim of the word was to reproduce itself whether it be 'in' or 'out' of its established context—regardless of composition.

Authorship revisited

Known authors of both cento and cut-up could be thought of as intellectuals. Burroughs can, in the antique sense of the word, be described as a polymath. The versatile nature of his knowledge base informs what he gleans from his alternative, cut-up narratives; but what his educated background tells us about the broader application and context of the cut-up form is generally understood as inconsequential. Alternatively, the decidedly *educated* vantage point from which we can consider known authors of Latin/Greek and/or Pagan/Christian cento tells us about the form and the function of Late Antique cento. The role that Virgil and other canonical authors played in Imperial and Late Antique Roman education cannot be overstated. One would have to be intensely familiar with Virgil, or any author, to slice the well-known lines into units only to alternately recompile them to tell a different topical story—in most cases from memory, and sometimes in front of a live audience. Cento can be placed squarely within a broader Roman performance culture as well as the more obvious areas of literary, rhetorical, and compositional culture. This experimental literary/poetic exercise cannot be practiced without a degree of formal education, which was substantially (but not solely) reserved for elite members of Roman society. Education was a viable way for those of variable and/or inferior social statuses (such as, the low-born or female) to obtain variable degrees of social mobility and perceived 'acceptableness.'

Petronius is a prime example of social mobility as gained through education in the Roman world. An early example of Virgilian cento was penned by the extremely ambitious Petronius (also a noted favorite satirist of Burroughs) who is described by his near-contemporary Tacitus (ca. second century CE) as a hedonistic, amoral, and highly witty character (Mikriammos 1984; Tacitus [1937] 16: 18–19). Petronius gained the favor of the notoriously fickle and lowly-curious emperor Nero. Not only was Petronius appointed governor of Bithynia, but he also became Nero's stylist (*arbiter elegantiae*) and penned the parodic novel *Satyricon*, which contains a brief example of Virgilian cento where Enclopius speaks harsh words to his (in this case flaccid) *mentula* (Latin for penis or 'cock') after a tryst gone awry (Petronius 138: 1; Petronius & Seneca 2020). Imperial favor, nonetheless, could be a double-edged sword under the Julio-Claudians: in 66 CE, Petronius was ordered by Nero to take his own life. Petronius did so in grand fashion by binding and reopening arterial wounds thus bleeding himself out slowly over the course of a party he planned himself. Regardless, Petronius is a notable example of extreme social mobility. In Roman society, applications of education *can* function to bring those from the perceived margins of broader Roman society into its mainstream. However, social mobility among educated men was not the only instance where this kind of perceived acceptability was achieved through formal education and mastery with words.

Women of certain classes were expected to be formally educated. Proba's aristocratic family background firmly places her in this realm of expectation. Despite non-universal access to traditional education, Roman women of the time who attained said education were *not* free to use it in the same manner as men. This extended well beyond obvious, inappropriate 'feminine' applications of their education in public life, and certainly affected the types of writing women could acceptably engage in and disseminate. For example, it was not considered acceptable for women to write recognizable historical literature, which was increasingly what cento represented whilst Christian faith and doctrine gained broader acceptance over the Later Imperial and Late Antique periods. Christian female authors took an early interest in composing cento. It was likely deemed suitable for educated women to engage cento in appropriate, traditional pagan/non-Christian contexts in the name of banal social amusements. The private manipulation of the genre over the fourth, fifth, and sixth centuries CE increasingly engaged female authors to espouse Christian concepts and agendas.

The role of the formal education system is identified as a factor influencing the authors themselves as well as the method and form of cento. Yet there is also speculation that education may too have played a role concerning the function of the genre as a didactic tool in light of female, Christian authorship. Scholarship suggests that cento may have played a role in the educational system itself. The second to fifth centuries CE was a time of intense theological, social, and cultural upheaval and schism, exemplified by the Imperial return to paganism under Julian a generation or so following Constantine's so-called 'conversion of the empire' to Christianity.[11] This return affected Roman educational structure by expulsion of all things Christian (including teachers) from the classroom by Imperial mandate in 362 CE. Adult basic catechesis, as one expects, continued to grow among segments of society, but *not* among Roman children who were educated by the suddenly pagan state, thereby leaving alternate religious Christian learning to be acquired at home. Aspects of formal education were supplemented at home by caregivers, which left the specifics as to 'what' largely to feminine discretion. Cento may have functioned through the period parallel to the female, Christian authorship as a means by which to go about a kind of 'traditional' evangelization of the next generation. Cento represents a deliberate tool by which to review aspects of the classic curricula while providing introductions in matters of Christian history and faith—it simultaneously supplied aspects of knowledge from the recognized canon by way of its manipulations from the margins.

The earliest of early Christian poetry from Late Antiquity, as represented by cento, tended toward the experimental. And the popular influence of Proba's cento was palpable. This can be discerned by the appearance of later imitations, subsequent quotations, *and* polemics against the genre—for example, Damasus (fourth century CE), Paulinus (mid-fourth century CE), and Jerome (fourth century CE). On the one hand, it is clear that it was acceptable for women to engage in a highly experimental (and generally dismissed) early subgenre of hybrid Christian poetry. On the other hand, it is also clear from available evidence that as the competence of Christian poets grew, and as Christian tastes developed more conceptually rigid sophistications, female authorship of such works was promptly sent back to the margins—to the zone of the unacceptable, according to shifting mainstream sensibilities. Authorship aside, it is the language and texts gained through formal education that are manipulated in hybrid forms like cento. McGill notes that 'cento appears on the fringes of the canon and curricula, where it resides amid other literary curiosities' (2002: 143), which is precisely from whence cento should be considered. Already-understood texts become viable secondary texts in their own right when manipulated and interpreted by persons speaking (and listening) from the margins about a faith system in the peripheries.

Reception revisited

Cut-up and cento are de facto collaborative literary forms. Both genres are collaborative in terms of authorship: source materials are often (or, in the case of cento, always) composed by an author separate from that of the secondarily orchestrated hybrid result. Beyond the proposed educational function of cento in Late Antiquity, it is hard to gauge the precise nature of collaboration with respect to the audience from an entertainment or performance perspective. In the case of cut-up and cento, we know that some contemporaries were quick to dismiss the forms as too amusing or too difficult. After all, Burroughs's cut-up work tends toward a type of pastiche reception that can alienate rather than empower his readership; similar sentiments likely affected cento's Late Antique reception as well. Regardless of potential variation in background, status, and understanding of the audience (collectively or individually), the texts of Virgil and Homer certainly functioned as language systems in their own right. Orally and literally, the texts contain familiar power structures that are viably manipulated to express alternative messages, as seen through their systematic manipulation in a hybrid poetic form like cento.

Early Christian scholarship suggests that Late Antique Christians essentially 'hijacked the powerful heritage [of traditional Roman/Pagan culture] and turned it to their own ends.' In fact, all concerns of fourth-century Roman Christianities (plural) seemed to focus on 'merging the value systems of two worlds' (Usher 1998: 329). It is generally accepted that cento may be read as a reconciliation of classical and biblical culture, each interpreted in terms of the other (Albu 2011: para. 9; Usher 1998: 329). Usher borrows Brecht's concept of 'defamiliarization' to contextualize the ultimate intent of cento: to deprive the ruling system of language of 'any self-evident, familiar, or obvious quality to produce instead astonishment or curiosity about' a decidedly different topic by way of manipulating already-established associational blocks (Usher 1998: 13; cf. Ong 1982: 34–54). It is likely that precisely because the themes of Virgil are so well-known, formulaic, and copious (as defined through rhetoric as 'abundant'[12]) that they could make clear to a subject what was illuminated as 'different' through manipulated tellings, non-referential allusion, juxtaposed allusion, and apposed allusion (cf. Pelttari 2015: 131–143). Traditional narratives increasingly function(ed) through the hybrid Late Antique form of cento so as to recontextualize classical concepts in order to convey decidedly different readings, particularly in later incarnations, as these relate to the emerging matters of a 'new' faith. Despite contemporary Western saturation in all things archetypally Christian, over the first 300 or so years of the common era, Christianities functioned in vying and multiple forms from the fringes and margins of Roman society in a variety of social and cultural ways. Through the likes of Virgil, who was (perhaps) 'inspired by the source of all truths' coupled with 'new' forms of representation, the reading of mainstream classical literature came to speak for the still-marginal Christ through alternative and experimental forms, and cento perhaps most notably (Meconi 2004: 112).

Despite cento composition prior to the articulation of the concept, the Derridean articulation of 'play' (or the liminal spaces that *play* creates) is alive and well in the experimental forms of cut-up and cento. Derrida (1967a/1978) suggests that *play* is a field of infinite substitutions in the closure of a finite ensemble. Liminal spaces exist in the fringes and margins of what can be identified as one thing or another. Literary pastiche and hybrid forms create their own liminal spaces: the form is less about dialectic oppositions than what comes from the space that exists between said oppositions. Language finds room to *play* at and in its points of articulation, like how the joints in one's hand allow fingers independent movements from the wrist and the arm (i.e. culture/heritage). Both cut-up and cento are identified as experimental, but what did their *play* really say to their audiences?

Experimental forms speak from the margins (in terms of authorship and content) and continue to speak to the margins until they are adopted by what is considered the mainstream, where established source materials meet their new canonical forms. As Land suggests, 'it is fairly obvious that language is dependent upon its recognition by others,' and through this recognition, language functions to define and therefore establish both dynamic and static identities (Land 2005: 455). In the case of cento, traditional and accepted Roman literature is determined by Christians in order to voice alternate Christian agendas. The expanded aura that resonates from cut-up and cento reveals variable levels of hostility against source materials themselves—specifically, how and what cento encoded as response to established power and governing language structures.

Systems of accepted power and control are reflected through language and its usage. Performativity, or the reiterative power of discourse to produce the phenomena that it regulates and constrains, doesn't just affect one's constructed identity. Social constructions shaping performative identities are reflected through the whole of language (Butler 1990, 1997). To a certain extent, who's calling who what, in a word, makes it so. Furthermore, according to Korzybski, one of the early fathers of semiotics who had a profound influence on Burroughs, 'either/or' distinctions do not exist and are better replaced with a 'both/and' classification; but, as Robinson suggests, this is seldom seen where language equals control. Those who control the language have the capacity to write history, which has a direct bearing on the future (Robinson 2006: 2). Cut-up and cento both attempt to restructure established (or legitimate) systems of power and control through the systematic deconstruction of established language systems already understood by their audiences. The language system manipulated through cento (based on whole canonical source materials, like Virgil) is in many ways more abstract than that manipulated by Burroughs and his cut-ups (i.e. language itself). They are both unavoidably, and methodologically, subversive by way of their emerging from/in the liminal spaces they created. This is certainly the case with cut-up, in its attempt to break down language's apparent coherence. If cento manipulated a system of language that entrenched its meaning most specifically through perceived traditional Roman associations, then the manipulation of these particular systems of power to express alternate Christian 'moral' and historical concerns could be seen as radical in intent. The language systems adopted may be different, but the results are surprisingly similar. Cut-up and cento function as instruments of a larger goal—that of disrupting the conventional narrative structures responsible for the established illusions (Benjamin 1936/2006; Dolan 1991: 537).

Despite perceived degrees of hostility against established power structures in cut-up and cento, the power intrinsic to the source texts on account of their entrenched and established language systems continues to emanate from the bastardized texts that result, regardless of whether the outcome was deliberate (cento) or aleatory (cut-up). Cut-up did not overly concern itself with notions of synthesis and the viability of manipulations—the cut-up method is an overstated subversive form. Cento, conversely, can be viewed as rooted in the synthesis of concepts and viable manipulation of what was understood as acceptable. Cento functioned in a more covert or subtextually subversive manner in order to affect the status quo from a place that existed, at the time, outside of it. It is clear that both poetic forms, in today's critical terms, deconstruct textual authority: each exposes the extension of Saussure's arbitrariness of the sign by problematizing origin/authority and closure/totality (cf. Derrida 1967b/1997). Classical scholars have recognized and engaged in more formal studies of cento, a form particularly apt for scholarship about reception, experience, and audience engagement. I embark on and apply said hybrid historical praxes actively with students and heritage tourists in my resource and cultural development work in the Canadian Rockies.

Coda

What is the end product of hybrid literary forms like cento and cut-up? Is it some resultant narrative? Merely the combined pieces of the 'original' narratives? Both? Neither? Perhaps, all and none simultaneously, which would make them not what they were prior or subsequent to the application of any respective 'patchwork' method. Cento and cut-up do not fall into a neat category of literary classification; nor does twenty-first-century research and presentation of hybrid history and craft culture in the Canadian Rockies. I am a trained classicist and ancient historian who has also become an early-twentieth-century historian focusing on resource and cultural development in the Rocky Mountains of Western Canada. This transition over the last decade has resulted in the development of many on-site programs, museum exhibits, and roadside heritage signs across southern Alberta, as well as direct engagement annually with thousands of students and heritage tourists on the Alberta side of the Canadian Rocky Mountains in Crowsnest Pass-Castle region, Canmore-Kananaskis region, and Banff National Park.

Like cut-up and cento, hybrid historical praxes are deliberate and systematic in their dismantling of source materials (i.e. historical 'facts') so as to recompose decidedly different narratives for audiences to receive and engage with. The range of consulted source materials is vast and results in the usage of a wide variety of facilitation techniques—oral, mnemonic, visual, and kinesthetic. It is not typical for any type of historian, ancient or modern, to describe what they are doing in research and presentation as analytic autoethnography, but that is one way to describe what I am doing, if I can appropriate Pace (2012: 3). The 'social world' and the 'informants' under consideration in most instances are not only in the here and now but also in the past. In my experience, good hybrid history results from this interplay—giving talks and tours, doing archival research, and spending time in tourist-directed built-heritage spaces, like historical cemeteries, breweries, hotels, and residences.

What genre is 'popular history'? In this context and in my experience, popular history is the result of hybrid historical praxes, ones carefully calculated as experiments in curating mixed media for contemporary audiences. The author is much like the late antique compilers of *compendia* and *brevaria* in that not everything is selected for inclusion or transmission in every instance. The intent is to select information aimed to encourage an experience. An effective heritage story is told by stitching discrepant pieces together from a wide variety of sources, and by tailoring the hybrid result to specific audience requirements. Like cento and cut-up, the composition of popular history is characterized by intertexuality and can be delivered/presented/offered as creative non-fiction, expository narrative, experiential learning activity, service-learning outreach, oral narratives/interpretive talk, museum exhibitions, or self-guided activities/outreach. Hybrid historical praxes can result in multiple products, all providing value and/or quality-added incentive to heritage tourists who are looking to transcend the social world under investigation through broader hybrid generalizations based on how regional facts are put together and presented to them (Pace 2012: 5–6).

Cultural tourism consists of many different activities, interests, and spaces (Ommundsen 2005). 'Writing,' here, is creative from the perspective of collecting and manipulating facts. At the same time, hybrid historical praxes effectively involve intertwining, say, telling the tale of liquor legislation trends in Western Canada while simultaneously elaborating on the history of resource development and tourism in the Canadian Rocky Mountains and Banff National Park. This form of hybrid interacting is accomplished via the use of countless 'found materials,' including what remains of the heritage buildings that continue to function as tourist spaces in Canada's oldest and busiest mountain park at Banff. Cultural heritage tends to be linked to national heritage and national identity, especially in the case study of Banff National Park. Current popular research sells out tours and talks, as people generally don't mind a bit of booze while they explore the history of the towns and wilderness of the Canadian Rockies.

Much like cut-up and cento, good hybrid historical praxes result in projects and programs that are accessible because they use familiar structures to effectively tell alternative stories. My 'classrooms' in the library, in the museum, or on the street are not always traditional classrooms, and that informs how I perform my various roles as a researcher and pedagogue. The function of heritage tourism is at least partially didactic, and through focused storytelling aimed at daily public consumption, this is achieved in hybrid ways. Importantly, hybrid history is designed and developed to increase the accessibility of the heritage content—the content that is found in less easily accessible spaces, like archival and museum collections. In 2016, I published a hybrid heritage book about heritage pub culture, vernacular architecture, and the tangential history of the Crowsnest Pass; *Booze and Bars: A Brief History of Pub Culture in the Crowsnest Pass* resulted from my development and facilitation of a series of historic pub tours over more than five years. Based on primary source research, building tours, and heritage tourism promotion, the stories I collect and disseminate both orally and in writing go from oral, to written, to oral, and back again (several times over).

We already covered the orality and performance aspects related to ancient hybrid poetic genres (like cento), and working hybrid historical method continues to be similar in that the performance aspects come in the storytelling. Several people who know me well, who have read my book, have told me, 'I can hear you talking while I'm reading it.' This is definitely a result of 'tour-scripts' acting as, and influencing, early drafts for many sections of what over time became the finished book. I developed a series of *Booze and Bars* heritage tours for annual Crowsnest Pass Doors Open and Heritage Festivals (2010–present) that focus on the vernacular architecture embodied by Rocky Mountain hotels, as well as tours of these same, still-operational heritage buildings. Depending on the broader festival theme and whether it is a coach or walking tour, several stops are made in the various towns of the Crowsnest Pass to visit hotels and their pubs, have a drink, and talk about some hybrid regional heritage. To prepare beyond the archives and literature review, not only do I also organize tours with knowledgeable proprietors/ managers, but I also spend some time talking to staff and patronizing the pub.[13] The cross-pollination of information exchanged between sites and circumstances cannot be underestimated with hybrid historical praxes. From school programs to drop-in (or, specifically developed) tours, all of this interplay leant itself to the creation of the finished *Booze and Bars* manuscript. My book sounds like me, because I spent so much time talking and researching directly and indirectly related heritage topics focused within similar geographical/geological regions. One result of this is the first *Booze and Bars* book, and there will no doubt be another.

One of the venues in Blairmore, Crowsnest Pass that is a chapter focus in *Booze and Bars* (Hamilton 2016) is the Alberta Hotel, which was owned by Emilio Picariello when he was convicted and hanged for his role in the shooting death of Alberta Provincial Police Constable Stephen O. Lawson during the prohibition era of Alberta's history, ca. 1916–1923. I have told the story of Emilio Picariello (and/or associated Crowsnest Pass rum-running tales) hundreds of times in a wide variety of ways[14]—the focus ranging from law-less to legitimate, largely depending on my purposes (tour, program, event) or whether the result of 'spontaneous' heritage engagement while working on-site at Frank Slide Interpretive Centre or Leitch Collieries Provincial His-toric Site. Of course, I included Pic's story in *Booze and Bars* (2016) because he owned the Alberta Hotel, but I included only a certain amount focused on Emilio Picariello in all his 'notoriousness,' because I didn't want for this *one* story to overshadow *everything* else—and let me tell you, it easily can—and there are so many other great Crowsnest Pass stories to tell![15] It turns out Pic bought the Alberta Hotel from a guy named Fritz Sick—a home-town hero to a girl who grew up in the Canadian prairie counting the bun-nies on Pilsner beer labels. Sick would create a brewing empire that stretched from the prairies to the west coast and by the time he died was renowned in Canada and the United States for brewing, likewise renowned, Old Style Pilsner and Rainier beer. Sick became an honest-to-god beer baron when he found himself in a position to buy out several nearly bankrupt breweries in dire financial straits post-prohibition in western Canada in the 1920s—a process repeated by his son Emil in the American West through the 1930s when prohibition was being repealed there. It was this type of historical hap-penstance related to hotel proprietorship trends in the second quarter of the twentieth century in Alberta that lead to inclusion of brewery information in *Booze and Bars* (Hamilton 2016).

The plot continues to thicken post-publication because the resources keep revealing layers of early connections between Fritz Sick and Emilio Picariello. What I have uncovered continues to be at once perpetually fas-cinating and illusive. For example, in the Alberta Hotel basement today, just adjacent to where Fritz Sick brewed beer when he owned the build-ing, Picariello's supposed 'rum-running tunnels' are still visible. The tunnels purportedly led to the CPR Station kitty-corner across Main Street from the hotel; but, based on information brought to me by a heritage-minded Crowsnest Pass local who attends the tour every time it is offered, the jury should be out as to whether this is a reasonable conclusion to come to—the 'tunnels' could simply represent alternative 'storage solutions' at the Alberta Hotel, ca. 1910s. Regardless, Emilio Picariello's 'rum-running' is only one of a million great stories, best told *in situ*, on site, or within a specific her-itage resource.[16] Over-subscribed tours developed for the 2017 and 2019 Doors Open and Heritage Festivals in Crowsnest Pass, Alberta, visited not only the Alberta Hotel, but also Sick's Lethbridge Brewing and Malting Co. Bottle Works just down the street. (Note: Picariello was sole distributor of Lethbridge Brewing products in Crowsnest Pass into the 1920s.) The building functions today as a real estate office and retains many original char-acter defining elements.[17] The 2017 and 2019 Door Open events (coupled with a similarly themed talk focused on 'Pic + Sick' presented to the general public at the Galt Museum in nearby Lethbridge, Alberta, to supplement a

traveling exhibit about Emilio Picariello, ca. 2017) were perfect opportunities to gather new intel to shed light on current research initiatives. Many
of the early dealings between Pic and Sick seem to have existed at the edges
of early twentieth-century law, especially as prohibition became a 'reality' in
Alberta post-1916—Pic became increasingly lawless while Sick became more
law-abiding. By the time Pic was convicted and hanged in 1923, most everyone had already forgotten that the ever-upright Fritz Sick had, not that long
ago, been a known business associate of Canada's most notorious rum-run-
ner (arguably), Emilio Picariello. The result of this specific interplay between
people, place, and resultant 'pearls' (as per Benjamin)[18] will continue to be
curated through the hybrid heritage feedback loop until they are ready to
appear in a forthcoming 'popular history.'

According to Pace (2012: 5), researchers are often visible in their narratives (which presents as consistent across time) and analytic autoethnography often engages in dialogues with a range of information systems and
informants. My process often involves broad collaborations across disciplines; I regularly engage with varieties of tradespersons, scientists, exhibit
designers, brewers/distillers, GIS and information specialists, trails specialists, and archaeologists. It all informs the outcome, be it interpretive
signage in southern Alberta's heritage spaces or books and tours focusing
on the evolution of pub culture in the Canadian west. Historiography's
approach to the archive can range from inhibiting (Steedman 2002: xi) to
the means by which systems are (re)established (Foucault 1982; Nelson
2015: 3). Sometimes described as methodological or critical dead ends,
hybrid genres and praxes can fall in and out of favor. What is most telling is
that highly intertextual hybrid genres continue to be reified, as aforementioned vis-à-vis cento and cut-up, in experimental, and in many instances
experiential, forms.

Popular history and hybrid historical praxes are not 'new,' but they are
not really 'old' either. Moving around the pieces to better illustrate a point is
what all ilk of educators do on a daily basis—with every person they engage
with! We all know there are numerous ways to demonstrate or illustrate any
one concept, and that despite designed intent, people take away what they
will at the end of a class, book, or site visit. This applies whether we are
referring to cento, cut-up, or twenty-first-century heritage tourism. Popular
histories should be hybrid; Concise and visual, they can take many forms:
interpretive signage, museum exhibits, building tours, site tours, and print
materials. It's worth noting again that none of this is anything new. It seems
that we collectively forget what we have learned from time to time, only to
rediscover what is suppressed and forgotten somehow—probably because
we need to learn it for ourselves in our own contexts. It may have always
been, may always be, and as a historian I nuance this polemic by Burroughs
in a variety of ways: 'We think of the past as being there unchangeable.
Actually, the past is ours to shape and change as we will' (Odier 1969: 35;
cf. Hutcheon 1988).

Notes

1 Note: 'cut-up' and 'cento' are both pronounced with the same hard 'c.'
2 It has been suggested by classical scholars and literary theorists that there is a need to engage in such an exercise. See: McGill 2005 (re: 60 pp. of footnotes in which numerous notes are made about the potential interconnections between cento and contemporary literary theory); Ehrling 2011 (re: cento may be a particularly apt genre by which to study subversive and/or humorous genres of Roman literary culture); and Pelttari 2015 (re: intertextuality and layers of meaning/non-referential allusion, the role of the reader as active player in text creation, and tolerance of contemporary literary theory).
3 Consider the 'oral v. textual' in light of Derrida's criticism of Saussure in his seminal work *Of Grammatology* (1967b/1997). In response to Saussure's system, where 'language and writing are two distinct systems of signs, the second exists for the sole purpose of representing the first,' Derrida suggests that written symbols are legitimate signifiers and should not be considered as secondary or derivative to speech. This is interesting as per historical methodology where oral sources generally function secondarily to written ones, largely because they are considered less quantifiable or authoritative than written texts. Of course, oral sources (which must be captured/heard somehow) provide different perspectives on the historical record—but all oral evidence from antiquity is gone. Text and material evidence are what is left by which to gain interpretations, making all of this methodologically interesting, but a relatively moot point.
4 Burroughs did not complete any of these graduate degrees. Educated in the 1920s and 1930s, Burroughs would have engaged in formal study of Latin and/or classics; therefore, he likely had at least accidental academic exposure to cento. Petronius was a known favorite of Burroughs, which means the latter definitely read the brief cento in *Satyricon*. Trying to assess whether or not he was aware of the genre of cento is harder to discern. I personally studied classics and ancient history for the better part of a decade before I specifically knew about these 'cento' works. Having said that, while translating thousands of lines of Latin and Greek over the same time ten-year timeframe, I certainly grew accustomed to seeing portions of recognizable, canonical texts being used outside of their original contexts in political speeches and treatises by philosophers *and* satirists alike.
5 Arguably, *Naked Lunch* is *not* a formal cut-up, though I might argue conversely for multiple reasons—most notably, the accidental aspects of syntax and literary method. Burroughs remembers the composition of *Naked Lunch* as being, 'not random, but arbitrary' (Acker interview, http://www.youtube.com/watch?v=axUc6Tt6SVQ). These sentiments also hold true with my earliest experiences with Burroughs over 25 years ago; for easily a year I carried *Naked Lunch* in my pack because it was, in my opinion, so versatile. I never engaged with this work sequentially, but always just opened it to any page and read. Personal communications over the years suggest that I am not alone in this type of hybrid approach and reception to Burroughs's work.
6 All authors from the time period under consideration (first to sixth centuries CE) were 'Roman' in the broader sense of the overarching, culturally dominant social and political system. The distinction made by the designation of Latin or Greek is based on language of composition alone. On a related note, designation of ancient authors as Christian or Pagan can be similarly useful when considering literature from this period; the designation intrinsically suggests a certain amount of information about the author and the work's historical context.
7 Gradations in 'quality' are also identified, in other ways, i.e. Greek v. Latin or partial v. whole—Homeric fragmentary examples are most often identified as thematically and grammatically subpar among various categories of cento.

8 What was long considered 'low' in traditional classical scholarship is actually seen among *all* ancient Roman classes. The Roman penchant for all manner of entertainments that have been long considered 'low' is becoming accepted as standard in all ancient Roman social strata. This especially is seen with respect to recent studies centered around ancient sport, spectacle, and performance culture (Christiansen 2014).

9 This is exemplified, for example, by the numerous literary compilations extant from antiquity. *Compendia* (i.e. Aulus Gellius, *Attic Nights*, ca. second century CE) and *lexica* (i.e. Pollux, *Onomasticon*, ca. second century CE) are collections of facts and descriptions on various subject matter gained through synthesis of source materials; whereas *brevaria* and chronicles are abbreviated military or political histories based on fuller histories; many of the latter do not exist today (i.e. Eutropius, *Breviarium*, ca. mid fourth century CE; & and Aurelius Victor, *De Ceasaribus*, ca. mid mid-fourth century CE). These types of works, in particular, became more prominent over the Later Imperial and Late Antique periods, ca. second to sixth centuries CE (Hinds 1998; Rohrbacher 2002; Scourfield 2007).

10 McGill 2002. For example, *De Panificio* (11 lines) and *De Alea* (112 lines) are about things people did daily, making bread and playing dice, respectively. Perhaps a better example of universal behavior is sex, since most people have it at some point in their lives. Regarding Ausionius's 'remarkably vivid' (McGill 2005) description of deflowering a virgin on her wedding night, 1919 translator Evelyn-White retains those lines of 'crude and brutal coarseness' in the original Latin un-translated (which was common practice at the time). Nearly 100 years later, McGill uses the words 'pornographic' and 'obscene' in consideration of Ausonius's cento (cf. Cullhead 2016). William Burroughs's texts likewise have been described as 'pornographic' and 'obscene.'

11 Constantine is known as the first Roman emperor to convert to Christianity. Constantine patronized several theologies and was not baptized Christian until he was on his deathbed (337 CE). Under his rule the Edict of Milan (313 CE) guaranteed religious tolerance for Christians, and when the Council of Nicaea (325 CE) was called to root out heresy among competing Christianities, a more solidified version of 'authorized' Christianity was set in place.

12 For example, *De Alea* (a 112-line cento about playing dice) is filled with martial imagery and themes from Virgil's *Aeneid*. Given the tradition in antiquity of describing dicing as a type of warfare (i.e. Juvenal, *Satires* 1.88–92; Juvenal and Persius 2004), the centonist effectively uses battles imagery lifted from Virgil's works to create an effective parody about the 'battles' engaged in when dicing.

13 I stayed at the Grand Union Hotel on a number of occasions, including when I brought photographer Frederick Burrogano-Bigras to the Crowsnest Pass to photograph the hotels included as "Appendix IV: Supporting Images Index" in *Booze and Bars* (Hamilton 2016). I am also a member of Alberta's first chartered Royal Canadian Legion in Coleman, as well as the Hillcrest Miner's Club. I have taken in live shows at 9 out of 10 of the venues examined in the first *Booze and Bars* book. Continued *Booze and Bars in the Bow Valley* research, conducted under the auspices of the Alberta Heritage Resources Foundation and the Lillian Agnes Jones Research Fellowship through the Whyte Museum of the Canadian Rockies, has further facilitated heritage pub culture research which resulted in my staying at a series of heritage Bow Valley hotels in 2019–2020. While staying at the Mount Royal Hotel in Banff in March 2020, I attended a burlesque show at the *Den and Meadow*, a bar in the basement; it was incredible, and so too is one of my favorite stories involving this same basement space and Rocky Mountain legend, Bill Peyto. The story goes, Bill was asked by the powers-that-be at the Banff Park Museum to acquire a lynx specimen for the zoo they were building. (The zoo no longer exists, but the Banff Park Museum does. It is full of taxidermal specimens of animals one might find in Banff

National Park, and access is complimentary with your National Parks Pass purchased at the Banff park gates.) Bill was an expert tracker, and he easily trapped and subdued the requested lynx, which he tied securely to his back before heading back to town. Bill decided to stop in at the pub at the Alberta Hotel (in the space mentioned earlier, known ca. 2020 as *Den and Meadow*) for a well-deserved drink after a long day subduing and transporting the lynx; but, upon seeing it was full of miners from Bankhead a few kilometers away, he released the lynx. Before long, he had the place to himself. Elements in the *Den and Meadow* that date back to the earlier beer parlor on the same site include: the fireplace, its monogrammed metal grates, and a bison mount. Giant murals hung on the walls for years and are now housed in the extensive art collection at the Whyte Museum of the Canadian Rockies.

14 Beyond 'prohibition topics' (Gray 1995; Pashley 2009) the heritage value of Emilio Picariello can be focused through a number of lenses including: immigration (Pic came from Italy to Canada in 1899), entrepreneurship (Pic's business interests beyond alcohol distribution and the Alberta Hotel included: ice cream, pasta, recycling, etc.), civic obligation (Pic was a municipal councilman in the town of Blairmore in the Crowsnest Pass); he is also well remembered as a generous philanthropist within the communities of the Crowsnest Pass and Elk Valley, especially during labor disputes and mine strikes, ca. early 1900s–1920s (Amantea 2007; Davies 2015).

15 Canada's deadliest rock slide at Frank—in 1901, over ninety million tons of limestone fell from Turtle Mountain in less than 90 seconds, which buried a 3 km square section of land, killing over 100 people (Kerr 2018). The Hillcrest Mine Disaster killed 189 men on 19 June 1914 and continues to be remembered as Canada's worst mine disaster/industrial accident (Hanon 2013). Crowsnest Pass also has a fascinating labor history, unique natural history, and wild-west-style shoot-outs (Wilson 2005). This was all captured on film by acclaimed western Canadian photographer, Thomas Gushul—archival and heritage collections at the Crowsnest Museum and Archives include over 10,000 Gushul negatives as well as hundreds of personal/photography artifacts.

16 Others include, for example, talking about early-twentieth-century coal mining at what was once an actual early-twentieth-century coal mine.

17 These elements include: local sandstone stonework, size and shape of fenestrations (or, windows), and exterior woodwork details. Original interior elements are also prominently featured since renovations/restorations, ca. 2005—including, the signatures of the men that originally constructed the interior walls of the building in 1906, which were revealed while replacing a front window.

18 See also, included in this volume, Jason S. Polley, "Smuggling creativity into the classroom" (Chapter 5).

References

Albu, Emily. (2011). "Fulgentius the Mythoclast: Cooling Pagan Passions in Christian Late Antiquity." In *Electronic Antiquity: Communicating the Classics*, Vol. 14, No. (1 November). pp. 81–94.

Amantea, Gisele, (2007). *The King v. Picariello and Lassandro*. Frank Iacobucci Centre for Italian Canadian Studies.

Ausonius. (1919). *Ausonius: Vols. I–II*. Trans. by Hugh G. Evelyn-White. Harvard University Press: Loeb Classical Library. (First published ca. fourth century CE).

Baker, Phil. (2010). *William S. Burroughs*. Reaktion Books.

Barthes, Roland. (1971/1979). "From Work to Text." In Josue V. Harari (ed.), *Textual Strategies: Perspectives in Poststructuralist Criticism*. Cornell University Press (pp. 73–81).

Benjamin, Walter. (1936/2006). "The Work of Art in the Age of Mechanical Reproduction." In Meenakshi Gigi Durham and Douglas M. Kellner (eds.), *Media and Cultural Studies* (pp. 18–40). Malden, MA: Blackwell.

Bloom, Harold. (1973). *The Anxiety of Influence*. Oxford University Press.

Butler, Judith. (1990). *Gender Trouble: Feminism and the Subversion of Identity*. Routledge.

Butler, Judith. (1997). *Excitable Speech: A Politics of the Performative*. Routledge.

Burroughs, William S. (1959/1992). *Naked Lunch*. Grove Press.

Burroughs, William S. (1961/1992). *Soft Machine*. Grove Press.

Burroughs, William S. (1962/1992). *The Ticket That Exploded*. Grove Press.

Burroughs, William S. (1964/1992). *Nova Express*. Grove Press.

Burroughs, William S. (1966/1973). *Exterminator*. Penguin Books USA.

Burroughs, William S. (1968). *Minutes To Go*. Beach Book, Texts & Documents.

Burroughs, William S. and Brion Gysin (1978). *The Third Mind*. The Viking Press.

Christiansen, Kyle (ed.). (2014). *A Companion to Sport and Spectacle in Greek and Roman antiquity*. Wiley and Sons.

Clark, Elizabeth A., and Diane F. Hatch. (1981). *The Golden Bough, the Oaken Cross: The Virgilian Cento of Faltonia Betitia Proba*. Scholars Press.

Cullhead, Sigrid Schottenius. (2016). "In Bed with Virgil: Ausonius' Wedding Cento and its Reception." In *Greece and Rome*, Vol. 63, No. 2, pp. 237–250.

Davies, Adriana A. (2015). *The Rise and Fall of Emilio Picariello*. Oolichan Books.

Derrida, Jacques. (1967a) "Structure, Sign, and Play in the Human Sciences." In *Writing and Difference*, Trans. by Alan Bass (pp. 278–294). Routledge.

Derrida, Jacques. (1967b). *Of Grammatology*. Trans. by Gayatri Spivak. Johns Hopkins University Press.

Dolan, Frederick M. (1991). "The Poetics of Postmodern Subversion: The Politics of Writing in William S. Burroughs's *The Western Lands*." In *Contemporary Literature*, Vol. 32, No. 4, pp. 534–551.

Eco, Umberto. (1967/1989). *The Open Work*. Harvard University Press.

Ehrling, Sara. (2011). *De Inconexis Continuum: A Study of Late Antique Latin Wedding Centos*. Goteborg universitet. Retrieved from http:/hdl.handle.net/2077/24990.

Foucault, Michel. (1982). *The Archaeology of Knowledge*. Random House.

Gray, James H. (1995). *Booze: When Whisky Ruled the West*. Fifth House Publishers. (First published 1972)

Green, R. P. H. (1995). "Proba's Cento: Its Date, Purpose, and Reception." In *The Classical Quarterly*, Vol. 45, No. 2, pp. 551–563.

Green, R. P. H. (1997). "Proba's Introduction to her Cento." In *The Classical Quarterly*, Vol. 47, No. 2, pp. 548–559.

Hamilton, Stephanie Laine. (2016). *Booze and Bars: A Brief History of Pub Culture in the Crowsnest Pass*. Crowsnest Historical Publishing.

Hanon, Steve. (2013). *The Devil's Breath: The Story of the Hillcrest Mine Disaster of 1914*. NeWest Press.

Hinds, Stephen. (1998). *Allusion and Intertext Dynamics of Appropriation in Roman Poetry*, Cambridge University Press.

Hutcheon, Linda. (1988). *A Poetics of Postmodernism: History, Theory, Fiction*. Routledge.

Juvenal and Persius. (2004). *Juvenal. Persius*. Trans. By Susanna Morton Braund. Harvard University Press. Loeb Classical Library 91. pp. 46–62

Kaster, Robert A. (1988). *Guardians of Language: The Grammarian and Society in Late Antiquity*. University of California Press.

Kerr, J. William. (2018). *Frank Slide*. Monica Field, Joey Ambrosi, and Stephanie Laine Hamilton (eds.). Government of Alberta. (First published 1990).

Knickerbocker, Conrad. (1965). "Interviews: William S. Burroughs, the Art of Fiction." In *The Paris Review*, No. 36, pp. 12–49.

Land, Christopher. (2005). "Apomorphine Silence: Cutting-up Burroughs' Theory of Language and Control." In *Ephemera: Theory and Politics*, Vol. 5, No. 3, pp. 450–471.

Lydenberg, Robin. (1987). *Word Cultures: Radical Theory and Practice in William S. Burroughs' Fiction*. University of Illinois Press.

McCutcheon, Mark A. (2012). "The Cento, Romanticism, and Copyright." In *ESC: English Studies in Canada*, Vol. 38, No. 2, pp. 77–101.

McGill, Scott. (2002). "Tragic Vergil: Rewriting Vergil as Tragedy in Cento Medea." In *The Classical World*, Vol. 95, No. 2, pp. 143–161.

McGill, Scott. (2005). *Virgil Recomposed: The Mythological and Secular Centos in Antiquity*. Oxford University Press.

Meconi, David Vincent. (2004). "The Christian Cento and the Evangelization of Classical Culture." In *Logos: A Journal of Catholic Thought and Culture*, Vol. 7, No. 4, pp. 109–132.

Mikriammos, Phillipe. (1984). "A Conversation with William Burroughs." In *The Review of Contemporary Fiction*. Vol. 4, No. 1 (Spring).

Miles, Barry. (2002). *William Burroughs: El Hombre Invisible*. Random House.

Miles, Barry. (2015). *Call Me Burroughs: A Life*. Twelve Books.

Murphy, Timothy S. (1997). *Wising Up the Marks: The Amodern William Burroughs*. University of California Press.

Nelson, Camilla. (2015, April). "Archival poetics: Writing history from the fragments." In C. Nelson and C. de Matos (eds.), *TEXT Special Issue 28: Fictional Histories and Historical Fiction: Writing History in the Twenty-first Century*. Retrieved from http://www.textjournal.com.au/speciss/issue28/Nelson.pdf

Odier, Daniel. (ed.). (1969). *The Job: Interviews with William S. Burroughs*. Penguin Group.

Ommundsen, Wenche. (2005, October). "'If It's Tuesday, This Must Be Jane Austen': Literary Tourism and the Heritage Industry." In Wenche Ommundsen and Takolander (eds.), *TEXT Special Issue No. 4*.

Ong, Walter J. (1982). *Orality and Literacy*. Routledge.

Pace, Steven. (2012, April). "Writing the Self into Research: Using Grounded Theory Analytic Strategies in Autoethnography." In McLoughlin and Brien (eds.), *TEXT Special Issue: Creativity: Cognitive, Social and Cultural Perspectives*. Retrieved from https://www.textjournal.com.au/speciss/issue13/Pace.pdf

Pashley, Nicholas. (2009). *Cheers! An Intemperate History of Beer in Canada*. Collins.

Pelttari, Aaron. (2015). *The Space that Remains: Reading Latin Poetry in Late Antiquity*. Cornell University Press.

Petronius and Seneca. (2020). *Satyricon. Apocolocyntosis*. Trans by Gareth Schmelling. Harvard University Press: Loeb Classical Library 15. pp. ix–436. (first published ca. first century CE).

Punday, Daniel. (2007). "Word Dust: William Burroughs's Multimedia Aesthetic." In *Mosaic*, 40(3), pp. 33–49.

Robinson, Edward. (2006). "Taking the Power Back: William S. Burroughs Use of the Cut-up as a Means of Challenging Social Orders and Power Structures." In *Quest*, Issue 4. Retrieved from http://www.qub.ac.uk/sites/QUEST/JournalIssues/.

Rohrbacher, David. (2002). *The Historians of Late Antiquity*. Routledge.

66   *Stephanie Laine Hamilton*

Scourfield, J. H. D. (ed.). (2007). *Texts and Culture in Late Antiquity: Inheritance, Authority, and Change*. Classical Press of Wales.

Sivan, Hagith. (1993). "Anician Women, the Cento of Proba, and Aristocratic Conversion in the Fourth Century." In *Virgiliae Christianae*, Vol. 47, No. 2, pp. 140–157.

Smolak, K. (1979). "Beobachtungen zur Darstellungsweise in den Homerzentonen." In *Jahrbuch de osterreichischen Byzantinistik* 28, pp. 29–49.

Sobieszek, Robert A. (1996). *Ports of Entry: William S. Burroughs and the Arts*. Thames and Hudson.

Steedman, Carolyn. (2002). *Dust: The Archives and Cultural History*. Rutgers University Press.

Tacitus. (1937). *Annals: Books 13–16*. Trans. by John Jackson. Harvard University Press: Loeb Classical Library 322. (First published ca. second century CE).

Usher, M. D. (1998). *Homeric Stitchings: The Homeric Centos of the Empress Eudocia*. Rowman and Littlefield.

Wilson, Diana (ed.). (2005). *Triumph and Tragedy in the Crowsnest Pass*. Heritage House Publishing.

Wilson-Kastner, Patricia. (1981). *A Lost Tradition: Women Writers of the Early Church*. University Press of America.

4 Expanding genre and identities in digital poems

Generating ethos and pathos through code-switching and shifting multimedia platforms[1]

Shirley Geok-lin Lim

Introduction: Making it new in the 21st century

In the turn from the 19th to the 20th century, British and U.S. poetry, composed chiefly in conventional forms, struggled to articulate the shift from tradition to modernity, what Henry Adams in 1900 had binarized as the Virgin and the Dynamo. My 1972 dissertation on American *fin-de-siècle* poetics concluded with Robert Frost, who remarked in his introduction to E.A. Robinson's collection *King Jasper* that Robinson's metrical verse composition was in fact 'an old way to be new.'[2] There came, of course, new ways to be new, as evidenced in Ezra Pound's Manifesto on Imagism and William Carlos Williams's practice of free verse via the strategies of the moveable foot. Jessica Pressman in 2014 argued that Poundian modernist strategies for 'making it new' in fact prefigured, if not laid the groundwork for, the poetics of New Media literary strategies that power digital works by major digital texts producers like Young-Hae Chang Heavy Industries.[3]

While Pressman's thesis offers a 21st-century expansion of literary traditions via close readings of electronic poetry, my more interruptive thesis argues that by the turn of the 21st century, these 'new' ways have themselves grown sclerotic, even as the concepts of stylistics, rhetoric, and features and characteristics that mark poetry—including dramatic tragedy and comedy, epic and lyric—limned in Aristotle's *Poetics* (circa 335 BC)—continue to signify contemporaneous aesthetic values for practitioners, readers, and teachers of poetry. Reading backward rather than forward, I argue that Modernism, Imagism, Surrealism, Free Verse, Language Poetry, etc., and the influence of non-European literary traditions that introduced Haiku, Tanka, pantun, and ghazal (to note some examples) have expanded the still-resonant Aristotelian typologies of poetry. Crucially, 20th- and 21st-century technologies—photography, film and video, music and audio recordings, and the entire multimedia platforms accessible via the Internet—offer opportunities for poets to shift, transform, generate, multiply, and complicate their poetic personae and to rethink the core issues of ethos and pathos that Aristotle was interested in in *Poetics*, resulting in a growing subfield categorized as Electronic Poetry.[4]

In 2008, Jan Baetens and Jan Van Looy published a very helpful introduction to Electronic Poetry (e-poetry for short), framing it not as a genre or medium but as a 'cultural practice,' or, as Raymond Williams theorized such phenomena, as a 'cultural form.'[5] To some extent still the case now as it was then, Baetens and Van Looy lamented the reductive approach to e-poetry as mere 'high-tech gadgetry.'[6] While advocating the cultural pertinence of e-poetry, their article is most relevant to scholars and creative writing instructors like me who attend to the intersections and permeable borders between print productions and e-poetry.

Twenty-first-century creative writing pedagogy: Hybridizing anglophone poetics

Speaking as a creative writing teacher, I will discuss some poems my creative writing students in Singapore and California have produced, not chiefly to critique the theories e-poetics scholars have promulgated, but to address pedagogical concerns in expanding the genre, as I introduce poetry composition to first-generation non-Native-English-speaking undergraduates. I will first summarize curricular goals and ideological threads that frame my assignments. Then I will analyze the students' print poems for linguistic strategies such as code-switching, multilingual stylistics, and the dialogic deployment of multiple registers to revitalize conventional poetic forms. Lastly, I will interpret their digitized texts as not simply an expansion but a transformation of the genre which has been infused with non-linguistic energies potent in multimedia creativity.

First, in assigning poetry composition to first-generation, non-Native-English speakers, I require they raise to consciousness a bifocal language dynamics, the required foundation in standard English (vocabulary, grammar, and syntactical abilities) and also their experiential quotidian, discursive range of oral speech, often multilingual, including non-English home languages (in Singapore: Hokkien, Malay, and Tamil; and in California: Spanish), registers of street and in-group slang, linguistic indices, and so forth. The student poets were encouraged to code-switch in their compositions, a prompt that initially confused them, as throughout their education they had been penalized for any non-standard English writing. In directing them to code-switch, I was building on the schema that Braj Kachru had constructed in his World Englishes thesis, which figured English not as a language of homogeneity but as heterogeneous tracks in a spectrum of Englishes.[7] Troping Kachru's thesis as spiraling circles with a core formed by native speakers, and moving through circles of English relatable to the core out to the furthest peripheral circles of English dialects hardly recognizable as English, Kachru's World Englishes theories helped illuminate something of the condition of English as daily oral communication among entire societies outside of Native-English-speaking nations and also among marginal communities within these nations. My Chinese Singapore and Hispanic California students grasped Kachru's schema as inclusive of the language worlds they inhabited. Second, just as this linguistic multiplicity did not excuse them from the task of mastering standard English, so it did not excuse them from undertaking the practice of writing in some traditional forms, such as ballads, sonnets, and villanelles.[8] Finally, they were asked to digitize one of their poems to expand the genre to incorporate 21st-century technologies that give rise to multimedia poetry, often abbreviated conceptually to digital, electronic, or e-poetry.

My curricular goals were nuanced by the historicized cultural contexts in which these postcolonial Singapore and minority U.S. students were embedded. Much of a global audience continues to perceive mastery of poetry in its Western and Anglophone forms as primary. While students were required to produce within specific poetic conventions, they were also asked to demonstrate deploying these language forms toward individual and social ends; that is, to indigenize the genre. This struggle between an apparent inherent or standard Anglophone poetic form—metrical, rhymed, patterned, figurative, etc.—and oral, local English of non-native-English-speaking poets was evident in the very earliest contact zones between Western colonialists and indigenous people. As Caliban famously countered to Prospero in Shakespeare's *The Tempest* (1610/11: 1.2. 368–370), a 'red plague' upon you 'For learning me your language!'[9]

Colonial and postcolonial stylistics:
The case of Singapore

Indeed, the position evolving in local universities in 1940s pre-Independence Malaysia/Singapore was that poetry would be 'the choice ... as the genre' 'for localizing the [English] language,' for, although a 'foreign language,' it 'had helped provide solidarity among the different cultural groups' and 'if infused with the right degree of local elements could become an adequate cultural vehicle.'[10] In short, the genre could be instrumental in producing 'a special Malaysian language,' 'an integration of the various local languages ... with the central, cementing influence being that of English.'[11]

This deliberately invented literary *Engmalchin,* a composite of English, Malay, and Chinese, failed. As Subramaniam noted, 'It emphasized language at too literal a level, sacrificing the demands of form, rhythm and metaphor for an immediate social integration. Language could not be synthesized overnight and nursed into sudden metaphorical expressiveness.'[12] That is, the genre was not receptive to social engineering but, as with all genres, must be an organic creation.

Post-Independence, more than a generation later, Arthur Yap's '2 mothers in a hdb playground'[13] exemplifies the genre as both localized and indigenized; poetry in which orality is dialogically sounded in the voices of two competitive mothers upstaging each other in a display of money and the academic standing of their sons.[14] I presented Yap's poem, currently taken by literary critics as canonical in Singapore's national literature (but which none of my Singapore students then had heard of—thus, demonstrating the neglect of the genre of poetry even in internationally high-ranked educational societies like Singapore's) as a concrete example of the genre's potential in tapping into code-switching, multilingual speech practices while still maintaining traditional form. The students responded with enthusiasm and impressive creative digitized poems, as reported in an online report on the semester's projects:

> Under the guidance of Professor Shirley Geok-lin Lim, students from the ULT2298E class have put together a collection of their poems titled *Red Pulse*. Singapore has often been called 'The Little Red Dot.' This term suggests that Singapore is static and unchanging—which could not be further from the truth. Singapore is constantly changing, fluxing and pulsing. It is with this idea that this collection of poems is titled *Red Pulse*. Videos of digitized poems will be shown during the book launch as well. Many of them are interesting re-interpretations of the written poems, brought to virtual life. *In This Book*, by Stella Goh, is a stop-motion video meditating on the meaning of books, knowledge and truth. Scott Png came up with *Dump Dwellers*, a digitized poem on social inequality and injustice.[15]

Ethos and pathos: Expanding the genre

In a more elaborated form, I analyze here one example of such a 'written' poem by a first-year undergraduate, Kevin Lam, who composed a traditional-form villanelle, generated after group brainstorming and two days of composition. Table 4.1 contains an annotated rendition of the villanelle (used with the author's written permission), together with relevant idiomatic expressions which also echo in Arthur Yap's poem. Lam's villanelle is localized—idiomatically and socioculturally. Nonetheless, the poem, re-scripted in Singlish, one of the many Englishes marking the creative genius of distinctive communal identities, may be viewed as a predictable evolution, signifying the confidence of nations seizing their place in the global economy. The poem takes its allegorical thrust from the annual Grand Prix held on the island nation-state (see note 14, timeframe 0:01–0:10, or Figure 4.1, an approximation), one that attracts a huge international following, closes much of the city down for the days it runs, and which is clearly a competition that pits drivers and cars against each other not simply on elements of skill and speed but also on courage, and on finance, on science, and on technology. That is, it is a competition not merely between individuals, but between finance-societal-technological corporate domains. The opening image of the Grand Prix, symbolizing a winner-take-all ethos, serves as the founding ironic critique of a nation in which the reader intuits the pathos of children caught up in the communal dogma: 'Die, die, cannot finish last!' (see Figures 4.2 and 4.3).

Kevin Lam's digitized version of the print poem, appearing as a rap rendition performed among his fellow poets, is posted on YouTube. His actual digitized poem/e-poem, created as the final assignment for my Poetics Mash-Up seminar in Fall 2012, was one of many screened in the same event of the launch of the students' print collection, *Red Pulse*, and exhibition of

Table 4.1 'The Singapore Grand Prix' (Annotated)

'The Singapore Grand Prix'		Idiomatic Expressions Resonating in '2 mothers in a hdb playground'	
Ferrari cars zooming past Padang, Nicoll Highway—Die die cannot finish last!*	(*A colloquial phrase that encapsulates the competitive ethos that Arthur Yap's poem thematized and that prevails as keenly a generation later)		
Ask *Ma*' help with arts and craft. Say 'cause you want go play Hot Wheels. Toy cars zooming past.	(*Hokkien for 'mother')		
Today, I a bit downcast—Heard *Ah Seng*' he got more pay. Die die cannot finish last!	(*A colloquial term for a generic Chinese Singaporean)	*my toa-soh*'	(*Hokkien for 'elder sister')
Last night party had a blast! Really went all the way; *Machiam*' sports car zooming past.	(*Malay word meaning 'just like')		
My boy *ah*,' knows 'chloroplast'— Tuition* there learn today. Die die cannot finish last!	(*A linguistic filler meaning 'you know') (*Afterschool private tuition)	your tuition teacher*	(*In competitive Asian societies, children receive expensive after-school private tuition to boost their scores in the national examinations)
Ah pa all his friends outlast, *Probly* better airway. But when hearse zooming past, Die die cannot finish last![a]		*to take you chya-hong*'	(*Literally, Hokkien for 'eat the wind,' idiom for 'getting some air/going for a drive')

[a] See Lam (2012). (Used with permission.)

Figure 4.1 The Singapore Grand Prix.

Figure 4.2 "Die Die Cannot Finish Last!" (Singapore MRT).

Figure 4.3 "Die Die Cannot Finish Last!" (Singapore Shoppers).

their individual chapbooks. In digitizing the original as a rap version, Lam made significant changes, as in introducing a secondary narrative of a male persona celebrating his test results that top those of a female classmate. The visuals underline a kind of *Bildungsroman* of the poet-persona, from desires associated with childhood, as in toys and Barbie dolls, to schooldays' triumphs in competition for high grades, to adolescent and adult social values in keeping up with the Joneses, boasting of wild parties, drinking, and sexual adventures, all of which are framed as constructed through a social ideology of hyper-competition and fears of being viewed as a loser.[16]

The repeated line, with its rhythmic 'die, die,' resounds as both comic and darkly threatening. It communicates the parental anxieties that pressure children to strive with the help of hours of expensive private tuition (see note 14, timeframe 0:52) not only to succeed academically, but also to 'top that class.' The dystopia of everyday life in densely urban Singapore is acutely visualized through images of commuters jostling to cram into the public transit system, the last in line perhaps missing the train should the doors close before they can board (see note 14, timeframe 0:19, or Figure 4.2, an approximation), and long lines of shoppers waiting to be served (see note 14, timeframe 0:38, or Figure 4.3, an approximation).

In assigning these Singapore undergraduates digitization of their indigenized poetic genre, I hoped to introduce them to a 21st-century manifestation of the genre. As Glazier noted 'of the language of the making of the new digital poetries,'

> From code to code, whether a Web page in Moscow, a speaking clock in Kentish Town, a computer-generated Buffalo, or a bot hiding in an archive in Melbourne, the making of poetry has established itself on a matrix of new shores. From hypertext through visual/kinetic text to writing in networked and programmable media, there is a tangible feel of arrival. ... New possibilities stand out as intriguing while technologies that once seemed futuristic now have all the timeliness of World War II bunkers.[17]

Kevin Lam's digitized text is visual and kinetic, exploiting networked and programmable media, using the most basic e-tools, an iPhone, and accessing resources—rap beats and visual images—available on the Internet. While the villanelle took over three days to complete, the digitized text, after the initial recording (combining the recording with the images, etc.) took about half a day.[18]

Crucially, the digitized text was *not* simply an expansion of the original poem; the genre itself was no longer recognizable as a traditional form but, dynamically, a different representation and hence a different poem—its features not simply additive but actually changed. For example, the villanelle was changed to four-line stanzas that lined up with a background rap-style beat. Lam dropped the last villanelle stanza, which he acknowledged was probably the most poignant part of the poem, but which I interpreted as unacceptable in a Chinese context, because it would have been taken as publicly foretelling, and so wishing, his father's death. The four-line stanzas in the digitized text enlarged on Yap's earlier generation domestic satire in 'Two Mothers' in order to subtly critique values encouraged in current state policies, crystallized in the all-pervasive national ethos of '*kiasi*' (i.e., submissiveness, fear of authority and social disapprobation) and '*kiasu*' (i.e., fear of losing out, a zero-sum approach to competition).[19]

E-Poetics/E-Politics: The case of California

In 2017, I taught a similar poetics mash-up seminar at the University of California, Santa Barbara, with many African American and Hispanic students. Pablo Robles, an American-born Chicano and first-generation college student, raised in gang-riddled, dangerous South Central Los Angeles, composed a poem[20] influenced by the Federal Government's current anti-immigrant, anti-Mexican policies, evidenced, for example, in the U.S. Immigration and Customs Enforcement (ICE) deportation of undocumented Hispanics:

BLACK ICE

> *In response to*
> *the Executive*
> *Order on*
> *Border Security*
> *and Immigration*
> *Enforcement*
> *Improvements*
> *under Trump*
> *Administration*

Do they know we got guns too?
Do they know we got names too?

> In 1940
> The World Wars littered the globe with corpses
> America needed Soldiers
> But Agriculture needed men to plow
> Lobbyist Extorting Congress
> Importing bodies from Mexico
> To the fields and factories
> These facts hardly get reported
> We the population are feeding this nation
> Accepting lower wages to get paid
> And take our families out of caves
> Not asking for a raise
> Just Citizenship
> What's this talk of independence?
> My people denied their medicine
> Folks this ain't television!

The president has tunnel vision.
I'm down the drain straight to prison!
ICE force deporting students
Man this wasn't in the course description
b/c the constitution is being rewritten
No need for children to inherit these chains
Mothers gone sterile protect fetuses from the pain
got me questioning how my time's spent
21 years old and feeling bold with a barrel
But the dead don't have consent
Executive orders harass you
White House just a corrupt castle
Cops drives slow and stare at you
　　　—asking for a green card
I think hard and remind 'em
The 13th letter of the alphabet is M
13 stripes on the flag
Splattered with our blood
Harvesting lettuce and tomatoes
So you could eat tomorrow
Please let us speak,
Do they know we got *words* too?

(Used with permission.)

Robles's poem, with its irregular yet strongly stressed rhymed lines, its metrically irregular yet heavily stressed phrases, and its first-person interrogative addresses that engage the reader bluntly, has much in common with rap poetry, albeit more in the way of instruction than entertainment, expressing a communal ethos triangulated within an 'I/we,' 'you,' and 'they' dynamic. His digitized version[21] of the print poem, although less subtle than Lam's, 'persuades' both through the oral pleasures of strong rhythm and rhyme, and through succinct instruction, offering a narrative history dramatized in visual form of the Chicano/a contributions to these United States of America, the community's patriotic sacrifices in military service, and as the labor force that feeds the country.

Unlike Lam's subtle social critique, Robles's poem is overtly and politically critical of U.S. immigration policies, and historicized to instruct ignorant readers of the social and political injustices that white supremacist America has inflicted on Mexicans who serve in the U.S. military and labor in the fields, and who are denied the benefits that citizens receive. This black and white image of braceros in the Library of Congress archives effectively historicizes the early movement of Mexican field labor (see note 21, timeframe 1:45, or Figure 4.4, an approximation). The nine men wearing the iconic straw sun hats that protect them from the intense sun pose with the crates of just-picked tomatoes. The men are lean, even thin, brown complexioned and generally unsmiling; they are paid cents for filling each crate, hard labor that U.S. farmers cannot find American citizens to do.[22]

Figure 4.4 Braceros.

The speaker legitimizes and authorizes this history; self-identifying as a student, his colloquial voice testifies to the convergence of academic and communal forms of knowing:

> ICE force deporting students
> Man, this wasn't in the course description
> b/c the constitution is being rewritten

This converging, double-layered point of view suggests an allusive play of images in the passage that follows:

> No need for children to inherit these chains
> Mothers gone sterile protect fetuses from the pain
> got me questioning how my time's spent
> 21 years old and feeling bold with a barrel

At the age usually taken as adulthood, the Chicano is socially constructed regressively as still playing with guns. '21 years old and feeling bold with a barrel,' a thought experiment pathetically underlined by the shocking black-and-white visual of a young Chicano boy holding a wooden gun looking into the camera with a gruesome skull in the foreground (see note 14, timeframe 1:16–1:21). What's more, this thought experiment is linked with the statement of Chicana mothers sterilizing themselves so as to save future children from the life of pain that awaits them, a subtle allusion to Toni Morrison's *Beloved*[23] and the pathological consequences of ethno-genocide in America.[24]

Unlike Lam's, Robles's digitized text did not depend only on Web resources. Robles videotaped South Central LA streets and scenes offer an insider's view of his Chicano/a community, generating an intimacy not so

Figure 4.5 Botello's "Virgin's Seed" Mural.

accessible to his audience. The video stream visualizes urban spaces that clarify how a so-called minority in fact owns its streets and is its own public in brown USA. While the earlier streaming video of cars driving down southeast Los Angeles passing by the exit to the penitentiary buildings, the destination for so many Chicanos trapped in poverty and crime, the digital poem, however, ends on a conciliatory note, with a large street mural of the Virgin's Seed (see note 21, timeframe 1:51–1:56 or Figure 4.5), photographed by Robles himself (used with permission), thus bringing into convergence the power of poetry and community values in resistance to state violence: 'Don't they know we have words too?'

The mural references first the Virgin of Guadalupe (in Spanish, *Nuestra Señora de Guadalupe*), the name Mexican Catholics gave to the Virgin Mary, whose image is enshrined in the Minor Basilica of Our Lady of Guadalupe in Mexico City, and taken as a symbol of Mexican indigenization of Catholicism.[25] The location of this magnificently elaborate mural in Los Angeles links the Chicano/a community, represented on the lower left-hand side as working class *Rasa* and on the upper right-hand side surreally as spirits, spatially and culturally with the original icon in Mexico City. The mural is heavily gendered, the Virgin dwarfed on either side by a looming male figure on the right bearing a bride in his left palm, with a fetus still attached to its umbilical cord seeming to fall from the bride's white gown. To the left of the Marian figure, an equally looming female figure gazes, like her almost twin male counterpart, not at the sacred icon but outwards, pensive and reflectively, her crossed arms bearing on the right palm the bridegroom and on her left palm what looks like an industrial factory. The mural is crowded with Aztec and Inca mythological figures, asserting, despite the Euro-Spanish physiognomy of many of the representational figures, its Indio-Latin-American cultural hybrid identity.[26]

Comparative critical poetics: Ethos and the transformed genre

In both digitized texts, arguably, a hierarchy of language rules—i.e. not simply words but words patterned by and into intensities of rhythmic sounds that signify diverse, even divergent and indeterminate, meanings. Brian Kim Stefans's essay on Seaman's 'Interactive Text and Recombinant Poetics'[27] offers an excellent survey of e-poetry theorists who take on an opposing definition of electronic poetry.

> The word is not valued in a hierarchy over other media elements. That is, electronic poetry celebrates not only the liberation of words but the breakdown of boundaries between the sign of the word and the sign of other media elements including video, sound, and still image.[28]

Contradicting e-poetry theorists such as Seaman, Lam's and Robles's respective reflections on differences between their print and digitized poems each placed words as primary. For Lam, the digitized text seemed to have been simply setting the original poem's words 'into music,' while, unlike Lam, Robles views the digital text as chiefly visual. Arguably, however, in both digitized poems, 'music' or rhythmic sound and visuals, including still photograph and video/moving visuals, emerge as digital script— 'ongoing, time-based summing of meaning forces,' a different writing that in effect creates a new poetic text that cannot otherwise have been created.

For example, Lam's digital poem changes the villanelle to highly rhythmic four-line stanzas with repeated rhymed lines (as in the playful, collaging, associative, allusive, visual punning of word, image, and cultural reference) in the stanza 'Last night party had a blast/Really went all the way./Lots of beer, vodka glass,/Macham sports car zooming past!' These words are the recitative to images that flash before us: a crowd of young revelers followed by a still of the iconic Merlion that stands on the Singapore River, a concrete statue invented by the Tourist Board to represent the island's mythical origin as one with lions but whose maritime prowess now powers its economic standing on the globe, and ending with the beer pitchers, vodka-filled glass, and sports car careening in the Grand Prix that the island hosts annually. The Merlion photographed with water gushing out of its mouth works as a *double entendre*; the phrase 'really went all the way' alludes to either an orgasmic or vomit-ive 'blast' that the words alone do not communicate. The visual pun is comic and satirical because in a nation notorious for encouraging prudish mores, the state-approved Merlion is deployed here to figure orgiastic, degenerate youths. The criticism of extreme academic, economic, social, and professional competitiveness, articulated in the repeated chants of '*Kiasi, Kiasu*, drive so fast, die die cannot finish last,' is visually encapsulated as the contradiction between state policies stipulating ethical mores while simultaneously pushing hedonist values to achieve high economic and materialist development.

As with Lam's digitized text, Robles's digital poem is linguistic-hierarchal; the closing line 'we have words too' epitomizes the genre's politico-moral charge, the ethos that makes the genre make what it makes. Robles, who continues to aspire to a writerly vocation, has an insight into the radical change when poetry as word-language is digitized. For him, the digitized text becomes a different form of writing, an e-poem that portends a shift in audience, hence an increased outreach:

> When you are writing a poem you develop a strong relationship to your words. ... [W]hen I write I feel an intense inward eye that is funneling emotions and experiences onto the page ... BUT what happens when you revisit a poem that you SEE and HEAR? Now you are *incorporating different sensory details, which will change what you write.* SO when you are doing a visual production it takes on another life because now you have to look at your poem from the audience's EYES! They will physically see your poem manifested on a screen and that is a different relationship than one being chanted out-loud or read on a page. I feel that I did not enjoy the digitized version AT FIRST, but now I love it ... because it's a great way to communicate in our world now. Many people do not like to read ... people respond more now to visuals so it is a great way to launch myself.[29]

While both students' e-poems crossed from print to computer-generated multimedia/audio-visual productions, they are, as Raymond Williams theorizes, both 'cultural forms.' Robles's Chicano utterance has its grounding in documentary *testimonia* and Lam's in satirical rap performance. In the transformation from print to multimedia platforms, did these texts shift in genre identity? Why and how does this question signify in 21st-century literary studies and for 21st-century creative mediums?

I am still thinking through how poetry as a genre is changed when the language text is digitized. (I do not study the e-poem when the e-text emerges without a time lapse or boundary between written language and electronic 'language.') I leave you instead with my unanswered questions. Yes, the digitized poem is a different poem, but is it also 'writing'? Or is it writing with a difference? Is the difference a mere additive expansiveness of the genre? Or is the genre itself so transformed that the assumed hierarchy of word in the genre no longer can stand? Instead, have multimedia technologies produced a genre still named poetry in which words and their significations may no longer mean, and if so, what happens to the way ethos can be made to mean for us humans?

Notes

1 My thanks to Jonkoping University, Sweden, for hosting the September 2018 conference 'Genres and Media Landscapes in Virtual-Physical Learning Spaces: Moving Frontiers,' where I presented the paper that would become this chapter. Thanks also to Stephen Sohn (University of California, Riverside) and Alan Liu (University of California, Santa Barbara) for valuable feedback on this foray into the sub-field of electronic poetics.

2 Dana Gioia (2013) notes that Frost himself attempted to find a way to link the deployment of traditional forms to Modernism; yet 'an 'old way to be new' [proved] so unobtrusively experimental that most critics and readers missed its sheer originality.'

3 Pressman (2014). Also, see Chang (n.d.).

4 See Craig Dvorkin's 'Poetry without Organs' (2007), Loss Pequeno Glazier's *Digital Poetics* (2002), and Brian Kim Stefans's *Fashionable Noise* (2003).

5 See 'cultural form' in Williams (1975).

6 Baetens and Van Looy (2008) see the evolution of e-poetry as the initial deployment of computers to 'generate [texts] by manipulating rules and variables.' Computers' 'graphical user interfaces' result in new forms of visual poetry while also enabling hypertextual—nonlinear and interactive—writing. See online examples in Pressman (2014) of such student digital essays generated in response to a course offered at San Diego State University:. https://www.jessicapressman.com/teaching/examples-of-student-projects/.

7 See Kachru (1976).

8 Both sets of undergraduates were required to read poetics spanning from Aristotle to Keats, and Coleridge, Wordsworth, Emerson, Charles Olson, Pound, Williams, and more.

9 See Shakespeare (1623)

10 Subramaniam (1977: 62–63); cited in Wong (1986: 97).

11 Wong (1986: 97–98).

12 Subramaniam (1977: 67–68); cited in Wong (1986: 97).

13 The acronym 'hdb' stands for Housing Development Board.

14 See Yap (1980); also, in the following section, I annotate student Kevin Lam's poem to indicate similar vernacular usages from Yap's poem. Yap's legacy reverberates through Lam.

15 See https://kentridgecommon.com/red-pulse-new-singapore-uspoetry/; also see http://www.youtube.com/watch?v=Qr-F4io-B8w

16 See http://www.youtube.com/user/USPPoets (Lam's official video, with words) as well as http://www.youtube.com/watch?v=MYCTIryBpZk (Lam performing with a classmate, with words).

17 See Glazier's introduction in *Digital Poetics* (Glazier 2002).

18 From an email interview with Kevin Lam (10 August 2018). The voices are those of three cousins (a 5- year-old female, a 10-year old male, and an 8-year-old male) combined with his own authorial commentary. The digitized text was recorded 'in one sitting when we visited our grandmother on Sunday (usual family gathering). Rehearsal was minimal (e.g., if they said something wrongly I just did the recording again). I did not coach them. The shooting was done in less than an hour.'

19 The Hokkien words 'Kiasi' and 'Kiasu' have gained near nationwide circulation, encapsulating the two traits that most Singaporeans accept as core to their sociocultural identity. 'Kiasi' (literally, a fear of dying) signifies a general fear of authority inculcated to regulate a law-abiding, obedient, non-questioning subject. 'Kiasu' (literally, a fear of losing) denotes an anxiety over losing out, not simply possessing a competitive spirit but a grasping psyche that not only keeps up with the Joneses but is vigilant to take advantage of any material gain that may be afforded to another; that is, signifying a zero-sum materialistic ethos.

20 The original written/print poem was submitted to me by Pablo Robles for the UCSB poetics mash-up seminar I taught. Presently, I retain the only copy of the print version.
21 See https://www.youtube.com/watch?v=d-NCEcnBayE
22 The history of the Mexican American Civil Rights Movement arguably was doubly powered by the National Farm Workers Association, organized by Cesar Chavez and Dolores Huerta, and the publication of *La Raza*, a community newspaper in Los Angeles in the 1960s. Chicano/a history is familiar across Mexican American generations both as oral histories and as curricula widely taught in California schools and universities. See also Rosales (1997).
23 See Yuniar Fatmasari's (2016) article, which mentions issues of forced sterilization in Morrison's *Beloved*.
24 The presence of Mexican American field hands in California, as the poem avers, may be explained as a result of the bracero program, with the Mexican Farm Labor Agreement with Mexico that the United States initiated in 1942 when World War II conscription of American citizens resulted in an urgent need for farm labor. It is the largest U.S. contract labor program, with 4.2 million contracts signed between 1942 and 1964. See also Gilmore and Gilmore (1963) for an overview of the bracero program.
25 The dominant iconic figure of the Virgin of Guadalupe, symbolizing the convergence of Mexican Catholic and national identity, in the mural is transmogrified by more pressing representations of human and nature fertility. The roses and birds, bride, groom, and fetus, the tree laden with oranges and working masses by the female side, overwhelm the single skeletal gray figure below the male. The Virgin of Seeds as a representation of female power has increased in popularity with women artists. See also Jacinto Quirarte (1992) on a study of Chicano art and its use of Our Lady of Guadalupe.
26 See Urton's analysis of the Virgin of Seeds figure as a synthesis of symbolic and metaphoric components drawn from Roman Catholicism and mytho-historical traditions, which he notes emerged as a complete blending and syncretism of rituals (1990: 118).
27 See Seaman (2004).
28 See Stefans (2005).
29 Pablo Robles (email interview, August 12, 2018).

References

Andersen, O., & Haarberg, J. (2001). *Making Sense of Aristotle: Essays in Poetics*. Gerald Duckworth & Burroughs, London.

Baetens, J. & J. Van Looy. (2008). "E-Poetry between Image and Performance: A Cultural Analysis." *E-Media Studies*, 1(1), 1–18. https://pdfs.semanticscholar.org/3ad2/ac713a81ba0f4d282339556f82ed69f56ab0.pdf

Chang, Y.-H. (n.d.). "Heavy Industries." https://yhchang.com/WANT_TO_DO_GOOD_KNOW_HOW_TO_SHOOT_A_SEMIAUTOMATIC_HANDGUN_V.html

Dvorkin, C. (2007). "Poetry without Organs." In R. Purves & S. Ladkin (Eds.), *Complicities: British Poetry 1945–2007*. *Litteraria Pragensia*. http://eclip-searchive.org/Editor/DworkinPWO.pdf

Gioia, D. (2013). "Robert Frost and the Modern Narrative." *Virginia Quarterly Review*, 89(3) (Spring), 186–193.

Gilmore, N. R., & G. W. Gilmore. (1963). "The Bracero in California." *The Pacific Historical Review*, 32(3), 265–282.

Glazier, L. P. (2002). *Digital Poetics: The Making of E-Poetries*. University of Alabama Press.

Fatmasari, Y. (2016). "Womb Control in Toni Morrison's *Beloved*." *Jurnal POETIKA*, 4(1), 22–32.

Kachru, Braj. (1976). "Models of English for the Third World: White Man's Linguistic Burden or Language Pragmatics?" *TESOL Quarterly*, 10, 221–239.

Lam, Kevin. (2012). "Singapore Grand Prix." In K. Lam & X. Y. Tan (Eds.), *Red Pulse: New Singapore USPoetry* (p. 23). The Gentleman's Press.

Pressman, Jessica. (2014). *Digital Modernism: Making It New in New Media*. Oxford University Press, New York.

Quirarte, J. (1992). Sources of Chicano Art: Our Lady of Guadalupe. *Explorations in Ethnic Studies*, 15(1), 13–26.

Rosales, F. A. (1997). *Chicano! The History of the Mexican American Civil Rights Movement*. Arte Público Press/University Press.

Seaman, Bill. (2004). "Interactive Text and Recombinant Poetics." *Electronic Book Review*. https://electronicbookreview.com/essay/approaches-to-interactive-text-and-recombinant-poetics/

Shakespeare, William. (1623). *The Tempest*. Composed in 1610–1611.

Stefans, Brian Kim. (circa 2003). *Fashionable Noise: On Digital Poetics*. Atelos Project, Berkeley.

Stefans, Brian Kim. (2005). "Privileging Language: The Text in Electronic Writing." *Electronic Book Review*. https://electronicbookreview.com/essay/privileging-language-the-text-in-electronic-writing/

Urton, Gary. (1990). *The History of a Myth: Pacariqtambo and the Origin of the Inkas*. University of Texas Press, Austin.

William S. 1984, *The Burroughs File*. City Lights Books, San Francisco.

Williams, Raymond. (1975). *Television: Technology and Cultural Form*. Schocken Books.

Wong, Irene. (1986). "The Search for a Localized Idiom in Malaysian English Literature." *ACLALS Bulletin*, 7(6), 97–110.

Yap, Arthur. (1980). *Down the Line*. Heineman Educational Books.

Part II

Catharsis: Collaboration as pedagogy

5 Smuggling creativity into the classroom

Jason S. Polley

Artificial boundaries

The working title of this chapter was 'Smuggling creativity ~~as Criticism onto the Syllabus and~~ into the ~~L2~~ classroom.' The strike-throughs aim to dismantle a dialectic. 'Criticism' and 'Syllabus' and 'L2' are all-the-more stressed by virtue of what Jacques Derrida would call their conspicuous absent-presence. Beyond contextualizing the Hong Kong English language, literature, and culture scene, and introducing the complication of any easy divide between creative writing in L1 (first language) and L2 (second language) classes, this chapter works, firstly, to de-privilege the purity of standard-English varieties vis-à-vis nonstandard ones, such as Hong Kong English (HKE). The essay, secondly, continues to address Hong Kong L2 as it aims to complicate the taken-for-granted formal writing requirements of the university classroom, which include the crippling burden of assigning high-stakes over low-stakes writing as well as the old guard privileging of 'critical' over 'creative' writing. I change t(r)ack in the last half of my chapter. My final two subsections, thirdly, place these liberating problematizations into suggestive rather than prescriptive practice by offering a reflective—and reflexive—evolving creative writing case study, one initially adopted for the local Filipina community in Hong Kong, then adapted for particular college and university participants in Hong Kong and the neighboring city of Zhuhai, in China.[1]

Likewise embedded in this experiential and, ergo, autoethnographic study are anecdotal accounts of and formalized responses to the fact that English literature courses in Hong Kong often elide the L2 issue. Some possible reasons for this patent omission, and how instructors can work around it, too are embedded herein. One of my main stakes, so the subtitle of this chapter suggests, concerns what Indigo Perry, referring to the space of creative writing instruction, styles as 'letting go of boundaries in our course design, teaching, and assessment' (quoted in Donnelly & Harper 2013: xxiv). Yet let me add a codicil. Perry's liberating 'letting go of boundaries'[2] should not be the purview of creative writing teachers *exclusively*. Nor, so other essays in this volume illustrate, should this horizon of deliverance[3] be limited to the province of literature instructors—or even just to humanities instructors more generally.

The strategies I discuss in this chapter do not merely aim to dismantle the difficult literariness of English literature. I plan also to dismantle what I see as an artificial boundary between creativity and criticism while also ensuring that instructors can satisfy the outcome-based interpellating of senior administrators forced to force us to fetishize key performance indicators, graduate attributes, and community impacts. 'Creativity,' I demonstrate, need not just be a buzzword that we educators pay lip service to. Pace Perry, we can ask our students to be more creative (in the service of the critical); we can ask ourselves to be more creative (and, by extension, more critical) in the design of English writing activities. Literariness (almost) always already comes off as necessarily high-stakes. High-stakes writing is therefore intuitively divorced from low-stakes writing, by which I mean the informal writing domains of text messages, emails, and conventional letters (if students write the last, beyond the cursory postcards that are the labor of holiday travel, anymore). As a result, literary or high-stakes writing tends to be understood in the Olympian arena of high risk, a situating that stifles learning by accentuating performance (results) instead of practice (process). Another stake in this chapter is the introduction of multiform low-stakes writing into the classroom so as to cultivate rather than constrain the creativity and criticism of student writers.

Herein, second language (L2) need not explicitly mean language classrooms, meaning a classroom where a second language is taught for the purpose of pragmatically acquiring the necessary skills to communicate in a particular language. For instance, for those of us teaching in Asia, and for my purposes Hong Kong explicitly—Hong Kong, a place where all eight public universities officially use *English* as their main *mode of instruction* (EMI)—most students in most classrooms are working in L2 or L3. So, whether a student is in the sciences or the social sciences or the humanities, whether in the chemistry classroom, the government and international relations one, or the music one, she is (officially, at least) in an L2 classroom. In the wider Hong Kong context, this colonial disciplining, this official transacting in English, also applies, albeit not universally. Take bank contracts, for instance. It says right there on my conventional English and Chinese bilingual bank-loan agreement that in cases of interpretative discrepancy, the English version is the default record. Not all legal documents in Hong Kong, however, are bilingual. The heterogeneity of linguistic power in Hong Kong, where the official language policy is trilingual (English, Cantonese, Mandarin) and biliterate (English, Chinese) presents a linguistic contact zone of conflict. 'Article 9' of the Basic Law, for example, allows that 'In addition to the Chinese language, English may also be used as an official language by the executive authorities, legislature and judiciary of the Hong Kong Special Administrative Region' (Hong Kong: Basic Law 1997: 3). Though not *the* preeminent semantic signifier in Hong Kong, English, we can carefully say, still occupies a privileged sociolinguistic place in the territory—this notwithstanding the handover to China over two decades ago in 1997, as well as the fact that according to the '2016 Population By-census' (Census and Statistics

Dept. Hong Kong 2017), 88.9 percent of the Hong Kong 'Population Aged 5 and Over' employs Cantonese as their 'Usual Spoken Language' (np).[4] Cantonese, it follows, is the mother tongue of the great majority of university students in Hong Kong. On average, 90% of my English literature students in Hong Kong are L1 Cantonese speakers.

The reason why the distinction between 'English' Instructor and 'English literature' Instructor, especially in light of creativity in the classroom, is important to me may at first seem paradoxical. When we think of the former, of 'English,' it conveys more concrete ideas of 'the basics,' of 'the practical,' and of 'interpersonal communication.' The latter, however, inculcates more abstract impressions of 'the literary and/or the poetic,' which may include more specialized field extenuations like 'Chaucerian or Shakespearian or Romanticist or High Modernist or Post-Structuralist.' Here we have a de facto dichotomy of simple versus complicated, of pragmatic versus philosophical. In 'Curriculum as Cultural Critique,' Eddie Tay (2014) describes this distinction as 'what one might call a prosaic as opposed to a poetic use of English' (111). 'The prosaic approach,' Tay explains, 'is an instrumentalist approach, one that regards language as a means to various ends' (Ibid). 'The poetic approach,' he continues, 'regards language as an end in itself—it is not necessarily about poetry, but it claims English as a subjective terrain from which one makes sense of the world' (Ibid). My main job, again as it pertains to creativity versus criticism, is to deconstruct this de facto dialectic, by which I really mean to destabilize the privilege always already accorded to one half of a binary pair (i.e. criticism > creativity; poetic > prosaic; philosophy > instrumentality). My strategy for doing so in the Hong Kong classroom involves dissolving what I will call 'the artificial boundary between creativity and criticism.' For me, it's stifling to think of literature as, well, conventionally literary in the sense of elitist, that is, in the Matthew Arnold (1994) way of a writer needing at once to 'delight and to instruct' his already-educated readers. Steve Healy (2013) correctly highlights how 'Matthew Arnold argued that the best literature could be a means for social progress and advancing civilization' (67). The problem, of course, concerns the endowment of interpretive agency. Who, in short, bestowed meaning to terms like 'progress' and 'civilization'? The answer to this rhetorical question, especially less than two decades before the height of the British Empire in 1888, should be obvious.[5] This 1869 *Culture and Anarchy*-dialectical type of thinking is stifling because it essentially discourages—or even prohibits—L2 English-language writing. It does this is by divorcing English writing from everyday communication. The 'prosaic,' pace Arnold, appears neither to delight nor to instruct. Such evolvement and refinement 'naturally' belongs in the province of the 'poetic.'

Additionally, *writing as edificatory duty* can also proscribe L1 learners from writing *properly*. I steal 'properly' from Xiaolu Guo's *A Concise Chinese-English Dictionary for Lovers* (2008). This English-language novel by an L2 learner opens with a brief, handwritten, rueful epigram. The reflexive author, who is by extension also speaking for her protagonist, apologizes 'for' her inept standard '*English*' (Guo 2008: n.p.). The adverb 'properly' humorously recurs as Guo's narrator, whose 'difficult' name Zhuang is abbreviated to 'Z' as she first studies in London then travels through several Schengen states, continues to fumble with culture-specific expressions and niceties even as her English improves. What Guo does here is expose the myth of any 'proper/preferred' standard(ized) English. It is because Zhuang speaks 'improperly' that she and her readers learn, improve, and are entertained. And improving can't ever end. L1 learners, in other words, too can improve—and must not be discouraged from writing in the first place on account of elitist or 'proper' or (I would argue) outdated literary/canonical strictures. If British conjures English and American English and Canadian English and Australian English, why not Filipino English, Indian English, Hong Kong English, and Singapore English? Indeed, why not Taglish, Hinglish, Singlish, and Chinglish?[6] In the Hong Kong context, we're almost 200 years removed from what Indian English novelist Amitav Ghosh characterized in the historical Ibis Trilogy (published in 2008, 2011, and 2012) as the 'pidgin' (arguably a corruption of 'business') of Opium War Guangzhou, where transactions occurred in a code-switching patois that combines a Cantonese grammar with predominantly 'English, Portuguese and Hindusthani' words (Ghosh 2011: 183).

Over the remainder of this chapter, I speak to polyvocalities, the varieties approach, and code-switching in my Hong Kong English (HKE) university classrooms—all in an effort to de-distance my students from the umbrella of world Englishes in the remaking around them. What I try to inculcate in my students is the agency to claim (an) ownership of English. I thus work towards embracing the humanistic optimism Dan Disney espouses in the final sentence of his essay 'Is this how it's supposed to work?' Speaking of the applicable range of L2 Creative Writing across 'a host of scientific and humanities-based disciplines,' Disney (2014) concludes by speaking at once to 'how we humanize language' as well as to 'how we understand [that] language humanizes us' (56).

Hong Kong English (HKE)

Like pidgin, the word *patois* has a negative nuance. So too does the designation *dialect*. To recall Yiddish sociolinguist Max Weinreich's famous quip, 'A language is a dialect with an army and a navy.' The arbitrariness of the binary distinction between a language and a dialect is especially germane to Hong Kong, where Beijing fiat has even Hong Kong Chief Executive Carrie Lam deflecting media questions concerning the future of Cantonese education in the territory. When 'lawmaker Shiu Ka-Chun, of the social welfare constituency, asked [Lam] what her mother tongue was,' the Chief Executive replied: 'We are speaking Cantonese every day, so this is a non-issue' (Su & Lok-kei 2018: n.p.). Shiu's duly diligent persistence left Lam lamely second-guessing the seriousness of Shiu's line of inquiry: 'Sorry, I don't answer silly questions' (Ibid). Setting top-down Chinese ideology and so-called Cantonese frivolity aside, English and Cantonese share a symbiotic relationship in Hong Kong. At least partly as a result of institutionalized English instruction in Hong Kong beginning in the 1970s (this alongside the official presence of the British and an increasing population of L1 and L2 English-speaking expats and tourists), the Cantonese spoken in Hong Kong differs from the one spoken in Guangdong. Ask almost any Hong Kong local, and that person can intuitively and immediately hear the difference between these two Cantonese varieties. One way that even a non-speaker of Cantonese may spot this linguistic variety is through simple observation at Starbucks, of which there are more than 170 in Hong Kong. Local Hong Kong clientele, or at least the high school, university, and youngish professional ones that Starbucks tends to attract, order their complex hot and cold beverages in English—or they at least code-switch between Cantonese and English when articulating their coffee and tea requests. English and English-inflected Chinese transactions are way less likely just over the mainland Chinese border. Even in Guangdong province, where some baristas address customers in Cantonese rather than in Mandarin, Cantonese-English code-switching is by no means *de rigueur*. English, so Li Yuting argues in her PhD thesis 'Early Cantonese Transliterations as a Phonological Basis for Modern Hong Kong English' (2019), is a parent-language of the Cantonese presently spoken in Hong Kong.

Code-switching in Hong Kong occurs at once in English and in Cantonese. University students, for instance, are inclined to refer to their supervisors as 'supervisors,' even when speaking Cantonese amongst Cantonese-speaking friends. On the surface, this may seem no different from the word for refrigerator in Tagalog: *pridyder*. This phonetic translation metonymically means the same as *repridyireytor*. These English loanwords transliterate Frigidaire and refrigerator. But no Tagalog speaker I have approached can think of the/any 'original' Tagalog word for 'refrigerator,' besides the abbreviation *ref* or the word *palamigan*, which more ambiguously means to chill things or make them cold (*malamig*). The point is that there do tend to be Cantonese equivalents to a number of the English words seamlessly code-switched into Cantonese, but Hong Kong Cantonese speakers tend to have normalized them—as with loanwords like 't-shirt,' 'bus,' and 'lift'—to the point that it's awkward or strange for the younger population to use 'older' Cantonese equivalents for these loanwords. English analogies may be the normalization of, for instance, the Cantonese dim sum (*dim sam*), ketchup (*ke jap*), Chop chop (*chuk chuk*), and coolie (*kuli*).[7]

I have anecdotally belabored this loanword point for two main reasons. On the one hand, I aim to debunk an elitist (and top-down normativized) myth about an unadulterated proper or standard form of English. On the other, and correlatively, I address the English that most university students in Hong Kong speak (and write). In terms of the HKE context, however, it also pays dividends to expose and interrogate the racist and classist assumptions that local students may have internalized on account of regional geopolitical positioning. What do I mean? In short, Hong Kong, not unlike

Singapore, is economically rich in comparison to its regional cousins. Witness the free-market proliferation of banks. Ergo, also, the large population of domestic helpers, most of whom originate from South Asia (predominantly the Philippines and Indonesia), as well as the number of residents and refugees from the Indian Subcontinent.[8] Ethnic-Chinese Hong Kong students, therefore, tend to be interpellated into a narrative where both darker-skinned labor/migrants from north of the Hong Kong-Chinese border and darker-skinned labor/refugees from other parts of Asia have less obvious/earned social endowments. An instructive way to expose this standardized negative valuation in the Hong Kong tertiary classroom is to write something like the following on the board without any framing preamble:

UK
Philippines
Australia
India
Canada
Singapore
USA

Follow this by asking students to select the top three countries where they would wish to study 'proper' English were money of no consequence. The quick task works best—if the few sheepish smiles and guilty nods and deadpan stares are any kind of accurate indicator—when you ask your students to *perform this* rationalizing *exercise in their heads only; no need to share your actual answers.*

Certainly, I am simplifying a whole range of understandings and motivations, many of which may transcend a student's personal impressions of class and race and move more directly towards questions of parental concern, demand, and duty, not to mention the hegemony of televisual romanticizing and journalistic (dis)information. Yet the intended value of the exercise is also to explode what local Hong Kong students may take for granted in respect to English and the expectations of speaking and writing and evaluating English properly—and/or English*es* conventionally. I am likewise overlooking employer expectations for Hong Kong university graduates, and particularly English Department graduates. This returns us to my early point about English degrees and pragmatism (what Tay aptly labels as 'prosaic'/'instrumental'). In terms of orthoepy, or phonetics, employers expect English graduates to speak more standard forms of English, which means complying to general 'British' or 'American' pronunciations.[9] Therefore, an L2 English or linguistics graduate in Hong Kong is expected to articulate the modern word for Turing machine as *computer* and not *kom-piu-ta*. So, irrespective of said applicant's appreciation of HKE as a linguistically legitimated English variety, she will likely defer to more standardized enunciations in the presence of potential future employers as well as in putatively 'polite society.' To not do so is at once paradoxically to do one or two or three different things.

The first is to boldly endorse HKE as a valid language variety. The second is to share a sort of in-joke with members of her interpretive community: unbeknownst to themselves, the elites who poo-poo HKE pronunciations are the dupes of outdated linguistic imperialism. The third is simply to speak the English variety that most local, public school-educated Hongkongers speak.

I realize that I am still mostly eliding the performative aspects that reflexively allow speakers to position themselves in public, professional, and other spheres. In terms of computer mediated conversation (CMC), for instance, a posted message is not always solely intended for the addressee. Instead, a message/messenger may use the platform of the ostensibly intended as a means to present oneself in a particular way to a particular collection of (future) users. This CMC personal positioning echoes how we represent ourselves in non-virtual spaces. Just as an informal text-message-concluding *lmfao* or *lolz* or *smh* or *imho* or *wtf* or *fwiw*[10] can mollify an argument by signaling level-headed solidarity, so too do word choices and how we choose to vocalize them indicate a rapprochement or willed-return to camaraderie when face-to-face. For example, pending vocal pauses, inflection, and the pacing of vowel elongation, the Cantonese (and HKE) request to a *ma fan* (high-maintenance) friend or family member to *fai di laaaaaa* ('hurry uuuuuuup') can be understood by the receiver to be more a statement of patient endearment than one of annoyed rebuke. The codes of interpersonal communication, virtual and non-, verbal and non-, depend upon with whom we're communicating, where we're communicating, how we're expected to communicate, whom we know might be or will be listening, and a host of other local determinations that expand upon any kind of all-encompassing standard lexicon. All of this is to say that L2 students should be encouraged (so my final case study section on creativity in the classroom and in community workshops endeavors to show) to expand upon whatever 'English' is when asked to write in 'English.' Their English/Englishes and how they use it/them ought to be at the heart of their writing, not anathema to it, not *not-serious enough* or *too too informal*. HKE certainly does include code-switching, just like Cantonese.[11]

Yes, seriously: L2 Learning through low-stakes (creative) writing

After an email back-and-forth lasting several days, the coordinator of the 'International EFL Conference for Creative Writing Instruction,' held at the University of Macau in November 2017, and I settled on the subtitle in the heading as the title of my plenary address. Kevin H. Maher dutifully had to ensure that my title would pass official muster—that it would be okayed by senior management, who too are positioned in a chain of command beholden to formal outcome bases made ready for university senate scrutiny.[12] Instructive here is the top-down narrative that trickles all the way into the classroom, or in this case, the conference hall. Alternate versions of this title (besides the one supra) included, for one, 'Yes, and: Second-language

Learning via Informal Creative Writing.' This version of the title first evokes the pillar of improv comedy, a performative art that requires its actors, some of whom may be randomly selected from the audience, to allow a story/ skit to continue developing by supplementing, instead of obstructing, its ongoing momentum. The same logic should be applied to writing, and academic writing specifically. Not that writing is a seamless ontological process. I, for one, spend more time backspacing and deliberating over word choices than I do actually moving forward in my writing. In this form-over-content interruptive process, I often lose the thread of my ideas, leaving me stuck between an impeccable word or turn of phrase and ... well, almost nothing— until the thought stubbornly returns, and I interrupt the writing process all over again. Recall Hemingway's agonizing toil to produce 500–1000 words per day. Interpret Lonoff's unending 'turning sentences around' in Philip Roth's *The Ghost Writer* (1979) literally instead of romantically; Lonoff is tortured, not inspired. Consider Joseph Grand in particular from Albert Camus's *The Plague* (1948). Grand comically agonizes over picture-perfect word and sentence usages. Even the idea of formal writing, before anything is said and done, tends to curtail the freer flow of words and ideas entailed by informal writing: texts, emails, social media posts, etc.

An earlier incarnation of my talk title shifted the emphasis from moving forward in the affirmative (rather than corrective) mode of improvisation to a re-prioritization of the conditions/demands of writing. This title read: 'Ya, actually, for real: Non-serious Writing Seriously Teaches.' The title attempts to be at once informal and localized. The informal 'Ya' harnesses the improv actor's spirit, albeit with the addition of an informal and/or sarcastic tone. The 'actually' democratizes the title for Cantonese students. The word *kei saat* translates to 'actually' and is much used in HKE. Locally, *kei saat* functions almost at the level of the vocal pause 'like,' passed from, like, American English to other Englishes around the globe. The 'for real,' along with the playful reproduction of the earnest root 'serious,' emboldens students to include familiar and unfamiliar expressions, tones, translations, and sentiments in their university writing. The goal, therefore, is to encourage students to consider really writing for/to their peers instead of for/to an authority figure (viz. the professor) who'll necessarily have serious formal requirements. When thinking of this approach by which to transcend the impasse of formal writing, I look laterally to a discussion Pulitzer Prize winner Adam Johnson delivered at Hong Kong Baptist University in the spring of 2016. Johnson sidestepped the paralyzing-for-some formality of writing when he drafted *The Orphan Master's Son* on a computer with a nonfunctional screen in a library with no Internet or phone signals. At the end of every thought, Johnson explained, he merely pressed *return* and continued typing. Cleaning up these line breaks, he went on to explain, proved remarkably painless. Johnson simply edited his spacing every morning over coffee. Johnson thereby changes the parameters of serious writing. He literally omits the formal urge to edit, which can interrupt the forward momentum of thinking in writing, by making his words invisible.

My goal is to offer my students a version of the same by blocking or at least softening the daunting gaze of the institutionalized evaluator. In the first half of this chapter (in the first two subsections), I endeavored to undo the artificial boundaries that tend to naturalize the favoring of one element or side of a binary pair. In the case of the university classroom, much of this normalized dialectical privileging has primarily to do with audience and affect. It can pay dividends, then, to have students shift their attention to their peers so that their work is not only formally aimed at their professors/assessors. As I discuss the ways in which I strategically encourage this democratizing (because multidirectional in lieu of unidirectional) gaze via experimental writing activities, I likewise continue to trouble the intuitive divide between creativity and criticism. Given the title of this chapter, it also remains for me to insinuate how my informal creative/critical writing exercises can be understood as hybrid poetry ones.

It's fruitful in certain situations to enable students to (i) write clandestine letters or confessions to idealized receivers. It's also instructive and rewarding for more advanced undergraduate students to (ii) respond to prompts that allow them to write sarcastic—or, better, satirical, parodical, and/or ironical—letters. Let me expand upon (ii), which entails creatively responding to a performative writing prompt, before I move onto (i), the clandestine-confession-to-an-ideal-reader exercise. I proceed in this fashion because the performative ironical letter assignment (ii) can also be translated into the clandestine confession exercise (i) upon which this 'smuggling creativity' chapter concludes.

One technique I use to impel students to write quickly and informally, which in this instance really means less painstakingly, is to assign a 15-minute entrance or exit paper. When applied at the opening of a class meeting, this low-stakes writing activity can also, of course, be used to reward punctual and prepared students, the latter meaning those pupils who have completed the assigned readings. When the writing activity is assigned near the end of a scheduled meeting, it simultaneously rewards punctual, prepared, and attentive students. And whether the informal paper is an entrance or an exit one, it can be applied in the renowned Wordsworthian sense of (a directed) 'spontaneous overflow' of sentiments to be later silently revisited. What I mean by this is that the informal writing assignment can be assigned, originally unbeknownst to students, as a 'spontaneous overflow' (i.e. an informal and preliminary rough draft) to be later silently revisited (i.e. edited and formalized later). Here's an example of an exit paper assignment for an undergraduate critical theory course:

> Write a ten-sentence letter to a friend/enemy/frenemy, whom you know you are smarter than, discoursing on a key Derridean term or technique or theory 'interpellating' you in class today.

The assignment invites students to 'play' with theory in a wealth of ironic and reflexive ways. What, for example, is a sentence? The paragraph-long ones of High Modernist Virginia Woolf in *To The Lighthouse* (1977)? The ten-page unpunctuated ones of her contemporary James Joyce in the

'Penelope' chapter of *Ulysses* (Joyce 1993)? The sporadic page-long ones of the High Modernist-influenced Korean writer Yi T'aejun (see, for instance, pp. 185–186 in 'Before and After Liberation' [Yi 2018])? The seven-page sentence that is the prologue of Jeet Thayil's 2012 Man Booker Prize-short-listed *Narcopolis*? The polished and precise prose of stylists like D.H. Lawrence and Margaret Laurence? The enthusiastic em-dash-separated fragments of Jack Kerouac's *Big Sur* (1962)? Burroughs's (1959) conceivably cento-modeled cut-up non-sequiturs?[13] Stephen King's vernacular vocal-pause evoking 'At least, not yet' in *Gerald's Game* (1992: 63)? Or the natural repetition of the same everyday four words, albeit with the order of the word pairs reversed, so the pedestrian short sentence hauntingly echoes back as it carries the same colloquial meaning (Ibid: 70)?[14] Or, deeper in the same novel, the reflective, telltale, nine-line sentence wherein protagonist Jessie recognizes that others, too, experience impenetrable interiority accidentally (Ibid: 211–212)? Does a student model her assigned sentences on Derrida's own Husserl- and Heidegger-informed brand of rigor combined with the deferral, difference, and deferring of *différance*? To wit: 'When we cannot take hold of or show the thing, let us say the present, the being-present, when the present does not present itself, then we signify, we go through the detour of signs' (Derrida 1968: 131). Or, and by extension, does the assiduous student sentenced by/to this letter-writing activity reproduce the *écriture féminine* of deconstructionist third-wave feminists like Luce Irigary—viz., 'If the female sex takes place by embracing itself, by endlessly sharing and exchanging its lips, its edges, its borders, and their 'content,' as it ceaselessly becomes other, no stability of essence is proper to her' (Irigary 1991: 86)? Not unlike any solid idea of 'the sentence,' this paragraph has, in Derridean fashion, problematized the expected (aesthetic) determinations of what 'the paragraph' ought to look like on the published page. With the exception of paragraph-length problematizers like Derrida generally, Virginia Woolf in *Three Guineas* (1998), Gabriel Garcia Marquez in *The Autumn of the Patriarch* (1978), Jonathan Littell in *The Kindly Ones* (2006), and Nikolai Grozni in *Claustrophobias* (2016), to name but a few rule-breakers, *most* every page in *most* every book has a paragraph break. But, then again, this paragraph does have something that resembles a block quotation; thus, it loosely conforms to given/standard book-page aesthetics' requirements that a page not simply be packed margin-to-margin with uninterrupted prose.

This Derridean 'Structure, Sign, and Play,' to borrow the key terms in the title of his famous 1968 essay,[15] can be applied to every word in my low-stakes writing prompt. The word 'sentence' in the sentence itself is pregnant. Here I am sentencing students to write, the 'you' itself literally interpellating each and every you, while literally or figuratively the 'friend/enemy/frenemy' is interpellated as yet another you: a mandatory interpellative activity that widens interpellation. One could question what a friend really is in contemporaneity. Someone whose Instagram posts you 'like' and who likes you back, even though you're both really posting on this forum because you're in competition cynically to attract the 'likes' of another person who also intermittently deigns to post on the forum? And what is it to be 'smarter'? Might I really think that I am less smart than my interpellated 'enemy' but use this assignment as a means to demonstrate my mastery of irony—or direct humor, or ironically adolescent sarcasm? And why the word discourse? Am I supposed to use jargon? And if I do, and if I am supposedly smarter than my interpellated receiver, then don't I have to (boringly? dutifully?) explain this jargon? 'Class today'? Is it being suggested that I encode Stanley Fish's contingencies concerning 'Texts' and 'Class' and 'Interpretive Communities' that we had to read for last week's class?[16] I mean, I know of three distinct definitions of 'class,' but my supposedly 'dumber friend,' who thinks in terms of secondary school and swimming lessons, doesn't know or care about Marx and the class system. Plus, this 'friend' still thinks of the class as a schoolroom. What's more, this 'friend' is unlikely to grasp in any meaningful way the sense that class can be as cultural as it is economic.

To interrupt and abbreviate the growing list of open-ended multiform questions my letter prompt invites, it's important to reinforce creativity. Though theoretically writing about theory, the student (like I just did) necessarily cycles through a variety of pronouns and alternate points of view. Here, she is compelled to think creatively about theory. Whether or not the 'letter' is a bona fide letter, it needs to read like one. The audience for the letter, then, is at once the friend and the professor. And if this is a Blackboard or Moodle assignment, if it's to be uploaded to an online forum that classmates will likewise have access to, then it's also a letter directed to these classmates. The audience of one is actually an audience of many. These concerns therefore take on the tenor of the aforementioned CMC (Computer Mediated Conversation). If student A wants to impress student B by wittily winning an unfinished argument with student C, then the assignment can complexly involve yet another creative factor. Let's say you're one of only two males in the 15-student class cohort and you feel that you've unjustly been labeled a masculinist. Well, this could be your chance to correct this general misreading with a letter that is clearly sympathetic to the overall feminist climate of the class. Or you might take it upon yourself to ironically redeem yourself by composing a preposterously masculinist mansplaining letter, one that will be read by the people who you feel matter as an apology for earlier ill-considered comments following *that student presentation and now-infamous question period*, or whatever. Perhaps you think your male feminist professor emasculates himself, and by extension, yourself, the other male in the class, and all males in academe, so you design your Moodle-public letter to impress upon your fellow students that a conscientious postmodernist can embrace feminism while simultaneously being 'properly' manly. All in all, under the guise of 'explaining theory or criticism,' the creative options of such an entrance or exit paper eventually formalize into a letter presenting students with a wealth of instructive writerly problems, all of which depend upon the devices of fiction (we can recall Wallace Stevens's famous 'poetry is the supreme fiction'), which first and foremost, especially for young creative/critical writers, involves interlocution and readerly reception.

Writing the unwritten, speaking the unspoken: Epistolary and poetry

Creative, critical, and collective thinking, writing, and receiving, however, need not carry the ultimately high stakes my Derridean 'Letter to a Friend' prompt smuggles in under the original low-stakes writing fiat. The 'Letter to a Friend' exit or entrance paper, alternatively, can simply remain a 10-minute entrance or exit paper—viz., continue to serve as a succinct in-class assignment that rewards prepared, punctual, and attentive students all the while troubling internalized myths about serious writing's privileging of formality over informality, standard Englishes over nonstandard ones, and the critical over the creative. A 'Letter to a Friend' writing prompt can also be used in the university classroom or college-level workshop in ways that eschew individual performance/performativity in favor of collaborative creative work, such as group found poems created over the course of an entire workshop or class meeting. In other words, the 'Letter to a Friend' writing model can, on the one hand, 'invit[e] the blurring of disciplinary boundaries' (Donnelly 2013: 6) in order to, so Paul Dawson offers, re-fashion 'literary and critical writing as complementary practices' (qtd in Donnelly 2013: Ibid). On the other hand, 'Letter to a Friend' creative-critical exercises furthermore furnish young writers with a contemporary corrective to romanticized myths about solitary genius and secluded authorship. In personal correspondences with Diane Donnelly and Graeme Harper, who co-edited the volume *Key Issues in Creative Writing*, J. Robert Lennon avers that 'the university environment does provide opportunities for students to discover, practice, and connect with a writing community' (quoted in Donnelly & Harper 2013: xiv). This sense of community proves instrumental on at least two levels. University administrators are increasingly tasked with qualifying and quantifying the community impacts of their government-funded institutions. At the personal level, individual writers can form productive connections with other developing writers, thus perhaps finding refuge not only in writing but also in collaborating. Community, here, can be as actual as it is imagined. I will presently veer away from the Derridean prompt in order to address these workshopped group found poems. In order to avoid any (local) confusion in terms of my specific workshop attendees, I will implement, and toggle between, the subsection titles 'Local Filipina Helpers' and 'Local Tertiary Students' (these being the two comparable workshops I primarily dilate upon). Finally, I will return to my Derridean letter prompt in order to suggest some germane collective, poetic modifications of/to it.

Local Filipina helpers

Over the past two years I have delivered a handful of versions of a workshop with a variation of this subsection's title. The first time I provided the workshop to a group of Filipina domestic helpers, some of whom were college graduates, in Hong Kong. I titled this initial *Cha* Writing Workshop, presented in association with the WIMLER Foundation of Hong Kong, 'Beyond *Tsismosa* and Before *Artista*: Imagined Letters to Imagined Friends—What I Don't Talk about When I Talk about My Hong Kong Everyday.' Actually, this was not the official title of my talk. The workshop poster disseminated online omitted the Filipinx/Latinx aspect of the title. Only the subtitle remained. This is because WIMLER, a Filipinx nonprofit dedicated to empowering impoverished minorities, rightly flagged the Tagalog designations *tsismosa* and *artista*. These nouns respectively translate to 'gossip, gossips, gossiper' and 'actor, liar, prevaricator.' They have precise connotations, ones that negatively stereotype women doubly since men who blather and betray are feminized as *tsismosas* and *artistas* (and not simply gendered as 'tsismosos' and 'artistes'). The male-gendered *tsismoso* has more recently come into fashion.[17] The feminized noun *artista*, however, remains—both for the value-neutral 'artist/actor' and for the negatively valued 'liar/prevaricator.' The open secret of this negative gender typing, of course, is something I designed the workshop to address; thus, the original sub-subtitle-officially-turned-subtitle: 'What I don't talk about when I talk about my Hong Kong everyday.' Thus, furthermore, the original subtitle-officially-turned title: 'Imagined Letters to Imagined Friends.' The point of the workshop was to empower or embolden the 25 female attendees through (i) individual catharsis, (ii) poetic wordplay, and (iii) group collaboration.[18]

Workshop participants implicitly connected through the shared experience of (i): almost every woman in the workshop noticed that almost every woman in the workshop was crying.[19] This seemed to prompt individual participants to collectively double down, to keep emotively confessing/revealing in a space ostensibly rendered immune from personal embarrassment. Poetic wordplay (ii) proved pivotal at once to the craft of writing and to the workshop overall because individual participants understood that they were required only to share 10 or so poetically modified pearls from their respective intimate letters. Enter, in other words, poetic play (which can euphemize 'revision') and audience awareness. Participants thereby can actively appreciate the (global)[20] payoffs of proofreading while they redirect their attentions from self to audience—as Stephen King suggests in *On Writing: A Memoir of the Craft*, draft one should be for the author herself; draft two for her Ideal Reader; and draft three for the general reader (2000). The aforementioned 'community' that J. Robert Lennon indexes manifests itself in (iii) group collaboration, where participants share their pearls in order to collectively create found poems. Each of these L2 English found poems encodes Filipina Hong Kong experience. Due to code-switching, and the 170-plus languages in the Philippines, each poem could too encode regional Filipina Hong Kong experience—one only readily readable to certain Filipinas, which returns us to issues involving linguistic identity, national identity, L2, and reader reception.

I delivered a similar tripartite-point-modeled workshop to a group of 50, comprised mainly of undergraduate English students, some English professors, and one Humanities Department administrator, at a sister campus of Hong Kong Baptist University (HKBU). The EMI institution, located near Hong Kong in Zhuhai, China, is commonly called United International College (UIC).²¹ My workshop was part of UIC's Department of Humanities and Social Sciences (DHSS) Lecture Series, an annual enterprise highlighting creative writing. With a similar primary psychoanalytic goal of exposing interiority, of revealing suppressions, the workshop title at UIC proved more general: 'Imagined Letters to Ideal Readers: What I don't talk about (and think about) when I talk about (and think about) my everyday.' The third incarnation of the workshop, which I will dilate upon forthwith to highlight poetry and/in tertiary pedagogy, was delivered at another HKBU affiliate, this one a Hong Kong EMI self-funded institution that grants associate degrees called the College of International Education (CIE).

Local tertiary students

With the same title as this book-chapter subsection, namely, 'Writing the Unwritten, Speaking the Unspoken: Epistolary & Poetry,' the workshop at CIE was part of the *Cha* Writing Workshop Series, like the Filipinx one.²² Allow me to appropriate from my own online reflection on the workshop: 'Writing the Unwritten, Speaking the Unspoken: Epistolary & Poetry' was delivered in partnership with the Hong Kong Poetry Festival Foundation and supported by the English Departments at Chinese University of Hong Kong (CUHK) and HKBU. The workshop began with a discussion of Anne Frank, who we know addressed the *Diary* (Frank 1990) of her early teenaged—and, sadly, final—years to an imagined ideal reader: 'Kitty.' In that spirit, I asked attendees to take 25 minutes to write a confessional letter (or epistle) to an ideal reader, to a reader they won't have to perform for, won't have to edit themselves for, and won't have to feel guilty for being deeply honest with (or, conversely, remorseful for being Hamletically 'cruel to be kind' to).

Local Filipina helpers

Perhaps for Filipina workshop attendees especially, a confidential confession to an ideal(ized) reader can prevent or mitigate the dangerous circulation of infectious/inherited trauma. I am thinking here of the traumatic inheritance Art Spiegelman speaks to in the National Book Award-winning *Maus* (1980–1991). In fact, *Maus* stylistically sanitizes the trauma that the young Artie first inherits from his father Vladek's stories of Auschwitz survival. Yes, Spiegelman does metatextually integrate his 1973 publication of 'The Prisoner of the Hell Planet: A Case History' (wherein the comic-artist is institutionalized following his mother Anja's Holocaust survival-guilt suicide in 1968) into *Maus* (Spiegelman 1986: 100–103). Yet the three-page 'Maus' (Spiegelman 2008), published alongside the republication of 'The Prisoner of the Hell Planet' (Spiegelman 2008) in *Breakdowns: Portrait of the Artist as a Young %@& *!*, depicts 'Artie' not as the adult 'Art' who reflexively sources his father's memoir of the Third Reich, but rather as the diminutive 'Artie' being told visceral bedtime stories of starvation, torture, and infiltration. The art here too proves more graphic, thereby less of a distantiation, less of a figurative (minor) remove by way of allegory. Anne Frank, in her *Diary*, at once insulates her family members, her neighbors, and herself from the unmitigated horrors of the Final Solution rising outside her Amsterdam hideaway and the escalating discomforts anyone would have after one year, and two years, and more, of young teenage confinement with disliked others. Frank engineers this insulation by creating a confidante, one who's infinitely compassionate—the ideal receiver you can neither disappoint nor injure. Domestic helpers in Hong Kong, not unlike migrant workers most anywhere, can find themselves in unimaginable contexts, circumstances that they neither report to their families 'back home' nor to their familiars in Hong Kong. We protect our parents, just as we do our children, just as we do ourselves—especially when we're far away, when we're strangers in a strange land, a land too often defined by manipulative work-placement agencies and self-protective survivors. Survival, sometimes, entails concealing discomfiting and dehumanizing experiences for fear of ironically losing whatever agency that diaspora nostalgically confers.

Their suppressed secrets (and often tears) 'spontaneously overflowed'—to return to Wordsworth—workshop participants are invited to revisit their just-completed confidential letters in search of favorite parts or lines. More specifically, I ask each individual to highlight and extract 5 to 10 'pearls' (to use Walter Benjamin's 'Found Poem' terminology for a 'beautiful line') from her unrepressed confession. Participants are then asked to poetically translate or encode or disguise each of these pearls with poetic devices, like homonymy, synonymy, antonymy, alliteration, and/or nonsense with the use of thesauri, dictionaries, their smartphones, and their brains.

Local tertiary students

This encoding complete, the 15 participants at Hong Kong's CIE (to unambiguously return to this workshop[23]) formed into three groups and collaborated on making collective found poems from their translated/disguised pearls. Especially befitting the trilingual and biliterate polyphony that is Hong Kong, each group collected their English found poems whilst interacting in a different language: one in Mandarin, another in Cantonese, and the last in English. Beginning in perplexity, followed first by tears, then by consternation, the increasingly animated workshop concluded in laughter (as did each of my 'Letter to an Ideal Friend' workshops). Here follow the unedited fruits of the confessional outpouring, poetic encoding, and collective production of 'the CIE 15' (Polley 2019) (used with permission):

'Love'
by Chiang Ching, Huang Yun Rong, Liu Mengqi, Chen Wan Yi, Li Shiqi

I act as a mute rubbish bin to restore all her piercing aggression
suggestions, not commands
cram smelly cells in your bloody brain

living in a pure and shining place,
that sick place full of violence, mess, hatred.
Freed me to wonderland;
pretend nothing happened to me.
It is fulfilling and strenuous at the same time.
You want to be the sun,
without being worried, frightened, angry at all.
Being defeated and never say die;
I enjoy.
The longest distance is that you don't love me.
This is a lie poem.
I love thee.
Our relationship is as pure as crystal
but stars out of your orbit can't be attracted.

'Fancy'
by Ng Yee Yan, Xiao Yu, Zou Minyan, Zhang Xinyi, Jian Haonan

The witch danced in the midnight.
Shinning, shimmering, covering the darkness at its back
she put her mask up high.
A sole mask with day and night
Black held it all, so dark, so calm
the bird is yelling.
She yelling through the moonlight
I am a rounded egg.

Open, feel it, warm it, spit it out.
I hold the knife toward myself
Quiet screaming. Stop it.
Peeking, relaxing. Panic. Breathe.
Break it before it hatches.
Thousand crisps, buried to the core.
Surrendering monster into riptide
vanished with those little crisps, leaving empty.
Strippers pretend to be angels.
Finding a crowded destination
for standing outside the fake strait
on the edge, hanging by a rope, swinging, struggling
to let everybody feel right.
I trust you, I trust you
loudly, stop shaking.
You won't be there, can't.

'Travel Around the World'
*by Zheng Cui Ting, Tang Ziyi, Nattapong Chan, Dr. Theresa Cunanan,
Ms. Sandy Chan*

50s virgins
with enormous wings,
wordless, helpless, speechless,
short, curt,
go outside to take in fresh air.
Sky is sea
choices are paradise.
Anvil from the sky,
a breather from the nightingale
choking youth.
All we can manage
Go out with friends to eat junk food.
Diva Drama
hating you dead with gluttony.
Ladies services
peel yourself off.
Hit the beach and enjoy sunshine.
Sand is lava.
Fair winds, Captain.
Will never rises.
Exercise is a great decompression method,
keep writing, keep thinking.
Blackout like you
Halloween on a wheelchair.

Conclusion

My chapter title and what follows it are meant to underscore the tug-of-war between institutional directives and practical outcomes. When we smuggle creativity into the classroom, we work to counterbalance official diktat with current practice, institutional protocol with lip service to it, and the contracted syllabus with evolving classroom dynamics. In this chapter, I have illustrated applied ways to make creativity practical in lieu of undefined and/or esoteric. I too have worked to show how criticism can be formally experimental (and fun) instead of traditionally expository (and 'boring'). I place 'boring' in quotation marks because I am quoting more than a decade's worth of first- and second-year English major students in Hong Kong (and I am sure elsewhere the world over) for whom 'boring' appears as a legitimate readerly response to certain engagements with literary studies. Like the word 'interesting,' I tell them, the word 'boring' is itself 'boring' because it reveals little more than a lack of reflective engagement on the part of the reader/interpreter.[24] Concluding simply that something is 'boring' or 'interesting,' without being able to explain why or how, is itself 'boring' and 'uninteresting.' Only the boring, I pontificate, get bored. Irrespective of my elitist and at least partly disingenuous (after all, I too, like you, do get bored) condemnation of uninspired affective student responses, the fact remains that certain secondary students do arrive to university with an innate sense that literature, criticism, difficulty, and boredom are intertwined—thus the pedagogical virtue of refreshing the study of English by breaking down artificial distinctions between criticism and creativity. 'Letter to a Friend' assignments and workshops can work to translate general boredom into personal enthusiasm, not least because 'Letter to a Friend' exercises complicate the top-down interpellation of teaching and learning by ensuring that the personal social realities of students aren't subsumed by the impersonal impositions classically associated to the disinterest or dispassion required of 'proper' criticism.

An instructive way to address this top-down complication is by way of Paulo Freire's elaboration of Erich Fromm's work on necrophily and biophily. As Eddie Tay (2014) explains, 'Necrophily refers to the preservation of the dead, the maintenance of socio-political culture, while biophily refers to a life consciousness and deliberation' (111). Tay goes on to say that 'creative writing,' so the reflections of his students at the Chinese University of Hong Kong show, 'regards the English language as a space of emergence and potentiality rather than solely as a passport to upward social mobility' (112). Creative writing, then, can problematize what Tay introduced in the essay 'Curriculum as Cultural Critique' as 'the instrumentalist attitude the average Hong Kong person[25] has towards the English language' (103). Instead of the 'prosaic' and 'instrumentalist' and 'necrophily' approaches Hongkongers tend to conjure vis-à-vis English studies as a field (where knowledge arrives from without), 'poetic' and 'emergent' and 'biophilic' methodologies implement a convergence of the creative and/as the critical in English studies (where knowledge can be produced from within).

I am of course ironically setting up boundaries just as I deconstruct them here. I am complicating the critical and the creative in order to collapse their formal distinctions. At the same time, I have seemingly set up a dialectic that simply reverses the normalized (in Hong Kong) privileging of the 'prosaic' over the 'poetic.' The collaborative 'creative' work of 'the UIC 15,' however, demonstrates, if anything, that the prosaic and the poetic, that necrophily and biophily, can and do converge. Take line 13 from 'Love' provided earlier. It reads: 'The longest distance is that you don't love me.' I recall what my Shakespeare professor said to a francophone class member after reading her *King Lear* paper: 'You don't *write* with a French accent.' To appropriate Professor Michael Bristol's smiling, jocoserious compliment to my Québecoise fellow student, 'The longest distance is that you don't love' reads more like Shakespeare than it does L2 English. We could say something similar of line 17 in 'Fancy' (also provided earlier). 'Strippers pretend to be angels' evokes the catalogs of Jack Kerouac and Allen Ginsberg. The first oxymoronic words of Line 11, 'Quiet screaming,' too suggest Beat Generation imagism and counter-culturalism over accepted/expected L2 language constructions. The closing lines of the sexually coded 'Travel Around the World' (Ibid)—viz., 'Blackout like you / Halloween on a wheelchair'—too evidence a confident experimentation with the malleability of English parts of speech.

Depending on whether the penultimate line is enjambed or end-stopped,[26] 'Halloween' can materialize as either a verb or a noun. So: it can be—it is!—both. This type of open-endedness bespeaks an L1-like comfort with the English language: that is, a refined understanding that we construct language (locally, biophylically; sousveillance from within) as much as language constructs us (canonically, necrophylically; surveillance from above).[27]

Even the gnomic and cryptic Derrida, and the intellectual machinations that a simple 'Letter to a Friend' about something about Derrida's deconstruction evokes, can be (on the face of it) de-intellectualized, or de-formalized or de-constructed, by simply having students go through the same multiform paces with the Derridean 'Letter to a Friend' as they do with the 'Imagined Letter to an Ideal Reader.' Here, the structure, the sign, and the play can literally happen collectively, an endless deferral of possibility—of creativity, of theory, of supplement, of agency. After all, what the poetic translation or beautification or uglification of pearls does is encode each pearl with a double entendre or portmanteau. Their words camouflaged, their words permitted to be amalgamated, a pregnant collage ensues, with each student effectively reading at least her contribution as 'double,' while understanding that every included line (or pearl) too carries a double meaning for another contributor/collaborator. What this does is instruct students not only in creativity, poetic techniques, and collaboration, but also in interpretive reading/writing. And this is critical thinking *tout court*.

Notes

1 I also offered a version of the workshop to English majors at Chaiduar College in Gohpur, Upper Assam, Northeast India. Yet this chapter focuses on Hong Kong's L2 cultural context.

2 Perry's point reflexively involves what Steve Healy, in 'Beyond the Literary,' sees as creative writing's spectacular 'liberation from the dehumanizing effects of capitalism' (Healy 2013: 77). Healy avails himself of Guy Debord's titular terminology from *The Society of the Spectacle* (Debord 1983) because the amorphous 'creative writing' designation models itself as 'some pure, transcendent space outside of the spectacle' (Healy 2013). The 'creative,' spectacularly commodified as non-spectacular, operates as 'an excellent tool for the spectacle' (Ibid). Inescapable marketplace forces also interpellate creative writing teachers and practitioners. In brief, alienation is all the more alienating when disguised as liberation.

3 Whether instituted naïvely or not.

4 Here are the other 2016 Census language categories. Each listed language is parenthetically followed by the percentage of its speakers aged 5 and older: 'Putonghua' (1.5%); 'Other Chinese dialects' (3.1%); 'English' (4.3%); and 'Other languages' (1.9%).

5 Shakespeare anticipates said colonial disciplining and punishment just a decade after the establishment of the East India Company in 1600. First performed in 1611, *The Tempest* (Shakespeare 1999) features a banished Italian duke shipwrecked on an unnamed island. He assumes control of the island by imprisoning Sycorax, the matrilineal ruler of the place, and by enslaving her son Caliban, whose name anagrammatically encodes the word cannibal, thus instantiating, in the style of *The Bible* (and, so, the Western canon), the dark other/outcaste as (uncivilized) 'savage' or 'barbarian.' See Shirley Lim's reference to *The Tempest* in this volume.

6 Were this a research essay mainly about the sociolinguistic realities of Hong Kong, in lieu of a critical pedagogy essay about breaking down naturalized top-down boundaries in the service of enhancing creativity in the tertiary L2 English class-room, I would turn to Kingsley Bolton's 'English in Asia, Asian Englishes, and the issue of proficiency' (2008). Bolton addresses the ongoing debate in the field of World Englishes, which has 'polarised researchers in second-language acquisition versus those employing a world Englishes approach' (2008: 11). Bolton notes that 'the challenge for second-language acquisition research is to recognise that, in many Asian contexts, individual language learning takes place in complex multilingual and functionally-differentiated settings' (Ibid). A marked contrast to the 'Asian context' is the American one, 'where a standard language ideology tends to view monolingualism as the default norm' (Ibid). For more on relevant regional debates in the field of World Englishes, see the essay volume *The Future of English in Asia: Perspectives on Language and Literature* (O'Sullivan et al. 2017).

7 For concentrated linguistic treatments of code-switching and mixing in Hong Kong, see Wakefield (2018). Wakefield's monograph *English Loanwords in Cantonese: How Their Meanings Have Changed* is forthcoming from Hong Kong University Press.

8 Auteur director Wong Kar-wai partly addresses Hong Kong's Indian Subcontinent population by virtue of the setting of his 1994 film *Chungking Express*. Chung King Mansions, located in Tsim Sha Tsui, Kowloon, is Hong Kong's de facto 'Little India.' For more on Chung King Mansions, see the long last sentence of footnote 29 (p. 244) in Polley (2018).

9 Bolton (2008: 9) cites Robert Phillipson in order to earmark the 'continuing linguistic imperialism of 'global English' and a related degradation of linguistic ecology.' Concerning the 'issue of [perceived] proficiency,' Bolton reminds us that 'Despite the patient explanations of many linguists, the use of such terms as 'Hong Kong English,' 'Indian English,' 'Malaysian English,' 'Philippine English,' and 'Singapore English' have typically evoked negative reactions from business and political leaders' (Ibid). See Bolton (2008: 9–12) for a brief over-view of the 'real-world issues' Asian businesses and tech enterprises face as glo-balization professionalizes Asian markets.

10 I like to think that my present and past students also half-jokingly use the abbre-viation *yhlgll*, which stands for *yung ha lei go lo la*. This is the only way I know how to say 'use your brain' in Cantonese.

11 Cantonese itself, and in Hong Kong especially, can be likened to the hip-hop of languages: it evolves quickly and in unexpected ways.

12 It behooves us to recall Steve Healy's point about the seductiveness of 'creative literacy' as fashioned as escape from capitalist alienation (cf. fn. 1 above). In 'Re-shaping Creative Writing,' Dianne Donnelly plainly attests to the establish-ment's interpellation of creative writing when she notes how 'Government imperatives challenge creative writers in the academy to substantiate how their work represents a body of research and contributes new knowledge to the fields' (2013: 21). Certainly, Mimi Thebo is right to apprehend that 'Creative writing has been slow to recognize the precedents set in the Fine and Performing Arts' (Thebo 2013: 44). 'In a way,' Thebo goes on to say, creative writing is 'marooned as the only practice-based subject in the humanities' (Ibid). There is a liberating quality to being academically unique, to participating in construc-tive academic development and implementation. Yet, again, said 'freedom' still spectacularly operates under the aegis of both state and global marketplace constraints.

13 See, included in this volume, Stephanie Laine Hamilton's wide-ranging and resourceful 'Trans-Contemporary Word Culture: Late Antique Cento, Twentieth Century Cut-up, and Craft Culture in the Canadian Rockies.'

14 The same four-word *sentence* also twice appears in Stephen King's *Dreamcatcher* (2001: 310, 325). In the second instance, however, the word pair is switched, the comma is removed, and the sentence serves as a chapter-ending *paragraph*.
15 See 'Structure, Sign and Play in the Discourse of the Human Sciences' (Derrida 1978: 278–293).
16 See, especially, the essay 'Is There a Text in This Class?' from the eponymous essay volume (Fish 1980).
17 The same applies in Spanish. A male who engages in *chisme* (*tsismis* in Tagalog) tends to be referred to as a *chismosa*. The masculine noun *chismoso* is gaining currency, however.
18 I begin outlining the specific requirements/processes of the workshop two paragraphs hence.
19 For anyone unfamiliar with the plights of female foreign domestic helpers in Hong Kong—whose official numbers projected close to 360,000 in 2017, a number almost evenly split between helpers from Indonesia and the Philippines, a number amounting to about 4% of the Hong Kong population in 2017 (Polley 2018: 237)—please see Hans J. Ladegaard's *The Discourse of Powerlessness and Repression: Life Stories of Domestic Migrant Workers in Hong Kong* (2017).
20 I modify payoffs with global because incremental or spot editing, in this case finding and reworking individual pearls, can/should be a lesson in revision overall. If I can 'improve' this line, I can also improve this one, and this one, and that one, etc. Plus, it's not a quest for *le mot juste*. Rather, it's the discovery of a landscape of variable *mots justes*—'right or fitting words' that, so the title of the workshop indicates, can encompass code-switching.
21 The official name of the institution is: Beijing Normal University & Hong Kong Baptist University United International College.
22 Published reflections on, with photos of, all *Cha* Writing Workshops are available for perusal at https://chajournal.blog/category/cha-writing-workshop -series/
23 College of International Education; the third incarnation of the workshop; cf. p. 132.
24 See Barthes's *Le plaisir du texte* [*The Pleasure of the Text*] (1973).
25 The designation 'Hong Kong person' certainly likewise applies to the average Hong Kong first- and second-year university English student, so my waxing on boredom is meant to evidence.
26 For instructive examples of this 'line-break' 'doubling,' see the sub-section 'A line is a line is a line?' in Disney (2014: 50–53).
27 See this inspiring 'testimony to biophily,' which 'transcends' linguistic, disciplinary, genre, and national borders, in the concluding subsection 'Creative Writing Pedagogy: Cultural Critique and Cultural as Resource' of Tay (2014: 114–118).

References

Arnold, Matthew. (1994). *Culture and Anarchy*. New Haven: Yale University Press. (First published 1869).
Barthes, Roland. (1973). *Le Plaisir du texte [The Pleasures of the Text]*. Paris: Editions du Seuil.
Bolton, Kingsley. (2008). "English in Asia, Asian Englishes, and the issue of proficiency." *English Today*, 24: 3–12.
Burroughs, William S. (1959). *Naked Lunch*. New York: Grove Press.
Camus, Albert. (1948). *The Plague*. Trans. Stuart Gilbert. New York: Modern Library.

Census and Statistics Dept. Hong Kong. (2017). "Population Aged 5 and Over by Usual Spoken Language and Year." *2016 Population By-census*. Hong Kong. Retrieved from https://www.bycensus2016.gov.hk/en/bc-mt.html

Debord, Guy. (1983). *The Society of the Spectacle*. Detroit: Black & Red. (First published 1967).

Derrida, Jacques. (1968). "Différance." In Neil Badmington and Julia Thomas (eds), *The Routledge Critical and Cultural Theory Reader* (pp. 126–148). New York: Routledge.

Derrida, Jacques. (1978). "Structure, Sign and Play in the Discourse of the Human Sciences." In *Writing and Différence* (pp. 278–293). Trans. Alan Bass. Chicago: University of Chicago Press. (First published 1968)

Disney, Dan. (2014). "Is This How It's Supposed to Work? Poetry as Radical Technology in L2 Creative Writing Classrooms." In Dan Disney (ed.), *Exploring Second Language Creative Writing: Beyond Babel* (pp. 41–56). Amsterdam: John Benjamins.

Donnelly, Dianne. (2013). "Reshaping Creative Writing: Power and Agency in the Academy." In Dianne Donnelly and Graeme Harper (eds.), *Key Issues in Creative Writing* (pp. 3–29). Multilingual Matters.

Donnelly, Dianne, and Graeme Harper. (2013). "Introduction: Key Issues and Global Perspectives in Creative Writing." In Dianne Donnelly and Graeme Harper (eds.), *Key Issues in Creative Writing* (pp. xiii–xxvi). Toronto: Multilingual Matters.

Fish, Stanley. (1980). *Is There a Text in this Class?* Cambridge, MA: Harvard University Press.

Frank, Anne. (1990). *The Diary of a Young Girl*. Trans. B. M. Mooyart-Doubleday. New York: Doubleday. (First published 1947).

Garcia Marquez, Gabriel. (1978). *The Autumn of the Patriarch*. Trans. Gregory Rabassa. New York: Picador.

Ghosh, Amitav. (2011). *River of Smoke*. London: John Murray.

Grozni, Nikolai. (2016). *Claustrophobias*. Sofia: Begemot.

Guo, Xiaolu. (2008). *A Concise Chinese-English Dictionary for Lovers*. New York: Anchor.

Healy, Steve. (2013). "Beyond the Literary: Why Creative Literacy Matters." In Dianne Donnelly and Graeme Harper (eds.), *Key Issues in Creative Writing* (pp. 61–78). Toronto: Multilingual Matters.

Hong Kong: Basic Law of the Hong Kong Special Administrative Region of the People's Republic of China. (1997). Retrieved from https://www.basiclaw.gov.hk/en/basiclawtext/images/basiclaw_full_text_en.pdf

Irigary, Luce. (1991). *Marine Lover of Friedrich Nietzsche*. Trans. Gillian C Gill. New York: Columbia University Press.

Joyce, James. (1993). *Ulysses*. Toronto: Oxford University Press. (First published 1921).

King, Stephen. (1992). *Gerald's Game*. London: Hodder.

King, Stephen. (2000). *On Writing: A Memoir of the Craft*. New York: Scribner.

King, Stephen. (2001). *Dreamcatcher*. London: Nel.

Kerouac, Jack. (1962). *Big Sur*. New York: Farrar, Strauss, & Cudahy.

Ladegaard, Hans J. (2017). *The Discourse of Powerlessness and Repression: Life Stories of Domestic Migrant Workers in Hong Kong*. New York: Routledge.

Li, Yuting. (2019). "Early Cantonese Transliterations as the Phonological Basis for Modern Hong Kong English." PhD Diss., Hong Kong Baptist U.

Littell, Jonathan. (2006). *Les Bienveillantes [The Kindly Ones]*. Paris: Gallimard.

O'Sullivan, Michael, David Huddart, and Carmen Lee (eds.). (2017). *The Future of English in Asia: Perspectives on Language and Literature*. New York: Routledge.

Polley, Jason S. (2018). "'I Didn't Think We'd Be Like Them"; or, Wong Kar Wai, Hongkonger." In Jason S. Polley, Vinton Poon, and Lian-Hee Wee (eds.), *Cultural Conflict in Hong Kong: Angles on a Coherent Imaginary* (pp. 235–255). Singapore: Palgrave MacMillan.

Polley, Jason S (2019). "Writing the Unwritten, Speaking the Unspoken: Epistolary & Poetry." *Cha*. N.p. Retrieved from https://chajournal.blog/2019/01/14/cie/

Roth, Philip. (1979). *The Ghost Writer*. New York: Ballantine.

Shakespeare, William. (1999). *The Tempest*. Mineola: Dover. (First published 1623).

Spiegelman, Art. (1986). *Maus I*. New York: Pantheon.

Spiegelman, Art. "Maus" (2008). In *Breakdowns: Portrait of the Artist as a Young %@& *!* (n.p.). New York: Pantheon.

Spiegelman, Art. "Prisoner on the Hell Planet." (2008). In *Breakdowns: Portrait of the Artist as a Young %@& *!* (n.p.). New York: Pantheon.

Su, Xinqi, and Sum Lok-kei. (2018). "Should Mandarin Replace Cantonese in Hong Kong? No, Says Carrie Lam." *South China Morning Post: Hong Kong*, 3 May. Retrieved from https://www.scmp.com/news/hong-kong/politics/article/2144578/should-mandarin-replace-cantonese-hong-kong-says-no

Tay, Eddie. (2014). "Curriculum as Cultural Critique: Creative Writing Pedagogy in Hong Kong." In Dan Disney (ed.), *Exploring Second Language Creative Writing: Beyond Babel* (pp. 103–118). Amsterdam: John Benjamins.

Thayil, Jeet. (2012). *Narcopolis*. New York: Penguin.

Thebo, Mimi. (2013). "Hey Babe, Take a Walk on the Wild Side—Creative Writing in Universities." In Dianne Donnelly and Graeme Harper (eds.), *Key Issues in Creative Writing* (pp. 30–47). Toronto: Multilingual Matters.

Wakefield, John. (2018) "Turning English into Cantonese: The Semantic Change of English Loanwords." In Jason S. Polley, Vinton Poon, and Lian-Hee Wee (eds.), *Cultural Conflict in Hong Kong: Angles on a Coherent Imaginary* (pp. 15–34). Singapore: Singapore: Palgrave MacMillan

Woolf, Virginia. (1977). *To The Lighthouse*. Hammersmith: Grafton. (First published 1927).

Woolf, Virginia. (1998). *Three Guineas*. In *A Room of One's Own/Three Guineas* (pp. 151–414). New York: Oxford University Press. (First published 1938).

Yi, T'aejun. (2018). "Before and after Liberation: A Writer's Notes." *Dust and Other Stories* (pp. 147–188). Trans. Janet Poole. New York: Columbia University Press. (First published 1946).

6 Using video poetry to teach biotechnology

Mary Jacob and Stephen Chapman

Affordances of digital poetry for writers and readers

By definition, any form of hybrid poetry involves bringing together two or more disparate elements, but what types of elements are combined? As co-editor of a substantive anthology of hybrid poetry (Swensen & St. John 2009), Cole Swensen (2009) describes hybrid poetry as an 'errance off the linear continuum that runs from the conventional to the experimental.' Matthew Hittinger (2007) defines hybrid form in terms of how it combines elements from different sources or genres, saying that it 'retains the elements of its two origins while being synthesized into something new.' Hittinger's model, with its emphasis on replacing 'either/or' with 'both/and,' echoes Pierre Joris's (2003) nomad poetics and the rhizomatic model provided by Deleuze and Guattari (1987), complete with its inherent parataxis. Hybrid poetry can include an exploration of the potential for ethnic, aesthetic, or cultural hybridity, as noted by Craig Santos Perez (2010). Hybrid poetry can include blends of media and words, and it can include blends of different types of language.

Given this broad range of available options, we find it useful to contextualize video poetry in a larger subset of hybrid poetry that incorporates digital elements. Digital elements have the potential to enable poetry to move across boundaries such as those separating so-called 'high art' and 'popular art,' and thus broaden the audience for poetry. Depending on how digital elements are used, they can alternatively push poetry even further into a zone where only those readers already accustomed to experimental poetry will find it accessible, or, conversely, bring poetry to a broader audience.

Image and word hybrids

Image and word can be created together as a hybrid digital artifact. For example, Welsh poet David Greenslade creates his own digitally altered image-poem combinations, as in the recent publications *Ubiquitext* and *Hamadryad*. An extract from *Hamadryad* as published in *Otoliths* (Greenslade 2018) is shown in Figure 6.1.

Under lock and key
I meditated wildly
lurching between space travel,
fireworks,
names of famous ships,
roofs I'd fallen from,
chrome blistering,
girlfriends,
doors opened,
doors shut in my face,
until a Hamadryad showed me how
to feel each Breath as it steals along
the groove between the border of my upper lip
and the margins of my nose.

Why should a Hamadryad be considerate?
No nervous system, outdoors all its life,
sucking minerals through clay and rock,
home to birds and insects?
Where's the Bodhisattva
in that? When it hits, it smacks
like a Mallet against Thin Skin.

Figure 6.1 Extract from **Hamadryad.**

Greenslade manipulates and combines images digitally, often starting with mundane photographs and then making them strange through serial alterations. Rather than writing poems inspired by pictures (as in traditional ekphrastic poetry) or creating an image as an illustration of a poem, his method involves an iterative process of parallel development in which both image and poem come into being together, each informing the other. Methods such as these in which there is a dialogic relationship between word and image extend the definition of ekphrastic poetry beyond the 'verbal representation of visual representation' (Heffernan 2004: 3). These hybrids can be described as verbo-visual poetic expressions that may or may not represent something outside of their own words and images. This phrasing puts the images and words on equal footing and highlights the potential for non- or low-referential works, thus moving away from a requirement of representation.

The rise of social media in the 21st century has led to the flourishing of new forms of poetry. The simple combination of photograph (or line drawing) and poem shared online via Instagram, for example, can reach a broad audience. Such poems tend to be short, because they must fit onto an image suitable for sharing via social media. Instagram poems are often more accessible than more experimental forms of hybrid poetry. Rupi Kaur attained fame in 2018 when her Instagram poetry went viral (Kaur [Instagram posts] 2020; see also Kaur 2018). As Hill and Yuan (2018) note, 'The 25-year-old Canadian poet outsold Homer two years ago: Her first collection, *milk & honey*, has been translated into 40 languages and has sold 3.5 million copies, stealing the position of best-selling poetry book from *The Odyssey*.' Rebecca Watts (2018), however, critiques social media poetry such as Kaur's for being overly accessible and contributing to the 'denigration of intellectual engagement and [a] rejection of craft,' with consumer-driven content and mass market appeal. Watts extends her critique to the popular British poets Holly McNish and Kate Tempest, who have both received the Ted Hughes Award for New Work in Poetry. Both McNish and Tempest used YouTube to spread their works in video form, thus reaching beyond a traditional poetry audience.

Watts's article sparked a lively controversy. Sarah Crown, director of literature at Arts Council England and former *Guardian* books editor, also notes that the controversy over Instapoets such as Kaur center around 'this notion of "accessibility"—and the question of whether heightened accessibility necessarily involves a blunting of the fine edge that is poetry's USP' (Crown 2019). Crown, however, celebrates this accessibility, noting that performance poetry is based on oral traditions. Crown goes on to discuss poet Anthony Anaxagorou, explaining that his hybrid poetry is a formulation of rich movements from the 1980s combined with the slam movement of the 1990s enriched with American sermonizing, employing language, ideology, performance, and intonation for effect. Furthermore, he argues that hybrid poetry is a fusion of traditions and approaches that all stem from the oral (Crown 2019).

Khaira-Hanks suggests that the controversy stems from the fact that social media poetry gives opportunities for poets who may otherwise be marginalized. Speaking of Kaur's popularity, Khaira-Hanks (2017) notes that, in a white- and male-dominated society, Kaur speaks a truth that the literary establishment is unlikely to understand. In the eyes of writers such as Khaira-Hanks, Crown, and Anaxagorou, it is the very hybrid nature of social media poetry that gives this hyphenated poetry value and expands its inclusivity, thus reaching audiences who might not otherwise fully engage with a purely text-based medium. The visuals can give audiences a way into the work. This process offers inclusion on the part of both creators and audience.

Hybrids with digital audio and video

With the growth in digital technology in this century, audio and video creation has become available to the general public through smartphones and tablets, which are easier to use and more pervasive than camcorders or dedicated audio recording equipment. As a result, a number of new platforms for digital poetry have arisen. Founded in 2017, the Visible Poetry Project (n.d.) website aims to make poetry accessible, by recreating poems through the medium of film. The International Video Poetry Festival (Void Network 2018) attempts to create an open public space for the creative expression of all tendencies and streams of contemporary visual poetry. It is organized by the Void Network, an activist collective based in Athens, London, and New York which aims to radicalize everyday life. US-based MotionPoems started with a collaboration between an animator and a poet in 2008 and has grown into a collection of videos including work by well-known and emerging poets. MotionPoems (n.d.) describes their aim as exploring the space between poets and other artists to create hybrid artworks that connect with modern audiences in new ways. They also offer resources for teachers. *Moving Poems Magazine* (n.d.) provides news and feature articles on video poetry. These are just a few examples to illustrate the growth and variety of video poetry in the 21st century.

In its simplest form, digital hybrid poetry can consist of audio recordings of poetry performances. Poetry podcasts and recordings can be found on platforms such as *The Poetry Society* (UK), *PennSound* (n.d.) (US), *The Poetry Foundation* (n.d.) (US/international), *Poetry Translation Centre* (n.d.) (international, with dual language poetry readings) and more. *The Poetry Exchange* (n.d.) (UK) was the British Podcast Awards 2018 Silver Award Winner for Most Original Podcast. They introduce their site with a quote from Elizabeth Alexander which concisely describes the site as a powerful and unique way to engage with poetry for wider audiences, thus reinforcing the power of podcasts to bring poetry to a new audience.

Besides just recording a poetry reading, digital audio and video can be used in experimental ways, incorporating non-verbal sound effects and digital sound alteration. William Burroughs and Brion Gysin pioneered the 'cut-up' artifact, including audio recordings and films. A video of Burroughs's *The Cut Ups* (1966), an early example of cut-up technique applied to film, can be viewed on YouTube. In his reappraisal of Burroughs's work, Rob Bridgett (2003) says that critics at the time overlooked the 'nihilistic aspects of the film and its confrontational approach to audience and language/logic as a control system.' Bridgett thus speaks to the social relevance of hybrid works.

More recently, Wales-based poet Zoë Skoulding performs hybrid poetry through live audio looping and digital alteration of spoken words and other sounds. When she performs extracts from her chapbook *Teint* (Skoulding 2016), for example, she uses live mixing, natural and digital generation of sounds, as well as pre-recorded audio clips, to bring out her central metaphor of underground rivers in a mysterious and evocative way. The chapbook itself is a hybrid form, featuring Skoulding's own photographs as an abstract counterpoint to her words. Skoulding's approach to inter-medial work produces a rich hybrid of digital and natural sound, voice, image, and word.

As suggested earlier, there is some overlap between social media poetry, digital video, and spoken word performance poetry. Social media poetry is any poetry shared on social media, which enables it to reach a wider, non-traditional (poetry) audience. Digital video enriches the language of poetry with moving visuals. It can easily be shared on social media thereby fitting into contemporary digital practices. Spoken word performance poetry is a hybrid of sound, physical presence, and word that is usually delivered live in person but can also be videoed for sharing on social media and other platforms.

Digital video poems afford various options to poet/creators, depending on mode. In the case of oral performance poetry, a video poem may be a straightforward video recording of a live poetry reading or poetry slam. The Poetry Slam organization, for example, runs a series of poetry/spoken word competitions, with videos available on their YouTube channel (Poetry Slam Inc. n.d.). The main Poetry Slam website (Poetry Slam Inc. n.d.) defines their mission in promoting the creation and performance of poetry that engages communities whilst providing a platform for voices to be heard beyond social, cultural, political, and economic barriers. The videos serve as a record of live performances, extending their reach globally through the internet.

Some videos are not linked to a live performance. They may consist of an audio narration supported by still images or short video clips that either support or establish tension vis-à-vis the content of the spoken word. The words may appear on screen or in an audio voice-over. Such works are easy to create using a mobile phone, and easy to share via social media. Other video poems are created as fully intermedial artifacts with the poems written (and often performed verbally) first, and the video created afterwards. These video poems often feature elaborate techniques such as animation, digital alteration of images, or an intense video montage effect, as in Kate Tempest's 'Europe Is Lost' (Tempest & Braun 2017). Tempest started her career as a rapper, and her poetry draws clearly on the verbal performance style of hip-hop and rap. In this politically oriented video, she recites her poem with passion, underpinned by a rapid-fire video montage. Some of the visual images serve as illustrations of the verbal image, while other images have a greater distance from the words, thus requiring the listener to engage a deeper/finer level of interpretation. A text transcript of Tempest's performance would create a fairly closed work that is straightforward to interpret. The use of images with some distance from the words, however, opens it up and makes her hybrid video poem both accessible and experimental.

Hybrid digital approaches have a different impact of poetry on both listener/viewer and poet/creator compared to poetry experienced through a traditional print-only medium or live in-person poetry reading. For poets/creators who spend time on social media anyway, it is a natural outgrowth of their practice to use content from their digital habitat to create hybrid poetry, often supplemented by critical cultural comments based on news or social media posts. Poets can pretty much combine anything with anything in their zone of experience. The free play of connections across sources and media that is enabled by digital hybridity is conducive to rhizomatic composition methods in which the work branches, loops back on itself, and moves into new verbal territory (Deleuze & Guattari 1987).

Images can communicate to audiences who may not be regular readers of poetry and thus may struggle with more traditional poetic forms. Depending on how the image is used, it can amplify the poem's message, narrowing down options for interpretation, or create a tension between word and image that makes the poem more open.

In summary, the visual elements of video poetry offer a diverse range of affordances:

1. Clarify the meaning of the words;
2. Draw the listener/viewer into more active interpretation than with words alone;
3. Enable the poet/creator to work with image and word in dialogic composition, where each influences the other, an approach that encourages rhizomatic branching and looping through visual and verbal associations that take the poem in unexpected directions;
4. Give poetic voice to members of underrepresented groups and to those who may be more comfortable expressing themselves through images than through words;
5. Reach broader audiences through the internet, so that the hybrid poems can be found easily through a search engine.

Because video poetry can reach beyond the traditional poetry audience, it is particularly useful for teaching non-humanities subjects such as biology and other STEM disciplines.

Affordances of video poetry for distance learners

The affordances of video poetry listed in the previous section can be used to help university students in disciplines that are not related to poetry. This is especially true for distance learners, as they have little or no face-to-face interaction with the instructor or their classmates. Video poetry can make the course content come alive in ways that aren't possible with a traditional lecture that has simply been recorded. When students take the role of listener/viewer and watch video poems created by others, having visuals in conjunction with words can bring potential meanings across more clearly, helping students to understand the content of the video. This affordance can be crucial for students in STEM courses and others where students must master a large number of new specialized terms and technical concepts.

Depending on the distance between word and image in the video, video poetry can also draw the students more deeply into interpretation, thus increasing their engagement with the learning material through interpretative task-based learning. This feature may be of most use to students in humanities and/or social sciences disciplines that focus on interpretive responses to literature and history or on creative production.

The real power of video poetry for education in disciplines other than literature, however, comes into play when students create their own videos. This type of activity promotes active learning and higher-order thinking, as students must conceptualize their video poems, synthesize what they have learned into a cohesive artifact, and critically evaluate both content and expression. The dialogic composition technique (allowing word and image to influence each other) opens up new channels of independent study and reflection as students individually explore the content, reflect, and then create. For students who do not already read a great deal of poetry, allowing them to use an intermedial word-image combination may help them in the articulation of their thoughts in more creative ways than in writing a report or even a traditional poem. Finally, the ability to share their videos publicly online (if desired/when required) can provide a powerful validating element to their studies. Unlike traditional coursework that takes the form of essays and reports, video poems are more likely to be shared, whether publicly or privately, with friends. These digital artifacts can also be used as part of a portfolio used in applying for jobs. This can be especially important for distance learners, who are often work-based students. The video poems may have a direct application to the tasks they are required to do in their careers.

Compared to more traditional approaches to education, the use of video poems offers students a chance to have fun and express themselves creatively. The result can be increased motivation, more time on task, and a shift from surface to deep learning. Speaking of poetry in general, Januchowski-Hartley et al. (2018) note the value of using poetry to teach science, saying, 'Across diverse scientific fields, students have expressed a sense of enhanced engagement and enjoyment when poetry is integrated with their core subject.' They go on to remark that poetry can help students overcome the potential barrier of the language of scholarly writing and come to grips with complex topics. This can help these students to better communicate complex scientific ideas to a more general public, which too is a useful workplace skill.

Building on the observation presented, digital video poetry allows a further expansion of poetry for teaching science. Januchowski-Hartley and Oester's (n.d.) own website, *Conservation Haiku*, offers a series of image-word hybrid haiku poems on conservation topics. Each post consists of a haiku written by one of the two scientists paired with an image in the accessible style of Instapoetry. The detailed explanation of the science behind the haiku gives viewers a chance to learn about the topic in depth.

These affordances can be especially empowering when video poems are used in scientific distance-learning courses. Having students make their own video poems can help teaching staff move away from the transmission model of teaching and attain transactional and even transformational learning and teaching. This tripartite model was first proposed by Miller and Seller (1985) and later developed by Miller in 1988 (second edition 2007).

Transmission-style teaching focuses on knowledge transfer from teacher to student. Miller notes that, in contrast to transmission-based teaching, 'transactional learning is more interactive, although the interaction is mainly cognitive,' and may require students to solve problems. In transformational learning, 'the student is not reduced to a set of learning competencies or thinking skills but is seen as a whole being' (Miller 2007: 10–11). This type of transformation is the aim of much meaningful teaching.

Traditionally, STEM subjects rely on a transmission-based teaching style to convey the building blocks of the subject, which may appear to be a battery of fact after fact. Knowledge transfer in these subjects may seem well suited to lecture halls and seminars, where many of the grounding theories and scientific breakthroughs can be disseminated quickly to large audiences. This transmission of knowledge, as noted by Miller (2007), is a teacher-led approach in which the teacher's responsibilities lie in enforcing academic truth, dispelling myth, and evaluating student learning. Transmission-style teaching does not entail the need to interact, engage, and reflect on course content, as academic achievement is measured by the students' abilities to demonstrate, replicate, or retransmit a body of knowledge through assessed work. As Dunlosky et al. (2013) note in their metastudy of the efficacy of various learning methods for retention of knowledge, evidence indicates that students retain knowledge better when they are actively involved in working with the content. Passive techniques may seem easier but are less effective for learning. Transmission of information alone is not enough for most students to retain what they learn.

Due to limited face-to-face contact between students and teaching staff, designers of distance learning often rely on a transmission model because more interactive classroom-based options are not available. Video poetry offers another pathway for teachers in distance-learning programs. Student creation of video poetry demands more of students than just passively absorbing information. The student must investigate the topic, expand beyond explicitly taught material, and draw upon personal experience to produce an artifact that effectively and concisely communicates their message. This gives students the chance to develop themselves holistically, realizing self-actualization in relating the material they are learning to their lives at the same time as developing digital skills and literacies. Teaching that develops the learner as a whole person reaches Miller's (2007) highest aim of teaching: transformation. Such situations can result in experiences that elicit greater understanding of one's self, others, and the environment. Creation of video poetry by distance learners gives students the chance to develop themselves holistically, relating the learning material to their lives and developing digital skills and literacies.

The explosion in the use of educational technology in the 21st century changed the landscape of education. The creation and sharing of videos has become widespread and, while some people may still be excluded, digital video no longer serves as a barrier for many. When students in distance-learning programs create and share their own video poems with peers, they form a community of shared practice and idea exchange. They can help each other learn, even across distances, and build independence from the teacher's transmission of information.

The number of distance learners has been increasing (Kupczynski et al. 2014), with over six million distance learners reported in 2015 in the United States alone (Allen & Seaman 2017). John Traxler (2018) notes the globalization of distance learning in conjunction with the increased use of mobile devices and student-created content, saying, 'mobile technology often empowers a more broadly-based demographic of creators, and empowers richer and diverse content, derived from the environment and the context, wherever people could take their mobiles.' The Open University surveyed online learning in the Middle East and Africa, reporting that 'innovations in the UK and elsewhere are based on adoption of emerging technologies and evolution in pedagogy, with many innovations focusing on increasing interactions between learners and educational materials, learners and teachers, or among the learners themselves' (Open University 2018). In such an educational landscape, it is increasingly important for teachers and educational designers to develop ways of teaching distance learners effectively.

Case study: Video poetry for teaching biotechnology

Our teaching intervention originated in a 2015 training session on digital storytelling for teaching in higher education. This session led to a collaboration between Stephen Chapman and Mary Jacob. Stephen is a researcher and lecturer in the distance-learning program offered by the Institute of Biological, Environmental and Rural Sciences at Aberystwyth University, while Mary is a poet and an Aberystwyth University lecturer in teaching and learning. Stephen has aimed to enrich the experience of his distance learners by actively engaging them with digital stories and video poems. Mary, inspired by this idea, offered further training and consultation in order to facilitate Stephen's implementation of the project across several of his distance-learning modules (courses) in taught MSc degrees. Mary, for her own part, likewise created one of the initial video poems for these distance-learning STEM students.

The literature on digital storytelling, especially work by Bernard Robin (2016) on the educational uses of digital storytelling, proved to be the initial inspiration for the project. Robin notes the rich opportunities for student-created digital stories to encourage creativity and draw connections between subject materials and students' own experiences. We realized there was very little opportunity for science students to engage with the subject through creative reflection. This is especially true for distance learners, who have limited or no face-to-face interaction with peers and instructors.

We started with the idea of using digital storytelling but soon shifted to video poetry because digital storytelling tends to be focused on the story of an individual, while the course content places greater emphasis on engagement with scientific concepts. Poetry allows students to bring in as much or as little personal content as they are comfortable with, and also allows scientists to generate new ideas through relaxed reflection. With poetry, both writer and reader can play with language, reframe concepts, and engage with topics in ways that are otherwise impossible with peer-reviewed articles.

The Institute of Biological, Environmental and Rural Sciences at Aberystwyth University operates a distance-learning program with modules including Ruminant Nutrition, Genetics and Genomics in Agriculture, and Industrial Biotechnology. Industrial Biotechnology (MSc) and Bioinnovation (MSc/MRes[1]) are modular degree programs composed of three core 20-credit modules: Conversion Technologies (BDM7720), Biobased Product Technologies (BDM7820), and Drivers of the Biobased Economy (BDM8520). These core modules are supplemented with several 20-credit optional modules and a 60-credit research element that students are required to take for full MSc accreditation.

Topics covered in these modules feature complex questions with no single answer. Answering these questions requires internalization of the question, identifying links to past experiences, and reflection. Some examples include:

- How should biorenewable feedstocks be grown to negate any unintentional consequences of producing sustainable energy?
- Are biodegradable materials such as paper better for the environment than fossil-fuel-derived plastics?

After confronting the science around the sustainability credentials between paper versus plastic, students may be surprised to learn that this is a nuanced issue without a single easy answer (Biona et al. 2015; Muthu et al. 2009). Questions such as these provide an ideal opportunity to introduce creative aspects of tuition alongside traditional lecture material, thus shifting from transmission-style teaching to transactional and transformative teaching.

Because the content is nuanced and complex, we felt that modules such as these would be well-suited to benefit from the use of video poetry. We carried out video poem teaching interventions for the modules BDM7720 Biorefining Technologies, BDM7820 Biobased Product Development, and BDM1320 Future Packaging. We aimed to bring in elements of transactional and transformative teaching to an otherwise transmission-based teaching style. In our first intervention (of the two addressed in what follows), we invited poets to create video poems for students to view and respond to. In the second intervention, we returned to our original digital storytelling inspiration and invited students to make their own videos. As with the first intervention, we provided the three original video poems as exemplars and as a stimulus to help students generate ideas.

Intervention 1

The first aim of this teaching intervention was to assess if viewing video poetry can make the science behind industrial biotechnology more accessible and engaging for distance learners. We aimed to use the poems to stimulate an interest in biotechnology, through the module (or course) BDM7720 Biorefining Technologies. Three (digital) poets—namely, Katya Johnson (2017), Linda Reinhardt (2017), and Mary Jacob (2017)—were recruited to make video poems for the three blocks (or sections) of the BDM7720 Biorefining Technologies module. The learning outcomes of the module were explained to the poets, and the key message of each respective video poem was agreed to in order to prevent any duplication in the poetic material. To ensure the poets had a strong working knowledge of the contents of the module, a field trip was arranged for the poets to observe biorefining facilities. This enabled them to capture images and meet key researchers active in biorefining. The poets then produced video poems using the WeVideo license for video editing provided by the CADARN Learning Portal. We implemented one video poem for each of the three blocks; each poet contributed one poem.

To address the aims of the first intervention, a survey was carried out composed of a series of Likert scale and short answer questions to allow for qualitative data collection. The students were made aware of the video poems and signposted to the survey during induction week and encouraged to fill out the survey once they were presented with the three video poems. The video poems were also placed in the module's Blackboard site to supplement and enrich the lecture content for each unit. The students reported back on what aspect of the video poetry they most enjoyed. Two anonymous comments from their feedback are:

> Good poetry says a lot with just a few short words and good pictures/video can say even more. I think the pace of the videos [was] great.

and

> To me, I liked the way all three poems though creative and beautifully written using appropriate technical terms seemed to also be written in a fun manner and not taking themselves too seriously. I also liked the optimism of some writers. It gives me motivation to succeed and contribute in this field for global benefit.

These student responses show that the emotive nature of video poetry did enhance their engagement with the module content. When we asked whether students would like to see video poetry used in upcoming modules, they gave us positive responses—which we'll again keep anonymous—such as:

I would recommend the use of digital poetry for up-coming modules. General themes can be good, but I think it would be good for specific ideas and techniques.

and

I would be open to a task whereby I would be required to work with my more literary [and] gifted colleagues to critique or even write my own poem.

These comments not only show that students like the activity, but they also provide insight into how the students want to interact further with such media. Comments like those just presented suggest that students want to see more video poetry of a more specialized nature, with specific biotechnological processes such as, for example, anaerobic digestion or pyrolysis. Furthermore, one participant reported a willingness to collaborate with colleagues to produce a video poem of their own.

The students professed that their preferred presentation format was to include a text transcript alongside the video. From an accessibility perspective, a text-plus-video format is also quite flexible, as it provides parallel channels for the same information. Visually impaired students can hear the poem by listening to the audio, while hearing-impaired students can read the words of the poem on screen. This principle is in accord with the Universal Design for Learning (UDL), whose guidelines are a 'framework to improve and optimize teaching and learning for all people based on scientific insights into how humans learn' (CAST 2018). The UDL guidelines are built around providing students with multiple means of engagement, representation, and action and expression.

Intervention 2

The second intervention investigated whether student creation of a video poem could improve retention of knowledge and drive deeper learning through a task-based activity. In particular, we were keen to see if video poetry improved learning by pushing students to the 'create' level in Anderson and Krathwohl's revision of Bloom's taxonomy of educational objectives. The levels fit into a hierarchy from lowest to highest as follows: remember, understand, apply, analyze, evaluate, create (Anderson & Krathwohl 2001). Working at the level of creating in most cases requires a transformational learning experience.

The same students who were instructed with the help of the video poems they 'analyzed' and 'evaluated' in BDM7720 Biorefining Technologies were asked to 'create' their very own video poems for the subsequent modules BDM7820 Biobased Product Development and BDM1320 Future Packaging. They were supplied with the three original—Johnson (2017), Reinhardt (2017), and Jacob (2017)—video poems as models, and they were required to create a video on a philosophical transaction. The assignment briefs are summarized as follows:

> **Assignment brief BDM1320:** Students are asked to create a video 'that tells the story of how we can improve the recycling rate of plastic packaging. In your digital story, you should comment on the benefits recycling brings, current recycling rates, and include a strategy that aims to improve recycling rates of plastic.'

and

> **Assignment brief BDM7820:** Students are asked to 'choose one type of bioplastic, be it biobased or biodegradable, and in the form of a digital story, explain the challenges facing the end of life options for your selected bioplastic type. Answer the emotive question "Are bio-plastics that much of a good thing?," and address what can be done to improve their end of life options.'

This second intervention was implemented at the same time as final assessments for the module are released, thereby adding gravitas to the assignment. All three reference video poems were included amongst the core lecture material for the unit, and guidance was given to the students on how to create their own video poems. Following submission of their videos, students were directed to an online survey.

In their survey responses, they said that creating their own video artifacts was a relevant and appropriate activity for a postgraduate module and reported that the weighting set for the assessment (9% of weighted total for the module) was 'perfect.' Importantly, the students felt the task of creating a video was 'enjoyable,' and when asked for further comment, one anonymous student described a process of overcoming initial ambivalence:

> Overall I was pretty ambivalent towards the assessment. It was enjoyable to do to a certain degree and I can see the value in it as a large part of biotechnology and green science should be dedicated to educating the public and informing policy makers. I think the story has a place in modules as a 'communications' assessment criteria.'

As suggested by Januchowski-Hartley et al. (2018), developing students' abilities to frame scientific content in a manner accessible for the general public is important for their future as scientists. As discussed earlier, some literary critics have viewed the accessibility of some digital hybrid poetry as a drawback, but in this STEM context, approachability is a strong asset. Creating video poems or digital stories can help students develop key digital and communication skills that will help them disseminate complex scientific ideas to a broad general audience.

We observed that video poetry has beneficial impacts on distance-learning education, especially when students create their own videos. Some of the artifacts created by students were outstanding in their clarity of expression and emotive connection with the content. The videos were often linked to the students' personal experience and workplace context. For example, one student applied the principles gained from biotechnology research at Aberystwyth University to his professional fieldwork in Hong Kong, adapting it to a very different environmental context. The students who created videos demonstrated greater retention of knowledge than those exposed to transmission-only teaching methods. They often also demonstrated the development of a passion for the subject. As teachers, we are delighted when we have the chance to ignite that spark.

Recommendations

We observed that students in the second intervention responded to the original video poems by appreciating the value of poetic language to communicate rich content vividly in some works; but in their own videos, they created narratives rather than poems. This is perhaps not surprising, as this was a workplace-based distance-learning module in which the students were working scientists and technicians. The aim of this learning activity was not to teach poetry, but to teach science. We noted that the students created high-quality videos, some of which were primarily informational in nature, while others told a personal story about their engagement with the science in a digital storytelling vein. The evidence supports the educational value of the activity.

For future iterations of teaching interventions based on this case study, however, there is scope for drawing out the impact of the videos' poetic qualities more explicitly. This would include analyzing imagery, prosody, poetic structure, and so on in connection with the visual images and the scientific content. This may encourage the students to attempt to make videos based on their own poems rather than on digital stories, and thus open up possibilities to explore poetry in its own right, beyond its use as a tool for learning science.

Conclusion

In the 21st century, digital literacy and skills are taking an ever more prominent role across the higher education sector. Digital skills are important workplace skills, so students need to develop them while in university. In 2017, the UK-based Higher Education Academy (now known as Advance HE) and Jisc jointly published *Digital Lens on the UK Professional Standards Framework* (UKPSF) to help staff who teach in digital environments. The UKPSF is a national standard for teaching at the tertiary level and has been used across the UK in its current form since 2011.

Through the teaching interventions in our case study, we have addressed the following items from the *Digital Lens* (Heacademy.ac.uk, 2017):

- Design opportunities for students to express ideas in digital media, especially if they can share those ideas publicly
- Design opportunities for students to record learning and achievements in digital media for reflection and review
- Design learning activities that support the development of students' general digital capabilities
- Design activities and programs for online and open learning
- Design assessment regimes that recognize relevant uses of digital technology on the part of students, or that allow a range of technologies to be used to achieve and evidence the outcomes
- Develop and make available digital resources to support learning, e.g., podcasts, screencasts, online presentations, video, open educational resources, reusable learning objects
- Assess learners' work in a range of formats including digital formats as appropriate, e.g., digital presentations apps, video, problem-solving, quizzes
- Value learners' own digital practices as resources for learning, and respect learners' desire to use their own digital devices and services.
- Provide learning materials in a range of media, wherever practicable

In our case study, student creation of video poems has promoted deep and independent learning, allowing students to connect the subject matter with their own lives and workplaces. When implemented in a thoughtful and reflective manner, video poetry can be a means for teachers to shift from transmission-style teaching to truly transformative student learning. The rapid expanse in available technology, matched with the relatively simple process of creating a digital poem, provides an easy way for students to create a meaningful digital artifact. The affordances of social media for sharing and disseminating video poems and other digital hybrid forms offer students an entrance to participate actively in a broader community of practice, one that extends across the globe. It is promising that such teaching interventions are supported and promoted by higher education frameworks. Digital forms of hybrid poetry have a great deal to offer teachers of subjects that extend beyond the creative arts.

Note

1 Respectively, Master of Science degree and Master of Research degree.

References

Allen, I. E., & Seaman, J. (2017). *Digital Learning Compass: Distance Education Enrollment Report, 2017*. Digital Learning Compass. Retrieved from https://onlinelearningsurvey.com/reports/digtiallearningcompassenrollment2017.pdf

Anderson, L. W., & Krathwohl, D. R. (2001). *A Taxonomy for Learning, Teaching and Assessing: A Revision of Bloom's Taxonomy of Educational Objectives*. New York, NY: Longman.

Biona, J. B. M. M., Gonzaga, J. A., Ubando, A. T., & Tan, H. C. (2015, December). *A Comparative Life Cycle Analysis of Plastic and Paper Packaging Bags in the Philippines*. In *2015 International Conference on Humanoid, Nanotechnology, Information Technology, Communication and Control, Environment and Management (HNICEM)*, USA, 1–6.

Bridgett, R. (2003, February 1). An Appraisal of the Films of William Burroughs, Brion Gysin, and Anthony Balch in terms of Recent Avant Garde Theory. *Bright Lights Film Journal*. Retrieved from https://brightlightsfilm.com/wp-content/cache/all/appraisal-films-william-burroughs-brion-gysin-anthony-balch-terms-recent-avant-garde-theory/#.XG18Ouj7SUk

Burroughs, W. S., & Gysin, B. (1966). The Cut-ups. Cinematography by Antony Balck. *YouTube*. Retrieved from https://www.youtube.com/watch?v=Uq_hztHJCM4

CAST. (2018). *Universal Design for Learning Guidelines Version 2.2*. Retrieved from http://udlguidelines.cast.org

Crown, S. (2019, February 16). Generation Next: The Rise—and Rise—of the New Poets. *The Guardian*. Retrieved from https://www.theguardian.com/books/2019/feb/16/rise-new-poets

Deleuze, G., & Guattari, F. (1987). *A Thousand Plateaus: Capitalism and Schizophrenia*. London, UK: Bloomsbury Academic.

Dunlosky, J., Rawson, K. A., Marsh, E. J., Nathan, M. J., & Willingham, D. T. (2013, January 1). Improving Students' Learning with Effective Learning Techniques: Promising Directions from Cognitive and Educational Psychology. *Psychological Science in the Public Interest*, 14(1), 4–58. Retrieved from http://www.indiana.edu/~pcl/rgoldsto/courses/dunloskyimprovinglearning.pdf

Greenslade, D. (2018, May). Extracts from *Hamadryad*. *Otoliths*. Retrieved from https://the-otolith.blogspot.com/2018/05/david-greenslade.html

Heacademy.ac.uk. (2017). Digital Lens on the UK Professional Standards Framework (UKPSF): Supporting the Digital Capabilities of Teaching Staff in UK Higher Education. Retrieved from https://www.heacademy.ac.uk/system/files/downloads/digital_lens_on_the_ukpsf.pdf

Heffernan, J. A. W. (2004). *Museum of Words: The Poetics of Ekphrasis from Homer to Ashbery*. Chicago, IL; London, UK: University of Chicago Press.

Hill, F., & Yuan, K. (2018, October 15). How Instagram Saved Poetry. *The Atlantic*. Retrieved from https://www.theatlantic.com/technology/archive/2018/10/rupi-kaur-instagram-poet-entrepreneur/572746/

Hittinger, M. (2007, February). On the Transformative Power of Hybrid Forms. *Memorius*. Retrieved from http://www.memorious.org/?id=157

Januchowski Hartley, & Oester, S. (n.d.). Conservation Haiku. Retrieved from https://conservationhaiku.org/

Januchowski-Hartley, S. R., Sopinka, N., Merkle, B. G., Lux, C., Zivian, A., Goff, P., & Oester, S. (2018, November 1). Poetry as a Creative Practice to Enhance Engagement and Learning in Conservation Science. *BioScience*, 68(11), 905–911. Retrieved from https://doi.org/10.1093/biosci/biy105

Joris, P. (2003). *A Nomad Poetics: Essays*. Hanover, NH: Wesleyan University Press.

Kaur, R. (2018). *Milk and Honey*. Kansas City, MO: Andrews McMeel Publishing.

Kaur, R. (2020). [Instagram posts]. Retrieved from https://www.instagram.com/rupikaur_/?hl=en

Khaira-Hanks, P. (2017, October 4). Rupi Kaur: The Inevitable Backlash against Instagram's Favourite Poet. *The Guardian*. Retrieved from https://www.theguardian.com/books/booksblog/2017/oct/04/rupi-kaur-instapoets-the-sun-and-her-flowers

Kupczynski, L., Brown, M., Holland, G., & Uriegas, B. (2014). The Relationship between Gender and Academic Success Online. *Journal of Educators Online*, 11(1), n1.

Miller, J. P. (2007) *The Holistic Curriculum*, 2nd edition. Toronto: University of Toronto Press.

Miller, J. P., & Seller, W. (1985). *Curriculum: Perspectives and Practice*. New York, NY: Longman.

MotionPoems. (n.d.). Retrieved from http://motionpoems.org/films/

Moving Poems Magazine. (n.d.). Retrieved from http://discussion.movingpoems.com/

Muthu, S. S., Li, Y., Hu, J. Y., & Mok, P. Y. (2009). An Exploratory Comparative Study on Eco-Impact of Paper and Plastic Bags. *Journal of Fiber Bioengineering and Informatics*, 1(4), 307–320.

Open University. (2018, November). Online Learning in Tertiary Education in the Middle East and North Africa. Retrieved from http://www.open.ac.uk/research/news/ou-predicts-increase-lifelong-learning-middle-east-and-north-africa

PennSound. (n.d.). Retrieved from http://writing.upenn.edu/pennsound/

Perez, C. S. (2010). Whitewashing American Hybrid Aesthetics. *Poetry Foundation*. Retrieved from https://www.poetryfoundation.org/harriet/2010/04/whitewashing-american-hybrid-aesthetics

Poetry Exchange. (n.d.). Retrieved from http://www.thepoetryexchange.co.uk/

Poetry Foundation. (n.d.). Listen. Retrieved from https://www.poetryfoundation.org/podcasts

Poetry Slam, Inc. (n.d.-a). Retrieved from https://poetryslam.com/

Poetry Slam, Inc. (n.d.-b). [YouTube channel]. Retrieved from https://www.youtube.com/user/thisispoetryslaminc/featured

The Poetry Society. (n.d.). Poetry and Podcasts to Listen To. Retrieved from https://poetrysociety.org.uk/projects/poetry-audio/

Poetry Translation Centre. (n.d.). Podcasts. Retrieved from https://www.poetrytranslation.org/podcasts

Robin, B. R. (2016, December). The Power of Digital Storytelling to Support Teaching and Learning. *Digital Education Review*, 30, 17–29. Retrieved from https://files.eric.ed.gov/fulltext/EJ1125504.pdf

Skoulding, Z. (2016). *Teint: For the Bièvre*. Swansea, UK: Hafan Books.

Swensen, C. (2009, April 21). An Interview with the Editors of American Hybrid. *Poems Out Loud*. Retrieved from http://poemsoutloud.net/columns/archive/an_interview_with_the_editors_of_american_hybrid

Swensen, C., & St. John, D. (2009). *American Hybrid: A Norton Anthology of New Poetry*. New York, NY: Norton.

Tempest, K., & Braun, M. (2017). Europe Is Lost. Retrieved from https://www.youtube.com/watch?v=QSVyyykaEOo

Traxler, J. (2018, March 8). Distance Learning—Predictions and Possibilities. *Education Sciences*, 8(1). Retrieved from https://www.mdpi.com/2227-7102/8/1/35

Visible Poetry Project. (n.d.). Retrieved from https://www.visiblepoetryproject.com/videos/

Void Network. (2018, August 19). 7th International Video Poetry Festival. Retrieved form http://voidnetwork.gr/2018/08/19/7th-international-video-poetry-festival/

Watts, R. (2018, January–February). The Cult of the Noble Amateur. *PN Review*, 44(3). Retrieved from https://www.pnreview.co.uk/cgi-bin/scribe?item_id=10090

Digital stories used in case study

Jacob, M. (2017). Miss Canthus. *Aberystwyth University*. Retrieved from https://vimeo.com/166030947

Johnson, K. (2017). Green Alchemy. *Aberystwyth University*. Retrieved from https://vimeo.com/164392472

Reinhardt, L. (2017) Life Cycle. *Aberystwyth University*. Retrieved from https://vimeo.com/166030495

7 An exploration of elliptic and hybrid poetry from a geomorphological viewpoint

W. Brian Whalley

Introduction

Geomorphology is the scientific study of landscapes, landforms, and their formative geological processes. It is more than looking at landscapes, as might be done on holiday, or taught in school as part of 'geography.' The art critic Göran Sörbom suggests that 'The picture of a landscape functions through its similarities to landscapes we are familiar with, and a poem describing a landscape arouses in the mind of the reader or listener a mental image of a landscape by means of words' (Sörbom 2002: 22). Here I want to delve deeper, in particular, to explore how scientific ideas can be used in poems and identify scientific approaches to poetry of the anthropocene and to 'elliptical poetry' (Hoagland 2006; Whalley 2014a). This is an area of developing interest in the arts via 'ecocriticism' (Clark 2015), contemporary 'nature poetry' (Gifford 1995) and 'eco-poetry' (Solnick 2016). From Wikipedia, we learn that 'the anthropocene is an informal period of geological time ... dating from the commencement of significant human impact on the Earth's geology and ecosystems.' I thus use anthropocene as an informal term in lowercase. In poetry, an introduction to the anthropocene is given by Solnick (2016) and is discussed subsequently here.

The term anthropocene in fact follows an earlier concept, that of 'environmentalism.' This has been a topic, sometimes disputed within academic geography (Beaumont & Philo 2004), that embraces ideas and practices related to the 'environment' involving not only science and engineering but also ethics and economics. As such, it is in current, often political, discourse—with reference to floods, soil erosion, water management, melting ice, and sea-level change—so it is very much part of a geomorphological purview. One form of this approach is the desire to place geomorphology within 'critical physical geography' (Lave et al. 2018), although this will not be pursued further. This chapter also starts to explore aspects of 'hybridity' with respect to visual imagery related to landscapes 'and landforms in and conveyed by poetry as part of semiotics; what is the 'meaning' of what we see, hear, and touch? I combine 'scientific' with 'literary' and some ways of transmitting poetic information (spoken, written, visual). How poetry might be communicated in hybrid forms is also touched upon as a means of increasing information. The information content and accessibility of scientific paper abstracts and the use of poetry has been discussed by Illingworth (2016). He quotes Purtill (1970): 'It is now generally accepted that the purpose, or at least the central purpose, of science is to explain, or perhaps to explain and predict.'

Here I shall take this notion for both scientists (here, earth scientists) and poets, with the addition that 'objective description' is a necessary prerequisite for good 'explanation.' Thus, 'Could poetry therefore be the medium with which to help encapsulate non-expert audiences with research findings? Science and poetry have much in common, both in terms of their use of metaphor and their embodiment of process' (Illingworth 2016). In terms of the American poet Robert Kelly's short poem 'Science' (2007): 'Science explains nothing yet science is the same as poetry' but only 'uses the wrong words' (Illingworth 2019: 174). Unfortunately, 'wrong' can often be differently interpreted. Hence, a scientific 'theory' means something rather different in lay terms, especially by engineering doubt as in, 'oh, it's just a theory.' The current COVID-19 pandemic has given rise to many misunderstandings, even if not willfully of misinterpretations, of specific scientific terms.

Illingworth (2016) asks, 'Could poetry therefore help scientists to choose their words more carefully, thereby helping them to avoid the academic dialect that so often ostracizes the non-expert?' The reverse is also true. Words help to explain the complexities of our existence, especially where equations fail to convey a complete explanation. Here I use geological words as part of scientific categories and communication, as part of 'object orientation' in geological mapping and data/information handling (Brodaric & Hastings 2002) rather than object-oriented ontology as seen by, for example, Harman (2011) and Morton (2012).

Enthusiasm for landscapes and science

This chapter is not conventional literary criticism (Clark 2010) or geographical analysis (Bristow 2015). But, taking my cue from Westcott and Spell (1999: 75), I try to instill enthusiasm for the study of landscape science in poetry, thereby increasing the appreciation of both landscape and poetry. Formerly, I did so with my students, in presenting a poetic point of view to an aspect of scenery; currently I do so by demonstrating geological viewpoints to audiences interested in poetry. For example, I have contributed geological terms to 'Word of the Month' of the Norman Nicholson Society's web pages and its magazine *Comet* in simplified geology and geomorphology (Whalley 2019a). Some tools and ideas from science illustrate how poems might communicate with readers, such as learning about the unfamiliar or shedding new light on the familiar. Herbert and Matthews (2004) speak to the 'anti-science' stance of much modern cultural geography. Yet poetry, in various guises, can promote a scientific mode of thinking and continue/ extend dialogues between the 'sciences' and the 'humanities,' as in Wilson's 'consilience' (Wilson 1998). The work of Miroslav Holub (2006a) is likewise important in this context. For poets to contribute to a better understanding of change in the anthropocene, and in the environment generally, a scientific appreciation of the way the world 'works' proves important. This approach is much narrower than most poems covered in Baker's 'Landscape Poetry' collection (Baker 2000).

Theoretical physicist Carlo Rovelli (2018) believes that 'The ability to understand something before it's observed is at the heart of scientific thinking.' Jack Oliver, one of the founders of plate tectonics, however, believed that 'All modern science is basically empirical, in essence merely the organization and comprehension of reliable observations' (Oliver 1996: 1). For Nobel laureate Albert Szent-Györgyi (1957), 'Research is to see what everybody else has seen, and to think what nobody has thought' (75). These deceptively simple statements hide different aspects of curiosity, creativity, and the conveying of ideas to an audience. This communication includes poetry. Perhaps Rovelli's statement may be correct for entities such as dark matter, but more generally, he ought to have said 'when' rather than 'before.' Geological curiosity might be dated from Neolithic people's search for suitable hand-axe materials, although geological understanding did not develop as a scientific discipline until the late 18th century where it was particularly concerned with paleontology and geohistory (Manning 2016; Rudwick 2005). Literary links with geology have been explored by, for example, Wyatt (1995) and Maddox (2017). Still, these links date from the study of landforms as a descriptive science. Davies's (1969) history of British geomorphology includes references to early enthusiasms for the popular mania of the early 19th century, including Wordsworth's mentions in 'The Excursion' ('Book III') and Scott's 'St. Ronan's Well' (Chapter 7). Davies also discusses the controversial ideas of the mid-19th century, including 'the glacial key' in the recognition that it 'had become generally accepted that glacier ice is one of Nature's most powerful geomorphic tools' (309). As we shall see, 'glacial action' is explicit in some poetic descriptions of upland Britain. This glacial emphasis perhaps reflects a general view that the uplands of the British Isles are formed by glaciers. This is an overemphasis. Weathering, slope movement, and river action were important before the 'ice age' and are still. Norman Nicholson's 'Beck' (Whalley 2014a) illustrates long-term processes acting today.

As Tinkler (1985) records, geomorphology started to be 'useful' in the Second World War—such as appraising landing beaches and coastal defenses, for example. Subsequently, especially as applied in engineering geomorphology, the subject has been concerned with measurement and prediction, particularly considering 'magnitude-frequency' (How big? How often?) concepts. Such investigations are concerned with how much (coastal recession takes place), when (a slope failure might occur) and how often (rivers will flood). Alongside concepts from physics, chemistry, biology, ecology, and engineering, geomorphology is an important way to study change in the anthropocene. Investigative tools, statistical concepts and techniques, and geographical information systems are as much a part of the earth sciences as are current interests in epidemiology.

This chapter considers a basic poetic landscape as a theatre stage 'landscape' with treatment of geomorphological processes progressively taking center stage. The examples largely arise from British Isles poetry of the last seventy years.

Figure 7.1 is sourced from Bunge's (1984) discussion of science and pseudo-science, included in Schumm's *To Interpret the Earth* (1991), where he discusses Bunge's (1984) 'attitudes and activities of scientists' in relation to geomorphology. The poetry field, of course, can interface with any other 'field,' but obscurantism should not intrude into fidelity of the appropriate use of language. Language also includes the formalism of mathematical representations of theory and reality. However, as 'scientific' areas have terminologies and usages of their own, precise statements, descriptions, and analogies from the earth sciences need to be used with care in poetic practice and analysis. Miroslav Holub, as a working scientist, provides many good medical examples (1990). Martin Malone's poems 'Mic-ing the Kit' and 'Haas Effect' (2011) have first sections dealing with technical aspects associated with his experience as a sound engineer before taking ideas further in subsequent lines. Another poem titled 'Geology' in Malone's collection integrates geological words into observations of a Cornish cove as a love poem.

An ellipse is a plane curve intersecting a cone and surrounding two focal points. Elliptic functions have a double periodicity and are defined by two vectors in a (complex) plane. Here, let's consider this very simply, regarding the plane to contain information that is taken from two points of view. Thus, in Figure 7.1, information from 'mathematics' maps closely to 'basic

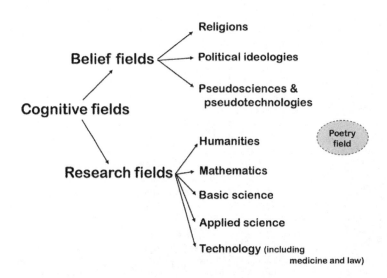

Figure 7.1 William Bunge's Cognitive Fields (1984) with an Additional Field of 'Poetry,' Which May Move Freely to Wherever the Poet Wants, Perhaps in Order to Link Subfields.

science.' Statistical techniques may help to explain aspects of language, not to mention some plays by Tom Stoppard which are related to scientific concepts. The poetry field of Figure 7.1 might be used to cover two points of view. I have used this approach (Whalley 2019b) to cast light on geomorphology content in landscape images.

In the following, I start to explore the use of geomorphological terms and terminology in poems, first dealing with general descriptions of landscapes through references to geomorphological processes and geological materials and leading to a 'sense of place' in poetry. Hybrid mixing of traditional poetic constraints can be amalgamated with the 'scientific' to enhance meaning and impact. Poetic comments about the anthropocene, climate, and environmental change may need to be couched with reference to earth surface events, such as flooding. I also start to explore the way in which the information content of poems might be enhanced by using typography and speech to convey hybrid presentations.

First view of a poetic geomorphological landscape

Poet Simon Armitage has an affinity with the landscape and people of his local area in the English Pennines. In this sense, he is not unlike Ted Hughes. In 2013, Armitage published 'Stanza Stones' (Armitage et al. 2013) about six poems cut into stone and rock.

Figure 7.2 shows one of these specially composed poems in its location. The poems are 'hybrid.' They combine the poet's words, the letter-carver's

Figure 7.2 'Dew,' One of Simon Armitage's 6 'Stanza Stones,' on the Southern Edge of Rombalds Moor, Upper Carboniferous Rocks of West Yorkshire. Letter-carving by Pip Hall. Photo: W. Brian Whalley CC BY-ND 2020

skills, and weather conditions at the time of a visit and reading. The rock slabs carved are local, in the landscape's gritstones. This helps to place the site psychologically as well as geomorphologically in the contexts of (i) 'place attachment' (Scannell & Gifford 2010) of person, (ii) place (here, 'Brontë Country') and (iii) process (seeing, reading, and perceiving generally). Gritstones are a type of coarse sandstone produced from the weathering of mountain ranges when the land mass of what is now the British Isles was over the equator in the Upper Carboniferous period (about 310 million years ago) (Leeder & Lawlor 2017). A poetic-geological description of gritstone is available in Mark Goodwin's (2019) 'The Geology Section from Stanage: The Definitive Guide' in his collection *Rock as Gloss*, where the name Stanage epitomizes English rock climbing on gritstone. The west-facing (Upper Carboniferous) crags of Stanage Edge, west of Sheffield, are also part of the climbing and geomorphological inheritance of the landscape for climber-poet Helen Mort. In 'Dear Alison,' Mort (2016: 27) writes, 'When I make slow patterns / on a route called Namenloss / I'm writing to you – // late afternoon / and Stanage is a postcard to your loss, / stamped with a daytime moon.' (Used with permission.) So too for Goodwin (2019), in his 'a 'Johnny Dawes' is a dot' where 'the poem focusses on Dawes's perception of friction as experienced on gritstone' (175).

Stratigraphically, 'gritstone' overlies (that is sediments were deposited after) the Carboniferous limestone evoked by W.H. Auden's 'In Praise of Limestone' (1979). The rock hears 'underground streams, what I see is a limestone landscape.' Auden appreciated the difference between limestone and gritstone, even if this is expressed in an allegorical love poem rather than in a geological poem. James Fenton's 'Terminal Moraine' (1972), notwithstanding the volume's quotation from Lyell's 'Principles of Geology' (1830–1833), incorporates a soliloquy rather than direct information about glacial geomorphology. These are explorations evoking Auden's 'concern for Nature's remotest aspects.' The 'geomorphological' title of a poem may implicate climate change, although it may not help to 'explain' it. Glacial examples include Lynne Wycherley's 'The Bøya Glacier' (Abbs 2002: 73) and Alyson Hallett's 'Erratic' (2007). Nick Drake's 'The Farewell Glacier' (2012) too is an evocation of Svalbard's exploration rather than an explanation of climate change per se.

Place, poetry, and geology

The general idea of 'Geological landscapes and the British peoples' (Leeder & Lawlor 2017) is to provide a geomorphological overview alongside geological depth together with the important human dimension in time. The text implements quotations of poetry lines as chapter headings. The 2012 compilation *Edgelands* by poets Paul Farley and Michael Symmons Roberts (2012) also provides a setting for poetry and literature in an English landscape, although geology and geomorphology remain largely overlooked within the anthropocene. Farley and Roberts 'know that an unseen, untouched English landscape is a myth' and that 'a long and complex inter-action between constant natural processes and more recent human activity has largely formed all the landscapes we can see today, and that landscape is indivisible from the human world' (2012: 26). The word 'landscape' here can refer to long-term geology or much shorter-time human modifications via land use change and occupancy. Fleshing out ideas of 'constant natural processes' alongside human interventions also provides links to the impor-tance of viewing the earth, its geology, geomorphology, and resources as integral to human history (Dartnell 2018). This geo-centeredness for hom-inin evolution and technology is explicit in Peter Redgrove's 'Everything Comes Out of the Cool Dark Mine'[1]—although this is not discussed in Bentley's (2002) critique of Redgrove.

Poets and landscapes can be closely linked, as with the Scottish poet Norman MacCaig and his affinity for landscapes (McCaig 2005: 286): 'Assynt [in NW Scotland] … its geology, a bamboozling complex of low hills sitting on a bed of Lewisian gneiss. It was the geology of this landscape that was the bones of its beauty' (McCaig 2005: xxxiv). MacCaig's Scot-tish contemporary Edwin Morgan had a similar affinity with geology, geo-morphology, and landscape as in his poem 'Slate' in *Sonnets from Scotland* (Morgan 1990: 437), which is, perhaps, a reference to founder of modern geology James Hutton's *Theory of the Earth* (1788). Auden also uses lime-stone in a general topographic sense as part of his discursive 'New Year Let-ter 1940.' These lines, however, are about affinity with landscapes rather than their ability to work or explain geomorphologically. We find other affinities in poems by Simon Armitage. In a climbing context, the work of Helen Mort (2016) and Mark Goodwin (2019), which place poetry and rock within the rock scenery of the British Isles (Turnbull 2009), have already been mentioned. Ted Hughes, for his part, is well known for his gritty poetry and sense of place.[2] In 'Remains of Elmet,' together with pho-tographer Fay Godwin (Hughes & Godwin 1979), Hughes links geology (usually of Upper Carboniferous sandstone) with scenery, buildings, and place. The glacier again recurs that 'Enlarged the long gullet of Calder.' This suggests that Hughes knew the basic geomorphology, enlarging a pre-existing valley, and that the last glaciers vanished from the southern Pennines 15,000 or more years ago.

Observation, description, and geomorphology

Scientists need to define and discuss terms, even if they do not necessarily know what these are precisely, as entities, or concepts, or time periods, such as 'Planck time' or 'Ediacaran.' Geomorphologists know what they mean by 'landscape'—even if others have their own ideas, such as phenomenology and archaeology (Tilley 2010), vernacular landscapes (Crawford 2002), or as a very idea of 'Englishness' (Matless 2016). Baker's (2000) landscape poetry collection reminds me mostly of a prettiness of scenery, as described by the geographer Vaughan Cornish for the Council for the Preservation of Rural

England (Cornish 1932). Baker, to be fair, does include poems by MacCaig in *The Faber Book of Landscape Poetry* (Baker 2000). He also integrates the piece 'Looking Down Glen Canisp,' also set in Assynt, as well as four poems by Norman Nicholson, of whom I'll speak more closely later in the chapter.

Although often treated descriptively, as, for example, at the high school level ('today we have the naming of parts'), modern geomorphology is concerned with the inter-connectedness of natural materials (M: soil, rock, water, ice), processes (P: slope failure, river or glacier action, flooding) and landform geometry (G: what landforms look like; river meander, moraine). These interactions can be represented by the functional expression:

$$\text{Landform L is 'explained' by considering}: L = f(M,P,G)$$

where M, P, and G are as above and the functionality (f) incorporates time and climatic effects, as well as human interventions (or effects). The simplicity of this expression hides many complexities—not least, that a landscape may consist of several landforms, each with its own functionality, especially over time.

Landforms and time

'Understanding' or 'explaining' landform evolution incorporates aspects of basic geological principles operating over millions of years as well as present-day (anthropocene) interactions, like floods, landslides, and coastal recession. The weathering of limestone (chiefly because this sedimentary rock dissolves in water) is more complex than can be 'measured' by Auden or in an A-level school text, and it operates in milliseconds on a small scale, even if the chemical reaction is 'far-from-equilibrium' (Jaeger & Liu: 2010) when viewed over long periods of time. This viewpoint, however, contrasts somewhat with T.S. Eliot's line in *Burnt Norton*, speaking to the end and the beginning having always been present, but is in line with James Hutton and makes Eliot's observations a compelling discussion point for students in respect to the perceived nature of time.

Timescales, as much as space and topography, are major research programs for earth scientists in general. Some events, such as floods and slope failures, are rapid and may alter local conditions—which is what gets them into the news. However, most landscape changes are small and incremental when looked at over 'long' periods of time. Conveying long time periods—the millions of years of 'deep time'—proves challenging. Goodwin (2014) includes the term in 'Forced Moment.' Tourists visiting 'old' landscapes, from the Grand Canyon to Scotland's Assynt, or to the Weald of southern England, may still have difficulty in appreciating James Hutton's (1788) memorable 'The result, therefore, of our present enquiry is, that we find *no vestige of a beginning, no prospect of an end*' (my emphasis). Although Edwin Morgan, in his poem 'Theory of the Earth,' did in fact find these vestiges (1990: 443).

As geomorphologist Bruce Rhoads (2006) indicates, 'Geomorphology as a science derives from research traditions grounded both in historical geology and in physical science, especially physics and chemistry.' Marr's *Scientific Study of Scenery* (1900) is descriptive rather than explanatory (as appropriate earth science tools were not available until the 1940s), with diagrams and photographs of a range of features (mountains, glaciers, volcanoes). Marr's approach differs markedly from a modern university text replete with equations, graphs, statistical analyses, and modelling of geomorphological processes and landform development over time. Rhoads (2006: 27) considers an excerpt from Shelley's 'Mont Blanc: Lines Written in the Vale of Chamouni' and compares this to a description from the scientific study by Ballendras and Jaillet (1996): 'In the Subatlantic period, and more particularly during the Little Ice Age, a recrudescence of torrentiality in relation with a phase of intense solifluxion on the slopes can be observed.' Rhoads remarks upon poetic and scientific perspectives of this area of the Alps.

Similarly, Alexander Pope's description 'Near Windsor Lock' (1711) is as 'sublime/beautiful' an observation as is Auden's of north country limestone. In the 21st century, we see things differently from Pope and Shelley—whether from the perspective of art, poetry, landscape aesthetics, geo-conservation, or geomorphology. This is a matter of cognition as much as it is of experience and the public understanding of science (although it can be approached via an object-orientated ontology [OOO]; Morton 2012). Yet 'recrudescence of torrentiality' amounts to what geomorphologists would term 'magnitude-frequency' and depicts the 'return period' of a flood statistically with more than half an eye on the anthropocene. Blake Morrison may have had an inkling of this, as his piece 'Flood' may demonstrate (Morrison 1996), where in dreams, not even sandbags can contain the floods within. The anthology of new Cumbrian poetry, *This Place I Know* (Darbishire et al. 2018), contains modern flooding references as in Debbie Mayes's 'Aftermath, Kendal,' where 'Stream becomes sea,' and Hilary Tatershall's 'Gote Bridge, Cockermouth, 5–8 December 2015,' which links the passage of Storm Desmond at this locality and its effects on the local population.

Some geomorphologists would consider this part of the 'critical' approach of some geographers that 'seeks to effect change not only through transformative insight but also through forms of progressive praxis … critical geographers want to make a difference' (Blomley 2006: 92). This is a movement towards 'critical physical geography' (Lave et al. 2014) as mentioned previously. It relates not only what physical geographers and geomorphologists practice, but also how science is practiced in a world of global environmental and climate change.[3]

Gifford's *Green Voices* (1995), in his chapter 'Some Versions of the Contemporary Pastoral,' compares the poetry of Norman Nicholson, George Mackay Brown, John Montague, and R.S. Thomas. Without arguing about the pastoral connotations reminiscent of Alexander Pope, Gifford quotes Eagleton's (1982) statement about Nicholson's 'Sea to the West' volume, which runs 'There isn't in this volume a great deal more than effective description.' But Nicholson *is* aware of developments in earth sciences (such as Continental Drift and plate tectonics) as witnessed in many of his poems, which often refer to 'time.' Nicholson's 'Scafell Pike,' included in Baker's Landscape collection in the 'Mountains, Hills and the View from Above' section, is much about the transitory nature of human existence in 'Scafell Pike' and its deep time persistence in the landscape. In 'Beck,' Nicholson's landscape description is scientific and explanatory (Whalley 2014a) in a way in which Auden is not; but Armitage's 'Beck' (Armitage et al. 2013) is evocative of the landscape, as in Figure 7.2. Indeed, Nicholson can be used to link a poetic voice to student analyses of landscape and communication skills (Whalley 2014b). Leeder and Lawlor's 'GeoBritannica' (2017) incorporates poetic quotations, including several by Nicholson, to introduce chapters viewing local geological regions. To a scene-setting overview of poetry and geomorphology, 'explanation' can be added to observation and description, or to processes and materials.

Poets, amongst other explorers and practitioners of the arts, have made links between earth sciences and human feelings: W.H. Auden, Edwin Morgan, and Norman Nicholson are good examples. Usually, this avoids tendencies towards pathetic fallacy by approaching subjects 'scientifically.' The most involved discussion of science and poetry to date, perhaps because the reading 'views' are collaborative, is Robert Crawford's edited volume *Contemporary Poetry and Contemporary Science* (2006). Simon Armitage suggests that scientific knowledge may imply, for the poet, 'the inability to engage with the subject at the approved and accepted level' (Ibid: 111). This may well be true for a hard-bitten scientific, reductionist, approach. As noted previously (Herbert & Matthews 2004), it is the reductionist view of the world which sets some against scientific viewpoints. Armitage is well aware of the problems of scientism and of the uses of metaphor, as we see in his 'Newton's Third Law' and the mimesis used to explain concepts. Miroslav Holub, in the same volume (Holub 2006b), indicates, however, that a scientist writing poetry must remain a scientist because that guarantees a 'scientific hard-centred approach.'

Landform poems, informationism, and information

As already quoted, Auden's 'In Praise of Limestone' is probably the best-known 'geological' poem—but it says nothing about science. A close runner-up is Hugh MacDiarmid's 'On a Raised Beach' of 1934 (Grieve & Scott 1972), which is his evocation of the Shetland landscape, of metaphysics, and of religion. However, the first lines are just de-contextualized names of specimens gathered together; Caen stone would not be found on a raised beach north of the English Channel! The words convey a poetic, rather than a geological, purpose. Regarding Hugh MacDiarmid, Edwin Morgan (2006) notes that 'almost all the information in MacDiarmid came at second hand, and could sometimes be wrong' (36). This contextualization is important in geology. A sample from Mark Goodwin's 'Forced Moment at El Torcal,

Andalucia' is at once evocative of the landscape while also true to geomorphology and geology:

> This is a high plateau where deep time fights stone.
> El Torcal is karst landscape—lime
> stone performed upon by water & wind. A
> medium
> of sea-bed micro-bones & ground shells. Sculpted or
> tortured?

(Used with permission.)

Herbert (2006) considers MacDiarmid's use of language in 'In Memoriam James Joyce' (2006). 'And did he know what precisely what a 'nunatak' was,' Herbert wonders, 'if not an assault by a nun? Perhaps not, but he knew it sounded good. The system of thought here is acquisitive and accretive, it is endlessly analogical' (Herbert 2006: 84). It is not clear what is analogue, what is metaphor, and what is simile. Herbert's 'testament and confessions of an informationist' show him part of this movement. 'One of the features of Informationist poetry,' Richard Price avers, in Alan Riach's review of Scottish literature and new media, is 'its engagement with and deliberate mixing of linguistic registers, and the interrogation of language's power-bearing qualities in the process' (Riach 2016). I posit, in the mode of Holub (2006b), Illingworth (2019), and Armitage (2006) that this is not a helpful use of the word 'information,' as it mixes modes rather than helps to distinguish ideas.

It is possible to think of a poem and a scientific paper, or an article in *Scientific American* or *New Scientist*, as a condensed form of communication—a conveying of distilled ideas of the imagination and intellect to a wider audience. From this point of view, we might consider the poem-paper as an information object (as in an image) as part of a semiotic triangle. Thus, the triangle of meaning (Ogden et al. 1923) from 'communicator' to the 'communicated to' via the symbol (word or image) and the 'referent' (the object or idea invoked) is complex. Some form of cognitive interpretation is almost certainly required. Geomorphologists are only just starting to grapple with this and to merge the semiotic triangle with information ontologies and digital mapping (Brodaric & Hastings 2002). For geomorphologists, Stanley Schumm's essay 'Badlands at Perth Amboy' (1956) is fundamental. Those with a poetic bent might associate the essay with Ted Hughes's 'The Badlands,' or even paintings by Georgia O'Keefe. The title-as-image may need interpretation. Such interpretations are a consequence of the need to consider cognitive psychology as much as semiotics. This approach invokes the 'sense of place' used in work on 'place attachment' (Manzo & Devine-Wright 2014; Scannell & Gifford 2010), and is seen especially in poems by Norman MacCaig (Assynt, Scotland), Norman Nicholson (Cumbria, England) and George Mackay Brown (Orkney Islands). Also spatially invoked are social justice, politics, and the landscapes of the highland clearances in the Gaelic poems of Somhairle

MacGill-Eain (Sorley MacLean), especially his 'Dàin do Eimhir' ('Poems to Eimhir') (MacLean 1971). The poems in the collection *This Place I Know* also come into this category (Darbishire et al. 2018).

Cognitive poetics is a relatively new area of literary criticism, linked to cognitive linguistics. Freeman (2003) suggests the following categories: descriptive, explanatory, theoretical, predictive, demonstrative, evaluative, and elegant. The last value elicits 'achieving simplicity in its ability to represent all the categories above' (279–280). Without extending this discussion, we can note that Freeman's list encapsulates most, if not all, of the aspects a scientist might wish for in producing a piece of work. Elegance might commonly also be associated with 'beauty.' This itself is 'a word full of resonance' (Reynolds 2016) that goes beyond tourist promotion of a place yet includes the quasi-religious-environmental views of Henry David Thoreau, who famously said 'A true poem is distinguished not so much by a felicitous expression, or any thought it suggests, as by the atmosphere which surrounds it.' This therefore relates to aesthetics and cognition. The linking of aesthetics to cognition is an area for further exploration in a poetic context.

Landscapes, literature, and the anthropocene movement

Literature and poetry have started to explore the concept of the anthropocene. A good introduction to the interrelated implications can be found in the opening chapter of Solnick (2016). Quotations from that introduction are useful to a framing of my discussion, although the topic is far too substantial to discuss further here. We shall look only at the geomorphological implications. 'Anthropocene,' Solnick explains, 'is a suggestive term which, while strikingly effective in communicating the impact of humanity on planetary systems, also risks becoming totalising and also encouraging a renewed anthropocentricism' (2016: 6). However, it is inevitable that anthropocentrism is significant as, in poetry at least, the juxtaposition of words is the communication itself. 'Science,' despite debates, is about sampling and the 'boundary conditions' of experiments; science does provide some objectivity. Debate, however, is not often part of some remits. Climate-change deniers, for instance, extend the field of discussion to where it may be difficult for poetics to follow. A geological and geomorphological view of landscape is presented in much of the work of Norman Nicholson, mentioned earlier.[4]

In various discussions and anthologies of 'anthropocene poetry' (Abbs 2002; Bristow 2015; Solnick 2016; Staples & King 2017), there is no mention of Nicholson. He too was omitted from *The Bloodaxe Book of 20th Century Poetry* from Britain and Ireland (2000). Although he died in 1987, so before the ongoing wave of 'eco-' prefaced literature, Nicholson set the scene in his own verse for the human activities that were developed on the upper coal measures of the west Cumbrian Coalfield as well as the iron ore deposits in the Lower Carboniferous. Thus, of worker and employer where, unusually, both coal and iron ore came from a shaft at Cleator Moor in Nicholson's poem of that name (Nicholson 1994: 16–17).

Nicholson, who suffered from TB as a teenager, was destined for university (to which he never went), rather than down into the pits or to the local ironworks. His later words are certainly not subscribing to Gifford's idea of the 'pastoral,' or of nature poetry (Nicholson 1994: 28). In 'Hodbarrow Flooded' (1994), Nicholson's eye travels from the geological setting of exploited resources through personal experiences: Nicholson's uncle Jack was killed underground by hematite ore being 'spilled onto his back' (Nicholson 1994: 279). The flooding refers to the mine shafts and adits[5] after the hematite extractions ceased during Nicholson's own lifetime.

The sea walls, built in 1888–1889 and 1900–1901, were intended to keep water from the mines at Hodbarrow Point, and are clearly seen from over-flying jets as testaments to anthropocene exploitation, even as their original purpose drifts away in time (but remain recorded in much of Nicholson's work). Millom's ironworks, and the reason for the founding of the town in 1850, are now seen only as trace fossils both in the landscape and in Nicholson's poetry such as 'On the Closing of Millom Ironworks, September 1968.' The movement of the poetry field of Figure 7.1 can be used to encompass contingent fields of geological existence. The boundary conditions of the poem change. Akin to what we see in Nicholson, Harriet Tarlo's recent reflection on the West Cumbrian coast, titled 'Particles' (Tarlo 2015), is a similar reflection on 'remains as reminders.'

In Nicholson's 'The Elm Decline,' we have statements about anthropogenic activity in Cumbria and the English Lake District by way of tree felling and destruction of the ancient forests of the British Isles. This poem presents a good overview of landscape alongside environmental change in the anthropocene—a period spanning seven thousand years from the early settlers to industrialization beginning in the late 19th century. The line 'valleys go under the tap' almost certainly refers to the flooding of specific Lake District valleys to provide water for expanding cities in the south. Haweswater (also the subject of Sarah Hall's novel of the same name) was formed in 1929 by flooding Mardale in order to supply water for Manchester. Similarly, valleys in the English Peak District and central and north Wales (Griffiths et al. 2017) were also flooded for water supplies to Sheffield, Nottingham, Liverpool, and Birmingham. The first verse of Griffith's poem 'Cwm Elan'/'Elan Valley' in Welsh and English remarks geomorphologically:

Mae'r ffrwd o'r ffridd a'r foryd yn pellhau,
ac yma yn yr haen o waddod du
ysgarwyd y ffynhonnau bach a'r bae.

and in Griffith's translation,

The hillside streams and estuaries estrange,
and down there in a layer of sediment
the sources and the sink are now divorced.

(in Griffiths et al. 2017)
(Used with permission.)

In this context, a brief mention should be given to the singular anthropocene event of the 20th century in the UK—Aberfan: 9:15 a.m., 21 October 1966. This disaster, an engineering geomorphology event, was the slope failure of a coal mine waste tip in south Wales. Political, economic, and social actions (or inactions) are a consequence of the local geology, geomorphology, and of the deaths in the pits themselves. Aberfan is commemorated by the Welsh poetry collection *Dagrau Tost* (James & James 2016). Climate change, of course, is not the only consequence of mankind's activities in the anthropocene.

Complexity, patterns, and emergent systems

In the landscape and geomorphological context, Favis-Mortlock and de Boer (2003, 127) examine the complexity of slope erosion: 'Here is an exercise for any physical geographer: stroll in the landscape of your choice, look around carefully, and then ask candidly, "How well can I explain what I see?"' In other words, just giving names to landforms is insufficient as an explanation. For geomorphologists, landscapes need to be measured and evaluated in scientific terms;[6] this tack also proves difficult for poets. Dynamical systems, such as in geomorphology, can be complicated, perhaps even 'difficult,' but also 'complex'; these systems are composed of many components which may/can interact with one another. 'Self-organization' is where some forms of order arise from local interactions. Frequently, these self-organized systems are visual in nature. Tom Stoppard's play *Arcadia* (1993) explores some of these issues in a historical context. A general discussion of said context can be found in Coveney and Highfield's (1995) overview. A discussion concerning artificial intelligence also holds in Mainzer (1997). Self-organizing geomorphological systems, such as meandering and braided rivers, can be tackled by simple rule-following models developed in space-time (Fonstad 2006). These replicate natural forms and behaviors. This is what probably happens when babies develop languages through the application of simple rules of grammar, syntax, and, ultimately, spelling and writing, not to mention signing. Visual observation of sentences respectively in English, German, and Finnish can be distinguished easily once these patterns are recognized/internalized. The language information content is encoded in the visual and supplemented by appropriate physico-mathematical models.

Verbal description is easier to accomplish than field experiments and numerical modelling—let alone visual comparisons (as noted in Figure 7.3). In geomorphological studies, language as information is usually combined with numbers and diagrams as the result of field or laboratory experiments. Favis-Mortlock & de Boer (2003) use simple models that can illustrate aspects of self-organization and complexity in fluvial landscapes. In other words, the model is set up with appropriate simple expressions that relate the soil slope (gradient) to a measure of 'erosion.' Model results are usually expressed as a single graph that may link a theoretical model with experimental results.

Figure 7.3 Scaling in Landforms and Landscapes, South California. Photos: W. Brian
        Whalley CC BY-ND 2020 *Note*: The same 'processes' (such as rainfall and
        its intensity, producing slope erosion) may act on different geologies. The
        landforms produced may be similar at a wide variety of scales from landscape
        (left) to small landforms (picture width at right approximately 2m).

This too may be what poets do: find words to describe some experiential
phenomenon (or result). Words alone may be insufficient; data may help, but
representing data dynamically, as it arrives on the data plot diagram, may be
better still. Yet this is hardly evident in print-on-paper journals and books.
This effect is discussed variously.[7] In general, when building models, we must
not forget that the aim is to understand something about the real world. Animating constituent data may be as helpful in comprehension as typography.

Edwin Morgan's essay 'Poetry and Virtual Realities' (2006) demonstrates
an interest in science. Morgan indeed compels his audience to relate to science.
We have already noted his interest in geology and geomorphology. A sequence
in 'The Moons of Jupiter' supplies lines that would add to any talk on planetary geology. Morgan also makes run-on comments about concrete poetry:

> Concrete poetry, insofar as it frequently makes use of structural elements
> of repetition, serial development, reversals and mirrorings, and precise
> counts of verbal or typographical or phonic components has recogniz-
> able though not readily definable links with the cybernetic age, and the
> 'pared down to the maximum' character of much of its approach may
> well appeal to the scientific as well as to the aesthetic sensibility.
>
> (2006, 38–39)

Richard Skelton (2015), for his part, shares these comments in his tribute to
the drystone walls in Cumbria:

XXVI
The legacy of ice is everywhere. A kind of savage
remixing. This very valley is an index of its last

movement—each spur and extremity a catalogue of
resistance

which includes 'towards a lithical vocabulary.' To wit:

limestone. mudstone sandstone
gneiss schist. slate
basalt dolerite. granite rhyolite

(Skelton 2015: 26)
(Used with permission.)

The geological impression of drystone walling here is static typography; it
is unlikely that a wall composed of these rocks could be found in reality. It
is, however, more of a 'geological poem' than is the aforementioned 'On a
Raised Beach.'

Animating poems: Typography and hybrid forms

Concrete poetry can provide strong visual clues or reinforcements of its
informative statement. Consider my poem 'BANDWIDTH' (Whalley 1990a):

Hr s sm nfrmtn
nnnnnnnnnnnnn
to ths whll take
oooooooooooooo
trbl to dcode t
iiiiiiiiiiiiiiiiiiiiiiiiiiiiiiiiiiii
mst f what u
ssssssssssssss
sy s rdndnt
eeeeeeeeeeeee

'BANDWIDTH' has elements of a puzzle, as, for example, in some work
by Edwin Morgan. But, how to evoke or communicate this puzzle? The
reader needs to work at my piece for it to convey something about language and information theory. Reading it out aloud is awkward. However,
two people reading in counterpoint might make it a more active experience, especially if the visual poem is projected to the audience/receivers.
It is an example of teaching about information theory (Soni & Goodman
2017).

In geomorphology, visualization is not only of and about landforms and
landscapes but a result of analyses of mathematical modelling. Armitage's
'Dew' (Armitage et al. 2013; pictured in Figure 7.2) is a poetic visualization, an environmental and cognitive model that deals with more than just
the words of the poem. The words of 'Dew' are clearly legible, those of his
'Beck' only on the printed page, the lettered boulder is disappearing under
mosses and lichen only seven years after cutting.

I now pose the question of whether it is possible to convey kinematics (movement), and dynamics (with respect to forces) in particular ways that also provide poetic form alongside visualization. The question, in short, concerns hybridity. Let's consider my piece titled 'Drops' (Whalley 1990b):

DROPS

A
drop
of rain
in its fall
from a thunder-
cloud reaches its
terminal velocity
and finally will
explode on
soil.

Millions of
events like this
wash soil
off
the
land
into the sea.........

'Drops' attempts to be a visual, geomorphological soil-poem. Reading can reinforce the visual effect; no real technical words are used, but the visual conveys additional meaning. People may have heard of soil erosion, even in the British Isles, but it may not have come to the general understanding of enhanced rainwater runoff, which affects fields in southern England (Boardman & Evans 2019). On the other hand, 'Drops' lacks the dynamic approach that Rhoads sponsors. There are numerous ways a hybrid might be attempted: several readers, audience interaction, and reading across a video that depicts soil erosion. A further possibility (which has yet to be performed) is for a reader to trigger an event, say, a drop falling, and thereby produce a data point in a mathematical model or a letter or word in the poem. The speaking rate could be varied at will in order to produce the threshold or erosive intensity of soil erosion. By altering the parameters of the model, it could be explored as a visual and audible hybrid. (I have now re-written this poem in an active form that can be performed by PowerPoint as a simple form of an animated hybrid sequence.) Some poets now do include audio versions of their poems. A good geological example is Mark Goodwin's 'She Sells' (2016).

We can now start to link in what might be called, for want of a better term, 'active' or 'kinematic' poetic forms with landscape descriptions that enable a sense of place. Kay Dunbar's (2005) volume *Landscape into Literature: A Writers' Anthology* has several poetic contributions of local landscapes in a local manner. This focus on the local was once evaluated as a negative poetic aspect ('the biographical fallacy'). Most poets, of course, have lived for years upon years in their 'homes'—and these are often identified in terms of their native homes. In geological terms, the word 'terrane' is an appropriate descriptor of this place-ness. In agriculture, the appropriate term is 'terroir.' Nicholson, MacCaig, George MacKay Brown, and Sorley MacLean, for instance, are Cumbrian and Scottish terrane examples, with strong landscape and cultural affinities, as noted previously. Alan Peacock, in 'Stone Gods,' makes this observation on place: 'My landscape, then, was to do with limestone, gritstone, water and sky; and I learned that stone was more than the geologist, artist or mountaineer saw' (in Dunbar 2005: 31). He continues, with a poem about a TV illustration of bending and fracture of rock and its time-dependence.

The poem can be said to speak to dynamic modelling possibilities expressed in, or by, poetic forms incorporated in a materials laboratory context. In fact, 'failure' entails a complex relationship in engineering and materials science. Poets have not linked such slow deformation (or rheology) of rock to the similar processes in glacier ice. The study of these behaviors is engineering rather than geography. Explanatory talks are available online—for example, Tonya Coffey's Materials Science course (Coffey 2017)—but ultimately, explanations are in the form of equations (Azizi 2007). Science, as explained in geomechanics, might also be applied in new poems or readings, and especially in performance-related visualizations utilizing wearable technology such as augmented reality (AR) glasses. The availability of AR apps on mobile devices is perhaps a rich area in which to develop further hybrid creativity. Conceptually, AR may also add a further attribute to William Carlos Williams's assertion that a poem is essentially a machine constructed of words (Poetry Foundation 2009).

Information and metadata

The information content of a poem depends upon what it means to reader and creator. Of increasing importance is the associated metadata. The concept of metadata is easily understood in relation to a digital image such as Figure 7.2; it covers geographic (UTM) coordinates, direction of view, time of day, as well as image on the recording device alongside the image's author. Further metadata might usefully be added for the poetry reader; Rombalds Moor is near the town of Ilkley (as in 'Ilkla Moor Baht 'at') and that the poem is one of six commissioned from Simon Armitage by the Ilkley Literature Festival. A poem's metadata might also include information about its antecedence and, in particular, performance details or directions to the reader as well as typographic information. In a digital world, metadata links to the analogue (that is, print on paper) poem need further exploration. Associated metadata might also include intellectual property rights (IPR) data in digital form attached to the image as well as geological information. Attribution and copyright information particularly need to be linked to new poems, as for instance with Goodwin's 'She Sells' on his website as a Creative Commons license (CC BY-NC-SA 3.0). In 1973 Edwin Morgan published 'The Computer's First Code Poem' (Morgan 1990: 277)—artificial intelligence (AI) and machine learning have come a long way since then. Taran et al. (2020) show natural-language generation such that text must have 'form' and 'content' components, again reminding us of Williams's 'machine made of words.' The research laboratory OpenAI recently released a version 3 of its language generator (GPT-3) allowing 'Jerome K Jerome' to compose 'The importance of being on Twitter' (Heaven 2020). This returns us to authorship, construction, and context.

Conclusion

This chapter has explored a few aspects of geomorphological science in poetry. New viewpoints change in any scientific discipline—and may reflect or be reflected in poetic insights. Viewpoints, thus interpretations, vary according to the scene, and such elliptic journeys with origin. 'Explaining' (as opposed to describing) landscape is difficult, especially in view of the physics of 'dynamic responses' and 'emergence.' Hybridization is one way of combining points of view (or fields; cf. Figure 7.1) in a poem. Location is a geomorphological feature that might invoke a particular feeling or a response after a signal event, such as a flood. A landscape feature or explanation can be used, non-exclusively, as:

- A poetic idiom
- An identifier of a mood or state of mind
- An identifier of place or location
- An environment, especially associated with anthropocene change
- A visual, data-driven form, augmenting reality.

The last, in particular, can help hybridize poems in collaboration with scientists, graphic artists, musicians, sculptors, and photographers so as to help elucidate and add information relating to 'change.' Hybrids increase information content, perhaps in the same way as Shaffer's (1998) 'third culture' suggests: 'The awareness of the element of creativity in science has done much both to place the arts and sciences on the same plane, to dispel the mystique of 'scientific method' as a mechanical and inexorable procedure' (6). Hybridization may also be associated with scientific ideas and data, a mixing of words and mathematics with statistics and visualization techniques applied to graphed data. This is an area ripe for investigation by poets of the anthropocene, just as it has been for graphic artists and scientists. It is associated with a sense of place as much as the language the poem is written in and translated into as perhaps the accent of the poet or reader. Griffiths's poem about flooding valleys in mid-Wales quoted earlier is a good example, as are the work of the climber poets of gritstone crags in the Pennines.

In our varied and interlinked world (only hinted at in Figure 7.1), students as well as the general public should benefit from poetic insights in science as well as poets learning from science. Graham Harman, originator of OOO approaches, avers, 'Unlike botanists, zoologists, linguists, and anthropologists, philosophers try to simplify the universe' (Harman 2011). The geology and geomorphology of the earth's surface is complex in four dimensions, but a better understanding of this complexity in and through poetry is a useful educational tool for all.

Acknowledgements

I thank Dr David Favis-Mortlock, Brian Lewis, and my referees for helpful comments on earlier versions of this chapter as well as the assistance of the editors. This chapter is dedicated to the late Peggy Troll, friend of Norman Nicholson, dedicatee of his poem 'Comet Come' and co-founder of the Norman Nicholson Society.

Notes

1 Though most mines are hot rather than cool.
2 That place being the West-riding of Yorkshire a few kilometres east of Simon Armitage's home in Marsden.
3 It is well beyond the scope of this chapter to explore this other than to point out the association with research in the anthropocene (Goudie & Viles 2016) and its ties with poetry (e.g. Solnick 2016).
4 See also Whalley (2014a).
5 Horizontal passages in mines for access and/or drainage.
6 See the functional expression description earlier in this chapter.
7 See, for instance, "effects of domain knowledge on mental model revision from animation" in Lowe and Schnotz (2008).

References

Abbs, P. (Ed.). (2002). *Earth Songs: A Resurgence Anthology of Contemporary Eco-Poetry*. Totnes, Devon: Green Books.
Armitage, S. (2006). Modelling the universe: Poetry, science, and the art of the metaphor. In R. Crawford (Ed.), *Contemporary Poetry and Contemporary Science* (pp. 110–122). Oxford: Oxford University Press.
Armitage, S., Hall, P., & Lonsdale, T. (2013). *Stanza Stones*. London: Enitharmon Press.
Auden, W.H. (1979). *Collected Poems*. London: Faber and Faber.
Azizi, F. (2007). *Engineering Aspects of Geomechanics, Glaciology and Geocryology*. Plymouth: Fethi Azizi.

Baker, K. (Ed.). (2000). *The Faber Book of Landscape Poetry*. London: Faber and Faber.

Ballendras, S., & Jaillet, S. (1996). Holocene chronology of catastrophic deposition in a high alpine valley; The case of basin filling in the northern French Alps. *Quaternaire*, 7, 85–96.

Beaumont, P., & Philo, C. (2004). Environmentalism and geography: The great debate? In J. A. Matthews & D. T. Herbert (Eds.), *Unifying Geography: Common Heritage, Shared Future* (pp. 94–116). London: Routledge.

Bentley, P. (2002). *Scientist of the Strange: The Poetry of Peter Redgrove*. London: Associated University Presses.

Blomley, N. (2006). Uncritical critical geography? *Progress in Human Geography*, 30(1), 87–94.

Boardman, J., & Evans, R. (2019). The measurement, estimation and monitoring of soil erosion by runoff at the field scale: Challenges and possibilities with particular reference to Britain. *Progress in Physical Geography: Earth and Environment*, 44, 31–49.

Bristow, T. (2015). *The Anthropocene Lyric: An Affective Geography of Poetry, Person, Place*. Basingstoke: Palgrave.

Brodaric, B., & Hastings, J. (2002). An object model for geologic map information. In D. E. Richardson & P. van Oosterom (Eds.), *Advances in Spatial Data Handling* (pp. 55–68). Berlin: Springer.

Bunge, M. (1984). What is pseudoscience. *The Skeptical Inquirer*, 9(1), 36–47.

Clark, T. (2010). Some climate change ironies: deconstruction, environmental politics and the closure of ecocriticism. *Oxford Literary Review*, 32(1), 131–149.

Clark, T. (2015). *Ecocriticism on the Edge: The Anthropocene as a Threshold Concept*. London: Bloomsbury Publishing.

Coffey, T. (2017). Materials science. *YouTube*. https://www.youtube.com/playlist?list=PLm2F3BtpcrEj7UsAGxjIli7R9qrgpwgXt

Cornish, V. (1932). *The Scenery of England: A Study of Harmonious Grouping in Town and Country*. London: Council for the Preservation of Rural England.

Coveney, P., & Highfield, R. (1995). *Frontiers of Complexity: The Search for Order in a Chaotic World*. London: Faber and Faber.

Crawford, R. (2002). *Poetry, Enclosure, and the Vernacular Landscape, 1700–1830*. Cambridge: Cambridge University Press.

Crawford, R. (2006). *Contemporary Poetry and Contemporary Science*. Oxford: Oxford University Press.

Darbishire, K., Moore, K., & Nuttall, L. (2018). *This Place I Know: A New Anthology of Cumbrian Poetry*. Dent, Cumbria: Handstand Press.

Dartnell, L. (2018). *Origins: How the Earth Made Us*. London: Bodley Head.

Davies, G. L. (1969). *The Earth in Decay: A History of British Geomorphology 1578–1878*. London: Macdonald Technical and Scientific.

Drake, N. (2012). *The Farewell Glacier*. Hexham: Bloodaxe Books.

Dunbar, K. (2005). *Landscape into Literature: A Writers' Anthology*. Dartington, Devon: Green Books.

Eagleton, T. (1982). Recent poetry. *Stand*, 23, 63.

Farley, P., & Roberts, M. S. (2012). *Edgelands: Journeys into England's True Wilderness*. London: Cape.

Favis-Mortlock, D., & De Boer, D. (2003). Simple at heart? Landscape as a self-organizing complex system. In S. T. Trudgill & A. Roy (Eds.), *Contemporary Meanings in Physical Geography: From What to Why* (pp. 127–171). London: Arnold.

Fenton, J. (1972). *Terminal Moraine*. London: Secker and Warburg.

Fonstad, M. A. (2006). Cellular automata as analysis and synthesis engines at the geomorphology–ecology interface. *Geomorphology*, 77(3–4), 217–234.

Freeman, M. (2003). Poetry and the scope of metaphor: Toward a cognitive theory of literature. In A. Barcelona (Ed.), *Metaphor and Metonymy at the Crossroads: A Cognitive Perspective* (pp. 253–283). New York: Mouton de Gruyter.

Gifford, T. (1995). *Green Voices: Underrstanding Contemporary Nature Poetry*. Manchester: Manchester University Press.

Goodwin, M. (2014). *Steps*. Sheffield: Longbarrow Press.

Goodwin, M. (2016). She Sells. https://markgoodwin-poet-soundartist.bandcamp. com/track/she-sells.

Goodwin, M. (2019). *Rock as Gloss*. Sheffield: Longbarrow Press.

Goudie, A. S., & Viles, H. A. (2016). *Geomorphology in the Anthropocene*. Cambridge: Cambridge University Press.

Grieve, M. & Scott, A. (Eds.) (1972). *The Hugh MacDiarmid Anthology*. London: Routledge.

Griffiths, H. M., Goodwin, G., Keevil, T., Salisbury, E., Tooth, S., & Roberts, D. J. G. (2017). Searching for an Anthropo (s) cene in the Uplands of Mid Wales. *GeoHumanities*, 3(2), 567–579.

Hallett, A. (2007). *The Stone Library*. Calstock, Cornwall: Peterloo Poets.

Harman G. (2011). *The Quadruple Object*. Alresford, Hampshire: Zero Books.

Heaven W. D. (2020). OpenAI's new language generator GPT-3 is shockingly good—and completely mindless. *MIT Technology Review*, 20 July. https:// www.technologyreview.com/2020/07/20/1005454/openai-machine-learning -language-generator-gpt-3-nlp/

Herbert, D. T., & Matthews, J. A. (2004). Introduction. In J. A. Matthews & D. T. Herbert (Eds.), *Unifying Geography: Common Heritage, Shared Future* (pp. 321–326). London: Routledge.

Herbert, W. (2006). Confession of an informationist. In R. Crawford (Ed.), *Contemporary Poetry and Contemporary Science* (pp. 72–87). Oxford: Oxford Univeristy Press.

Hoagland, T. (2006). Fear of narrative and the skittery poem of our moment. *Poetry*, 187(6), 508–519.

Holub, M. (2006a). *Poems Before and After* (Expanded Edition). Hexham: Bloodaxe.

Holub, M. (2006b). Rampage, or science in poetry. In R. Crawford (Ed.), *Contemporary Poetry and Contemporary Science* (pp. 11–24). Oxford: Oxford University Press.

Hughes, T., & Godwin, F. (1979). *Remains of Elmet: A Pennine Sequence*. London: Faber and Faber.

Hutton, J. (1788). Theory of the Earth. *Royal Society Edinburgh, Transactions*, 1, 209–304.

Illingworth, S. (2016). Are scientific abstracts written in poetic verse an effective representation of the underlying research? *F1000Research*, 5.

Illingworth, S. (2019). *A Sonnet to Science. Scientists and Their Poetry*. Manchester: Manchester University Press.

Jaeger, H. M., & Liu, A. J. (2010). Far-from-equilibrium physics: An overview. arXiv preprint arXiv:1009.4874.

James, E. W., & James, C. (2016). *Dagrau Tost—Cerddi Aber-Fan (Poems of Aber-fan)*. Cardiff: Cyhoeddiadau Bardddas.

Kelly, R. (2007). *May Day*. Newry, Canada: Parsifal Press p. 44.

Lave, R., Biermann, C., & Lane, S. N. (2018). Introducing critical physical geography. In *The Palgrave Handbook of Critical Physical Geography* (pp. 3–21). Cham, Switzerland: Springer.

Lave, R., Wilson, M. W., Barron, E. S., Biermann, C., Carey, M. A., Duvall, C. S., Johnson, L., Lane, K. M., McClintock, N., & Munroe, D. (2014). Intervention: Critical physical geography. *The Canadian Geographer/Le Géographe canadien*, 58(1), 1-10.

Leeder, M., & Lawlor, J. (2017). *GeoBritannica*. Edinburgh: Dunedin.

Lowe, R., & Schnotz, W. (Eds.). (2008). *Learning with Animation: Research Implications for Design*. Cambridge: Cambridge University Press.

Maclean, S. (1971). *Poems to Eimhir* (I. C. Smith, Trans.). Newcastle on Tyne: Northern House.

Maddox, B. (2017). *Reading the Rocks: How Victorian Geologists Discovered the Secret of Life*. London: Bloomsbury.

Mainzer, K. (1997). *Thinking in Complexity. The Complex Dynamics of Matter, Mind and Mankind*. Berlin: Springer.

Malone, M. (2011). *The Waiting Hillside*. Matlock, Derbyshire: Templar Poetry.

Manning, P. M. (2016). Charles Lyell's geological imagination. *Literature Compass*, 13(10), 646–654.

Manzo, L. C., & Devine-Wright, P. (Eds.). (2014). *Place Attachment: Advances in Theory, Methods and Applications*. London: Routledge.

Marr, J. E. (1900). *The Scientific Study of Scenery*. London: Methuen.

Matless, D. (2016). *Landscape and Englishness*. London: Reaktion Books.

McCaig, E. (Ed.). (2005). *The Poems of Norman MacCaig*. Edinburgh: Polygon.

Morgan, E. (1990). *Collected Poems 1949–1987*. Carcanet.

Morgan, E. (2006). Poetry and virtual realities. In R. Crawford (Ed.), *Contemporary Poetry and Contemporary Science* (pp. 27–47). Oxford: Oxford University Press.

Morrison, B. (1996). *Pendle Witches*. London: Enitharmon.

Mort, H. (2016). *No Map Could Show Them*. LondonChatto and Windus.

Morton, T. (2012). An object-oriented defense of poetry. *New Literary History*, 43(2), 205–224.

Nicholson, N. (1994). *Collected Poems*. London: Faber and Faber.

Ogden, C. K., Richards, I. A., Malinowski, B., & Crookshank, F. G. (1923). *The Meaning of Meaning*. London: Kegan Paul.

Oliver, J. (1996). *Shocks and Rocks: Seismology in the Plate Tectonics Revolution*. Washington, DC: American Geophysical Union.

Poetry Foundation. (2009). *Introduction to The Wedge, by William Carlos Williams*. (In Collections, An Introduction to Modernism, Poetic Essays). The Poetry Foundation. (Original work published 1954), https://www.poetryfoundation. org/articles/69410/introduction-to-the-wedge

Pope, A. (1711). *Windsor Forest*. In D. Brooks-Davies (Ed.), *Alexander Pope* (Everyman poets). London: Phoenix.

Purtill, R. (1970). The purpose of science. *Philosophy of Science*, 37(2), 301–306.

Reynolds, F. (2016). *The Fight for Beauty*. London: Oneworld.

Rhoads, B. L. (2006). The dynamic basis of geomorphology reenvisioned. *Annals of the Association of American Geographers*, 96(1), 14–30.

Riach, A. (2016). "Things are never fixed, finally formed and closed": Alan Riach on Scotland's literature media. *National* (9 December). Available from http:// eprints.gla.ac.uk/161520/).

Rovelli, C. (2018). *The Order of Time*. Harmondsworth: Allen Lane.

Rudwick, M. J. (2005). *Bursting the Limits of Time: The Reconstruction of Geohistory in the Age of Revolution*. London: University of Chicago Press.

Scannell, L., & Gifford, R. (2010). Defining place attachment: A tripartite organizing framework. *Journal of Environmental Psychology*, 30(1), 1–10.

Schumm, S. A. (1956). Evolution of drainage systems and slopes in badlands at Perth Amboy, New Jersey. *Geological Society of America Bulletin*, 67(5), 597–646.

Schumm, S. A. (1991). *To Interpret the Earth: Ten Ways to Be Wrong*. Cambridge: Cambridge University Press.

Shaffer, E. S. (1998). *The Third Culture: Literature and Science*. Berlin: Walter de Gruyter.

Skelton, R. (2015). *Beyond the Fell Wall*. Toller Fratrum, Dorset: Little Toller Books.

Solnick, S. (2016). *Poetry and the Anthropocene: Ecology, Biology and Technology in Contemporary British and Irish Poetry*. London: Routledge.

Soni, J., Goodman, R. (2017). How information got re-invented: The story behind the birth of the information age. *Nautilus*, 10 August, Limits/how-information-got-re_invented.

Sörbom, G. (2002). The classical concept of mimesis. In P. Smith & C. Wilde (Eds.), *A Companion to Art Theory* (pp. 19–28). Blackwell.

Staples, H. L., & King, A. (Eds.). (2017). *Big Energy Poets: Ecopoetry Thinks Climate change*. Kenmore, NY: BlazeVox.

Stoppard, T. (1993). *Arcadia*. London: Faber.

Szent-Györgyi, A. (1957). *Bioenergetics*. New York: Academic Press.

Taran, M., Revunkov, G. & Gapanyuk, Y. (2020). The hybrid intelligent information system for poems generation. In Kryzhanovsky, B, Dunin-Barkowski, W, Redko, V. & Tiumentsev, Y. (Eds.) *Advances in Neural Computation, Machine Learning, and Cognitive Research III*. (pp. 78–86). Cham: Springer Nature Switzerland.

Tarlo, H. (2015). *Poems 2004–2014*. Bristol: Shearsman Books.

Tilley, C. (2010). *Interpreting Landscapes: Geologies, Topographies, Identities; Explorations in Landscape Phenomenology 3*. Walnut Creek, CA: Left Coast Press.

Tinkler, K. J. (1985). *A Short History of Geomorphology*. Totowa, NJ: Barnes & Noble.

Turnbull, R. (2009). *Granite and Grit: A Walkers' Guide to the Geology of British Mountains*. London: Frances Lincoln.

Westcott, W. B., & Spell, J. E. (1999). Tearing down the wall: Literature and science. *The English Journal*, 89(2), 70–76.

Whalley, W.B. (1990a). BANDWIDTH [unpublished poem]. CC BY-NC-ND 2020.

Whalley, W.B. (1990b). Drops [unpublished poem]. CC BY-NC-ND 2020.

Whalley, W. B. (2014a). Norman Nicholson (1914–1987): a geologist's poet. *Geoscientist*, October, https://www.geolsoc.org.uk/Geoscientist/Archive/October-2014/Norman-Nicholson-a-geologists-poet.

Whalley, W.B. (2014b). On Beck. In S. Matthews & N. Curry (Eds.), *Norman Nicholson at 100: Essays and Memoirs* (pp. 102–107). Carlisle: Bookcase.

Whalley, W.B. (2019a). Rocks and landsscapes in the west (part 3), *Comet*, 14(1), 11–15.

Whalley, W.B. (2019b). Drawing as pattern information extraction: linking geomorphology and art. *Drawing: Research, Theory and Practice*, 4(1), 29–53.

Wilson, E. O. (1998). *Consilience: The Unity of Knowledge*. London: Vintage Books.

Wyatt, J. (1995). *Wordsworth and the Geologists*. Cambridge: Cambridge University Press.

Part III
Mimesis: Exploration as pedagogy

8 Found poetry and communal memory-making in the L2 classroom

Jason E. H. Lee

Introduction

If the contemporary age has become an image-saturated one, replete with data and information overload, it has also created a dilemma in terms of how we read notions of craft and authenticity in the field of creative writing today. Given the common refrain that everyone is now an author and everything has already been said, we are now said to be living in the age of the 'insta-poet,' the serial 'copy-and-paste' plagiarizer, where the pithy sound bite, the Twitterverse, and the status update have been made readily digestible for a younger, social media-ingrained global readership.

Though some of us may express that familiar lament over the death of creativity and contemporary poets' waning 'anxiety of influence' (Bloom 1997), we must be careful not to fall into the trap of reductive binary thinking by forming rigid distinctions between, on the one hand, original, authentic poetic craft, and, on the other, mechanically reproduced, soulless art. For instance, in discussing the move from a lyrical or confessional poetics to a citational or constraint-bound one, Marjorie Perloff (2010) wrote of an emergent 'unoriginal genius' in the context of twenty-first-century experimental poetics, whereby the language of citation 'has found a new lease on life in our own information age. It is a commonplace that in the world of digital discourse, of the Internet, e-mail, cell phone, and Facebook, communication has been radically transformed both temporally and spatially' (4). Drawing on works of Walter Benjamin, Charles Bernstein, and Kenneth Goldsmith, Perloff maps the trajectory of an experimental, modernist aesthetic through to its twenty-first-century iteration, finding new possibilities in the interplay between found texts, new media, the internet, and their impact upon modes of cognition and creative process.

Perloff's theoretical position is supported by Goldsmith's (2011) own pedagogical commitment to 'uncreative writing' in the university classroom. Paradoxically, rather than signal the death of authentic writing, Goldsmith's approach suggests a renewed commitment to close, analytical reading. For example, he describes how the British artist Simon Morris, in retyping Jack Kerouac's *On the Road* over a 400-day period (that is, a page every day), was able to gain a heightened appreciation for the Beat poet's language—it's rhythms, cadences, and idiosyncrasies. Goldsmith claims that Morris's act 'shows us that appropriation need not be a mere passing along of information but, in fact, moving information can inspire a different sort of creativity in the author, producing different versions and additions—remixes even—of an existing text' (153). In extolling the virtues of copying, Goldsmith connects his findings to his earlier luminary Benjamin (1978), who had some decades before stated that 'the copied text commands the soul of him who is occupied by it, whereas the mere reader never discovers the new aspects of his inner self that are opened by the text' (66). Tellingly, Goldsmith brings up the example of a student who, after a semester of sanctioned plagiarizing and transcribing, admits that 'by not being "creative," she produced the most creative body of writing in her life' (9). Goldsmith's (un)creative writing opens up a space for all kinds of innovative pedagogy, a supervised classroom environment where copying, stitching, writing over, or writing through is prioritized over the nominally authentic. Ethical questions aside, the virtue of copying can be applied directly to the practice of found poetry, particularly as it allows the student to engage in more analytical processes that extend their appreciation of the possibilities opened by the text.

For Jena Osman (2006), found poetry is akin to detective work or 'gumshoe poetry,' 'because it encourages an investigation into language where the reader and/or writer (as detective) discovers new logics beneath the surface, and thus creates a renewed picture of the textual (and consequently nontextual) world' (240). One consequence of this is that 'The control of the poems shifts from the author to a reader-centred creativity produced through the act of finding' (241). The student is recast as an investigator, mining the text for clues, and forcing out of the language some kind of hidden revelation. The students' interactions can be said to take on extra-literary significance; for example, reading both within and outside the frame of the text, they channel an awareness of how it functions as a historical document, but also how its past significance can be underwritten by their present-day imaginings. In doing so, they find ways of focalizing the mundane, everyday object, defamiliarizing them, deconstructing them, and, consequently, memorializing them as artifacts.

Found poetry for L2 learners across the disciplines

Found poetry has been used in ELT experimental practices since at least the 1980s (Gorrell 1989), primarily as literacy scaffolding, but also as a strategy to balance student rule-based linguistic 'input' with their own creative language 'output.' In negotiating the formal structures of language acquisition and stretching learners' understanding of different cultural contexts of English via found poetry, Dan Disney (2012) found that his L2 tertiary students demonstrated 'increased aptitudes for linguistic variety and complexity, as well as a developing breadth of vision and new or substantially improved insightfulness' (5). Despite these myriad breakthroughs in ELT-based pedagogies, found poetry remains stubbornly associated with the avant-garde, and academic instructors, especially those of a non-creative bent, may feel reticent in applying these ideas to the L2 tertiary classroom. Yet, as I hope to show, so-called 'avant-gardist' forms of poetry need not be difficult for students to adopt, and the demystification process can often be achieved with step-by-step writing exercises which make the tricky process of putting words down on paper easier. Not only does this override the pressures of conforming to certain forms or diction that come with studying the traditional Anglo-American poetic canon, but it also allows students from different disciplinary backgrounds and varying language competencies to experiment with the material at hand.

Hazel Smith's *The Writing Experiment: Strategies for Innovative Creative Writing* (2005) offers one such working model for how short, incremental exercises can help students get their writing off the ground by fostering a love for play and experimentation. Her strategy of using language as the starting point for textual creation is predicated on the belief that 'Language creates the world rather than the other way round … Playing with language allows us to construct our own world, and question some of the ways in which reality is normally perceived' (3). Smith distinguishes between language-based and referent-based strategies to show how any word, object, or issue can serve as a focal point in the initial stages of experimental writing. For instance, language and script-based strategies alleviate the pressure on students to create something from nothing. Word association, sound association, pooling words into arbitrary compounds—all of these exercises stimulate creativity by utilizing students' existing vocabulary banks and can be combined to form longer writing projects. Engaging in endless Derridean play on both signifier and signified components, students' choice of words or phrases can serve as a template for other forms of associative meaning. As words are inherently polysemic, carrying a number of different combinations and meanings which conflict with and occasionally contradict each other, L2 learners may delight in the handicap provided by these exercises, being free from the restrictions of having to invent their own fictional settings, plots, characters, or viewpoints, or infusing their writing with any logical meaning-creation.

Likewise, referent-based strategies, which typically take an object, issue, or emotion as its basis, can often stimulate other forms of narrative writing, and in this the found text offers students a ready-made context for them to build upon. A found text contains its original contextual meaning, but it can be overlaid with additional writing which may interrupt or alter the original narrative flow, whether in the form of paratexts, intertexts, or hypertexts. One other benefit found poetry has for L2 learners outside of immersive language acquisition pedagogies is its ability to connect different language scripts, especially where they appear side by side in translation. Forms of exophonic writing (i.e. writing in one's non-native tongue) may strengthen students' own bilingual competency whilst connecting them to other language communities, especially when they code-switch using a combination of speech and text-based references, allowing them to experiment with English and non-English scripts, amalgamating and superimposing them over one another.

While there are sound pedagogical practices for experimenting with found poetry in the L2 ELT and creative writing classroom, it is only recently that their application across multidisciplinary academic settings has been discussed. For example, the role of poetry within the social sciences went through much critical revision in the 1990s, when educational scholars like Elliott W. Eisner (1991) pioneered the field of arts-based qualitative research. Expanding on this earlier work, Lynn Butler-Kisber (2002) promoted research-led poetry as a performative act that would allow researchers to more adequately map out the full range and complexity of human behaviour, such as by using the lyric form to better mimic interview respondents' expressive language, whilst at the same time allowing the researcher to individualize and make personal their own interventions into social praxis. Likewise, for Melisa Cahnmann (2003), qualitative researchers are able to present recorded data differently via the poetic form. The heightened sense of language, rhythm, the pauses, reflections, and tone of the conversations and dialogues, suggest that formats beyond conventional transcripts may be preferable, whilst at the same time fostering a more humane, collaborative relationship between respondent and interviewer.

Similarly, the affective turn and the focus back towards the academic's own writerly self has led to new formations within the discipline—what Norman K. Denzin (2018) has called 'performance autoethnography,' where

> There is no separation between the writer, the ethnographer, the performer and the world ... It is transgressive. It is resistance. It is dialogical. It is ethical. It is political, personal, embodied, collaborative, imaginative, artistic, creative, a form of intervention, a plea for social justice. ('Preface')

Such autoethnographic practices performed by the creative writing instructor/researcher can be readily passed on to students, who come to understand their own role in the socially constructed world that the text provides, and to intercede with that text as necessary, balancing the technical and artistic aspects of their training.

Given these developments, I argue that found poetry functions not only as a useful prompt within the L2 creative-writing classroom, but also as a potential archival and memory-making tool that can bridge the creative disciplines with the humanities and social sciences via what Monica Prendergast et al. (2009) have termed 'performative ethnography.' Elements of found poetry, which can encompass styles ranging from William Burroughs and Brion Gysin's famous cut-up technique (1978) to the recent erasure poetry of Tracy K. Smith's polemic 'Declarations' in *Wade in the Water* (2018), enable practitioners to open up the artifice of poetry and re-contextualize existing blocks of text by assembling their own forms of innovative and/or subversive meaning-making, but also by using found texts and images as concrete matter to represent their communities' experiences and concerns.

Taking 'Declarations' (Smith 2018: 19) as an example of contemporary social-minded found poetry, Smith overlays the American Declaration of Independence with her own invisible erasures, leaving the reader to ponder over her intent, as well as the relationship between poet, narrator, and addressee. Taking a lesser-known tract of the famous Declaration text, Smith strips away the voice of its celebrated authors Jefferson and Adams, replacing them with the marginalized figure whose rhetorical protest is consistently cut short at critical moments. No doubt there is a presumption among many contemporary readers that Smith has substituted the text's grievances against King George III for a recent occupant of the White House, but I think the more crucial point Smith makes is that critical intervention where she brings the historical inflections of the initial Declaration into sharp focus with the present. Placing Smith's poem against its unedited original positions the works as co-texts; their reflections and echoes inform and illuminate one another.

I cite Smith's poem to show, firstly, how the collective trauma of an embattled community lamenting the failure of twenty-first-century America to live up to its ideals can result in such a subversive response, and secondly, to demonstrate how the text (and the collection as a whole) offers potential avenues for further practice-led research—or what Smith and Dean (2009) call 'practice leading to research insights' (5). Such implications not only enable a community-minded writing practice to occur (Lahman & Richard 2014), they also show how found poetry, besides adding value for those engaging in more typical ethnographic and research-intensive methodologies, can work across that practice/research divide extant in the university setting.

Hong Kong and communal memory-making in the L2 classroom

Having outlined some of these pedagogical developments and experimental writing processes across the practice/research divide, I now want to apply these concepts more properly to the L2 tertiary-level classroom. Taking examples from Hong Kong Anglophone poetry, I offer a number of approaches to crafting experiential learning activities for L2 students that allow them to appreciate and respond to their local environment. The familiar surroundings, texts, and formats that found poetry builds upon not only aids students' poetry-writing ability, enabling them as L2 learners to store and retrieve memories and images through these forms, but also allows them to use poetry more reflexively as a way to engage with their perpetually changing environment.

My reasons for choosing Hong Kong as my case study come down to a number of interesting and overlapping issues: (1) the environment has spawned a number of impressive, varied, and growing Anglophone poetic voices in recent years; (2) Hong Kong is a location where English is spoken by the majority of its population as a second or third language, but remains the primary medium of instruction in most tertiary programmes (which include foreign-exchange students, who themselves use English as an L1, L2, or even L3), making Hong Kong an ideal site for innovative L2 (and L3) English classroom pedagogies; and (3) the absence of stable placemarkers and the constant change driven by the accelerative thrust of neoliberal capitalism has sometimes left the community prone to fits of collective amnesia and bereft of meaningful self-identification.

Hong Kong has often been proclaimed as a constantly emptied-out place, or, to use the well-known phrase by Ackbar Abbas (1997), a 'culture whose appearance is accompanied by a sense of the imminence of its disappearance' (71). Given the constant designation of Hong Kong as a *borrowed* place on *borrowed* time, it would seem natural to use *borrowed* texts and *borrowed* lines to capture the city in all its elusive glory. By using found material, which can be as wide-ranging as interview data, photos, ciphers, maps, posters, street signs, official transcripts, and newspapers or graffiti, students and researchers can become involved in recreating the texture of everyday life in Hong Kong, turning the fabric of the city into a living, speaking entity. Borrowing from the interrelated concepts of place and space in human geography by Yi-Fu Tuan (1977), we can say that the poet's conceptual rearrangement of texts, images, and objects helps to recreate, however imperfectly, a history of that grounded place. These artistic representations of place, via a place's various textures and liminalities, are what permit the students to engage in this creative act of communal memory-making, albeit as predominantly local, Hong Kong Chinese individuals have their own ways of engaging with the English and Chinese languages.

The exterior spaces of Hong Kong are thus mediated via the L2 student's creative acts of memorialization, which are added to an already existing network of past memories. The physical world serves as an anchor upon which we shape these communal memories, but as Paul Ricoeur (2006) reminds us, these experiences are also intersubjective, insofar as private and public memories are simultaneously created. However, while collective remembering is useful in solidifying certain group identities, it cannot aim for objective representations of the past, especially if we consider communal memory as an aggregate of individual memory, which can itself be fallible, subject to revision, and the occasional blurring between imagination and reality.

One thinks here of Henry Wei Leung's award-winning *Goddess of Democracy: An Occupy Lyric* (2017), which uses the hybrid form to create an autoethnographic account and sociohistorical document of an important moment in Hong Kong's post-Handover history, the 79-day street protest in 2014 known popularly as the Occupy or Umbrella Movement. Leung's use of textual erasures, timelines, reproductions of banners, signs, translations, and other paraphernalia related to the protest demonstrates how found materials can be used in multiple ways to write back to or against any dominant narrative of the Occupy Movement. While the world media and most Hongkongers' collective memory of the event is suffused with stock images of, for instance, yellow umbrellas, tear gas, the Lennon Wall, *and* concept artwork that was set up on the streets, Leung's collection is at times sparse, punctuated by white spaces and full of fragments, forcing the reader to excavate the text and reconstruct it again into a narrative whole. In this way, Leung's collection also suggests a form of remembrance which goes against the all-encompassing spectacle of the event which, as Guy Debord (1995) noted, is used to mediate our everyday reality: 'The spectacle is not a collection of images; rather, it is a social relationship between people mediated by images' (4).

Similarly, the street-level view that Leung provides is problematized by his own constant self-examination of the protests' aims and their potential repercussions, particularly insofar as the poet's narrative 'I' / (eye) finds itself caught up in the maelstrom of the Occupy protest site while, simultaneously, trying to remain detached from it. In 'Translation Poem for Hong Kong,' Leung includes a translated (and vulgar) Chinese-language document lamenting the negative impact of the protest on businesses and warning the protesters to leave. The poet's attempt to 'translate the other' (43), however, cannot fully reconcile the insurmountable gap that separates these opposing camps. Instead, Leung arranges his collection in such a way as to encompass conflicting perspectives, thus addressing different reading communities' textual interpretations of erasures and signs in innovative and culturally significant ways.

As a collection, Leung's work serves as a useful model for what can be achieved over a period of time—the documentarian and poet tandem in Leung can be used as one such template for future writing projects that seek to bridge creative writing with community building in a space like Hong Kong. In the following section, I offer two such exercises based on found poetry that utilize (1) image-text relations and (2) literary-language structures, which can be adapted for cross-disciplinary purposes in the university classroom. In doing so, I show how these exercises can prompt students to rethink their relationship with their immediate physical environment, raise their awareness of social issues, and finally, through the act of crafting poetry, demonstrate their own agency in challenging (or reproducing) any clichéd or preconceived views of their local community.

Found images as visual props: Eddie Tay's *Dreaming Cities*

As it pertains to focalizing text-image relations in poetry, a number of recent publications by Eddie Tay come to mind, especially his use of street photography as found 'texts' on which to base artistic responses. Tay, a Singaporean native and long-term Hong Kong resident, has published four collections of poetry, with the latter two, *The Mental Life of Cities* (2010) and *Dreaming Cities* (2016a), combining English and Chinese bilingual writing with sustained meditations on the urban condition. Drawing inspiration from urban study scholars like Georg Simmel (1950) and Michel de Certeau (2011) in his own reflections on creative practice, *Anything You Can Get Away With* (2018), Tay's primary goal is to absorb 'urban spaces into the mental space of creative practice, transforming everyday public scenes into an existential domain that is productive to thought, agency and meaning creation' (5). The agency given to the photographer is nevertheless tempered by a realization that the medium remains at best a copy, an imitation of a scene that stands transfixed in time.

As Susan Sontag (1977) reminds us: 'To photograph is to appropriate the thing photographed. It means putting oneself into a certain relation to the world that feels like knowledge—and, therefore, like power' (4). While Sontag's remarks are important insofar as she cautions against the visual image being seen as a wholly 'truthful' representation, it is worth pointing out the respective dynamics of the street photograph, which is almost wholly unplanned, is spontaneous, and doesn't seek to create a total narrativizing gaze. These distinctions are irretrievably blurred when the image begins to take on a documentary role, but whereas the explicitly documentary photograph might sit preserved in an archive or museum, as a witness to official events in history, the street photograph aspires to a micronarrative of everyday observance, the unofficial counternarrative that passes undetected by the street's inhabitants.

For Tay, street photography 'aspires to the condition of found poetry in its search for the readymade scene. It is not the street scene that awaits the arrival of the photographer, but the photographer who designates the street as such' (17). One positive consequence of this act of self-designation is that students taking photos with their cameras or smartphones are able to control the frame and angle of the found scene or object, which in turn makes the style or content of their poem distinguishable from the work of others. The budding poet-photographer draws upon the experience that led to the taking of the photograph, or, failing that, that residue of experience that informs their interpretation of the 'image-world' developing in front of them.

To take one such example, consider this found photo-poem called 'Groundwork' presented in Tay's collection side-by-side as a text-image coupling (Tay 2018: 14–15):

there is power in granite
not of your choice,
earth-deposits of a history of money.

so today you are digging
out of the pavement a strength
you already possess,
a faith in stone.

i wonder what would happen
if you find a fish gasping in the dust,
or if a hundred-year-old turtle crawls out
to proclaim the good news.

i am waiting for a minotaur
to emerge to start a fresh flood.
we imagine ourselves to be trees
in the thick sulphur of this city

where no one needs to speak.
maybe you're waiting to tell a story
of an underground government
of broken bodies.

who are our leaders,
that they would stay quiet?

these are eruptions
too deep in the ground,
metaphors of stone,
groundwork of hands.

Figure 8.1 'Groundwork'.

The photo in Figure 8.1, shot in monochrome, takes a relatively banal scene featuring construction workers in some indeterminate part of Hong Kong. By itself, it may not evoke any particular emotive response, but combined with Tay's own poetic intercession, it helps to 'excavate' a psychology of the streets, one that is passively acknowledged yet rarely confronted by the passer-by. As the text is created in response to the photo, creating what

Roland Barthes (1997) would call a form of 'anchorage,' the poem becomes yet another version of the original scene, this time twice removed from reality. Text and image are seen operating in an unequal semiotic relationship; the poem connotes rather than denotes the photograph: 'the text constitutes a parasitic message designed to connote the image … the image no longer illustrates the words' (Barthes 1997: 25).

However, rather than dismantling the material world, the poem sets it up anew in its ethereal otherworldliness. The poem's surrealist imagery, replete with a fish, turtle, and minotaur, expands the universe of that 'image-world,' whilst the 'earth-deposits of a history of money' and 'metaphors of stone' help connect the concrete material in the photograph with the abstract thoughts of the poet-photographer. The photograph's object permanence, not to mention its aesthetic power, helps to memorialize the event, but it is through the students' individual creative storytelling that they intervene with their own act of communal memory-making.

To show how found images and poetry can be directly deployed as an experiential learning activity, I take concrete examples from one off-campus excursion, where selected finalists and awardees of the 2015–2016 Hong Kong Budding Poets Scheme (Polley 2017), were taken to the small, rustic island of Cheung Chau, located some 20 km off Hong Kong island. The students, consisting of mixed-age groups from upper primary to all secondary year levels, were sent round the island and asked to compose their own found poems using Tay's various photo-poems on Cheung Chau as prompts (Tay 2016b).[1] To the stated learning outcomes—namely, combining found texts and digital photography, responding to place, people and objects with a heightened awareness, transposing these responses to more familiar everyday locales—was added the more significant act of memorializing a part of Hong Kong that had largely escaped the urban development and reclamation that has made the city one of the most densely populated areas on the planet.

Through this combination of text and image snapshots (which they were indeed encouraged to conglomerate on the page), students were able to recreate their own past and present narrative journeys of Cheung Chau and the city environs in general, whether in linear or non-linear fashion, as a collage, storyboard, or as cut-out fragments. Furthermore, that joy of rediscovery students experienced when they stumbled across some of the locations Tay had photographed elicited further, often contrastive, responses to the original photo prompt, as the students began to rely more on their experiential learning by sensing, seeing, and feeling their way through the scene presented. The exercises enabled these advanced learners to become psycho-geographers (much like Tay himself), aware of the object world around them, and jolting them out of the habitual perceptions they may have had of their surrounding cityscape. These off-campus excursions looking for found material could also be supplemented by additional writing exercises within the classroom proper, by juxtaposing old and new pictographic representations of Hong Kong's streets and asking students to compose their own responses to these changes. Another exercise involved reversing the photo-led prompt and instead asking students to take (or find) snapshots in response to a poem about Hong Kong. Students were presented with one final wrap-up activity that featured more lines of Tay's photo-poems (Tay 2016c), but with his photos omitted, and they were asked to fill in the gaps between the lines with the photos they had taken. On this occasion, I used Tay's text as a 'relay' for their own photos, encouraging students to complete their visual essay of the prompt-poem using the images they had captured while meandering around the island.

Found text and literature-language games: Tammy Ho's 'How the narratives of Hong Kong are written with China in sight'

Whereas Tay's poems and the aforementioned prompt exercises might be used to bring out students' own interactions with the image-text, I also want to draw upon examples that would stretch their appreciation with the phrases/words within a given text. Written during the Umbrella Protests, Tammy Lai-Ming Ho's list poem borrows the opening lines from classical English texts and suffuses them with political statements, jarring their meanings and loading them with intertextual allusions:

1. Call me One Country, Two Systems.
2. It is a truth universally acknowledged that the democracy fighters in Hong Kong must be genomically modified by the West.
3. Hong Kong and democracy—it was love at first sight.
4. An order from the PRC comes and never leaves.
5. Many years later, as the Hong Kong people remembered the 'generosity' of the Chinese government for not shooting them or overrunning them with tanks, they would be forced to cry in gratitude.
6. China, non-light of my life, non-fire of my loins.
7. Happy cities are all alike; every unhappy city is unhappy in its own way. Hong Kong is unhappy because it wants happiness too much. It believes that the right to vote for its own leader would contribute to its happiness. It believes.
8. democracyriverrun, past Mongkok, Causeway Bay, Admiralty and Central...
9. Hot days in September. Some rainy nights in October. Tick-tock tick-tock tick-tock the clocks were striking and Big Brother was watching. Let him watch. Let the whole world watch.
10. It was the best of times. It was the age of wisdom. It was the epoch of belief. It was the season of Light. It was the spring of hope. We had everything before us—in short, the period was so far like the present period, that some of its noisiest Chinese authorities insisted on its being received, for good or for evil, in the superlative degree of comparison only.
11. You are about to begin reading the story of Hong Kong, 'One Country, Two Systems,' when you realise that such a story doesn't exist.

Keep the 'country,' remove the plural marker in 'systems' and replace 'two' by 'one,' then you are truly beginning to read the story of Hong Kong. (One and one is always one.)

12. Someone must have slandered Joshua Wong ... for one evening, without having done anything outrageously wrong, he was arrested.
13. Whether Hong Kong shall turn out to be the hero of the international fight for democracy, or whether it will be utterly defeated, the pages of history must show.
14. It was a broken promise that started it. The students returned to the streets day after day. And the voice on the other side of the border responded with contempt, scorn.
15. Through the facial masks, between the crooked handles of umbrellas, people could be seen fighting, in their own way, which is the best way.
16. 689 was spiteful.
17. In the beginning there was the Party and the Party was with the Country and the Party was the Country.
18. There is a spectre haunting China—the spectre of Umbrellaism.
19. The Hong Kong people said they would fight for the city's future themselves and they would bring umbrellas.
20. They say the past is a foreign country and people do things differently there. We say the past is always upon us.
21. Hong Kong was born many times: first, as a fishing village; and then, as a British colony. After that, it became a Special Administrative Region. And then one summer, it became very special indeed.
22. Where now? Who now? When now? Hong Kong now. We now. Now now.

(Ho 2014) (Used with permission.)

If Ho's poem employs pastiche to represent the Umbrella protests via the spectre of some of English literature's most famous lines, it also frames an emergent subaltern voice that speaks back to an assumed dominant narrative centre (in this case, the Chinese Communist Party). What at first seems to be a comic, humorous opening, appropriating the lines of Herman Melville's *Moby Dick* and Jane Austen's *Pride and Prejudice*, takes on a more serious tone—the poet's own struggle to articulate a position that might resist this totalizing, alternative 'official' narrative. Ho's response, fittingly, is to enact an ironic double appropriation, using some of the statements originally conceptualized by that dominant power, such as 'democracy fighters in Hong Kong must be genomically modified by the West' or 'the Party was the Country.'

Using Ho's poem as a template, students can manipulate their own foun'd phrases, whether they take their source texts from educational materials, leaflets, posters, recipes, menus, billboards, or other signs, reordering the main lexical units, substituting nouns, verbs, adjectives, as they prefer, whilst keeping the rhetorical structure of the sentence intact. Their purposes may be sociopolitical critique, lamenting the hyper-capitalist nature of Hong Kong public life perhaps (by using advertising slogans), or something more innocuous, poking fun at a system of teaching that relies on rote learning (by scrambling words from a cloze text). The operation remains the same: to find amongst the bric-a-brac statements some kind of unified meaning which can help the students to think laterally across a variety of textual formats and to synthesize and connect blocs of information in ways that might not seem readily apparent.

Another language game example: in one recent collaborative open-call project entitled 'HK Vanity Poems' conducted with the artistic director and advertising professional Michele Salati, participants were invited to craft found poems out of a list of car vanity plates in Hong Kong extracted from Salati's own street photo collection. As the lexicon of vanity plates ranged from English and Cantonese names and affiliations, to loanwords and slang, to abbreviations, acronyms, and numeronyms (replacing letters for numbers), there were plenty of opportunities to play on the web of signifiers available through their various collocations, as one poem by Tom Kwan Ee Chan, 'CARNIVAL LOOKS' demonstrates:

I
BIG FISH | ROLLER
LIV2LUV | GLAMOUR | CITY LIFE.

II
GOLDRUSH | MERCHANT | HAV IT | TOO EASY
THE CEO | KIDS | ROCK ON | DREAMER | MERCEDES

III
10 CENTS | WEALTH
LE POET | JOKE | MOONWLAK | REFORM

IV
20K | MONK | SELL | FORTUNA | PROMISE
JAPAN KOI | ORACLE | RECYCLE | XMAS | BLISS

(Chan 2020)
(Used with permission.)

Unlike erasure poetry, which requires students to limit their vocabulary based on what individual phrases, words, or letters are available, or ekphrastic poetry, which assumes a semiotic connection between the text and another creative medium, this form frees the students to experiment with almost endless combinations of words, ideas, or meanings. Chan's submission, like many others, contains an ironic social critique which imitates the many humorous if cringeworthy declarations to free-market capitalism in Hong Kong, and his juxtaposition of the two vanity plates 'HAV IT' and 'TOO EASY' no doubt exemplifies what many observers feel when they see cars containing owners of these vanity plates hurtling down Hong Kong's roads at high speed.

As part of the project's stated output, the individual words and phrases of the poems themselves were then matched with their respective image and compiled into a GIF file (Salati & Lee 2019), with plans made for further dissemination of the poems virtually on Instagram, as well as a featured exhibition with live readings. Predictably, once the individual vanity plate images were paired together, an additional layer of visual effect was created. The sight of these found vanity plates, sans punctuation, line breaks, or other syntactic markers, produced an altogether different reading of the poem. As the moving digital images provided a fluctuating assortment of backdrops of Hong Kong's elevated highways, cluttered alleyways, and leafy suburbs, they also sensitized viewers to their own cognitive schemata and memories of these places.

I reference the HK Vanity Poems project not only to show the efficacy of found poetry at recalling the textures of everyday urban life, but also because it can be used as an embarkation point for more expansive writing exercises. By incorporating other thematic exercises in their writing, students can compose longer and more ambitious pieces that might form the backbone of a creative/research-writing portfolio. Students can start with one line or segment from a particular found text (for example, a billboard, a street sign), progressing onto other texts and forming layers of narratives that cross over and inform one another (Leung 2017). They could also take a more randomized sample of found extracts, working in groups or individually, to arrange and rearrange the material until a cohesive unity starts to form. This strategy works across English or other languages, whether they are translated or left in their original script. Elements of classical or canonical English and non-English literature can be used, as can pieces of colloquial writing, slang, or jargon, which stretch students' bilingual, translation, as well as code-mixing skills.

After reconstructing their chosen found text, students may be given the task of reappraising a similarly completed text as critical readers. When reading their classmates' work, students may have fun trying to guess the origins of these redacted lines (as with the vanity plates exercise), googling certain collocations and trying to piece together, like detectives, their original contexts and meanings. In retracing their steps back to the original source text, students are necessarily forced to recollect their physical environment and dip into their own memory banks. This act, however, requires more than just a passive recollection of already-existing texts, as students have to actively sift through the evidence closely, wading through the detritus or clutter contained in the new found poem. As a result, their interpretation becomes less habitual and more alive to the variations of syntax or choice of wordplay—a process which again recollects Goldsmith's earlier celebration of re-copying a text and subjecting it to a more critical gaze.

Conclusion

By using locally produced texts and images, combining or reconfiguring them in multiple ways, students are trained to think both creatively and conceptually about the material that they encounter on a day-to-day basis and to appreciate the found texts and objects that proliferate their cityscape (or other suburban/rural environment). These writing exercises can be tailored for students across the creative and non-creative disciplines, where they might help offset the tedium that comes with imitating poetic form or transcribing datasets, allowing students to gain a wider picture of the social impacts of their disciplinary subfield. When these varied Anglophone (or mixed-language) found poems are used as an entry point to students' own exercises, the process consolidates their knowledge and appreciation of their own locally produced cultural imaginary. More importantly, by actively engaging with works created by local arts practitioners, as well as the social concerns that they inevitably take as their subject matter, students may also come to see their own potential for interceding on behalf of their community. As the state of tertiary instruction shifts further towards measuring research impact upon the local community, found poetry methodologies may yet play a greater role in service and experiential learning activities. In a digital world where students have become increasingly disconnected from their own communities, the turn towards performative ethnography may yet engage them to think about their role as agents of social change. Through the endless recycling of images, ideas, and clichéd statements, they may yet find a way of preserving something akin to a communal memory of their physical environment.

Note

1 The students were workshop-prepped for the remote island visit. They were also provided, in groups, with a suggestive photo-poem pamphlet. Each group was also accompanied by a workshop instructor/mentor.

References

Abbas, Ackbar (1997). *Hong Kong: Culture and the Politics of Disappearance.* Minneapolis, MN: University of Minnesota Press.
Barthes, Roland (1997). The Photographic Message. In Roland Barthes (Ed.), *Image-Music-Text* (pp. 15–31). London: Fontana. (Original work published in 1961).
Benjamin, Walter (1978). *Reflections.* New York, NY: Schocken.
Bloom, Harold (1997). *The Anxiety of Influence: A Theory of Poetry* (2nd ed.). New York, NY: Oxford University Press.
Burroughs, William S., & Gysin, Brion (1978). *The Third Mind.* New York, NY: The Viking Press.
Butler-Kisber, Lynn (2002). Artful Portrayals in Qualitative Inquiry: The Road to Found Poetry and Beyond. *Alberta Journal of Educational Research* 48(3), 229–239.
Cahnmann, Melisa (2003). The Craft, Practice, and Possibility of Poetry in Educational Research. *Educational Researcher,* 32(3), 29–36.
Certeau, Michel de. (2011). *The Practice of Everyday Life* (3rd ed.). Berkeley: University of California Press.
Chan, Tom K. E. (2020). "CARNIVAL LOOKS" [Unpublished poem].
Debord, Guy (1995). *The Society of the Spectacle* (Donald Nicholson-Smith, Trans.). New York, NY: Zone Books. (Original work published 1967)
Denzin, Norman K. (2018). *Performance Autoethnography: Critical Pedagogy and the Politics of Culture.* New York, NY: Routledge.

Disney, Dan. (2012). "Is This How It's Supposed to Work?": Poetry as a Radical Technology in L2 Creative Writing Classrooms. *New Writing*, 9(1), 4–16.

Eisner, Elliott W. (1991). *The Enlightened Eye: Qualitative Inquiry and the Enhancement of Educational Practice*. New York, NY: Macmillan.

Goldsmith, Kenneth. (2011). *Uncreative Writing: Managing Language in the Digital Age*. Columbia, NY: Columbia University Press.

Gorrell, Nancy (1989). Let Found Poetry Help Your Students Find Poetry. *The English Journal*, 78(2), 30–34.

Ho, Tammy L. M. (2014). How the Narratives of Hong Kong Are Written with China in Sight. *Radius*. Retrieved from http://www.radiuslit.org/2014/10/06/poem-by-tammy-ho-lai-ming-4/

Lahman, Maria K. E., & Richard, Veronica M. (2014). Appropriated Poetry: Archival Poetry in Research. *Qualitative Inquiry*, 20(3), 344–355.

Leung, Henry Wei (2017). *Goddess of Democracy: An Occupy Lyric*. Oakland, CA: Omnidawn Press.

Osman, Jena (2006). Gumshoe Poetry. In Joan Retallack & Juliana Spahr (Eds.), *Poetry and Pedagogy: The Challenge of the Contemporary* (pp. 239–250). New York, NY: Palgrave Macmillan.

Perloff, Marjorie (2010). *Unoriginal Genius: Poetry by Other Means in the New Century*. Chicago, IL: University of Chicago Press.

Polley, Jason S., Ho, Tammy Lai Ming, & Lee, Jason E. H., eds. (2017). *Words Are Worlds: The Magic of Hong Kong's Local. Hong Kong Budding Poet's English Award 2015–16 Anthology*. Hong Kong: Government Logistics Dept.

Prendergast, Monica, Leggo, C., & Sameshima, P. (Eds.). (2009). *Poetic Inquiry: Vibrant Voices in the Social Sciences*. Rotterdam: Sense Publishers.

Ricoeur, Paul (2006). *Memory, History, Forgetting* (Kathleen Blamey & David Pellauer, Trans.). Chicago, IL: University of Chicago Press.

Salati, Michele, & Lee, Jason E. H. (2019, December 4). *HK Vanity Poems* [Video File]. *Facebook*. Retrieved from https://www.facebook.com/842590122839240/

Simmel, Georg (1950). *The Sociology of George Simmel* (Kurt H. Wolff, Trans.). Chicago, IL: The Free Press.

Smith, Hazel (2005). *The Writing Experiment: Strategies for Innovative Creative Writing*. Crows Nest: Allen and Unwin.

Smith, Hazel, & Dean, Roger T. (Eds.). (2009). *Practice-led Research, Research-led Practice in the Creative Arts*. Edinburgh: Edinburgh University Press.

Smith, Tracy K. (2018). *Wade in the Water*. Minneapolis, MI: Graywolf Press.

Sontag, Susan (1977). *On Photography*. New York, NY: Penguin Books.

Tay, Eddie (2010). *The Mental Life of Cities*. Hong Kong: Chameleon Press.

Tay, Eddie (2016a). *Dreaming Cities*. Singapore: Math Paper Press.

Tay, Eddie (2016b, January). *Cheung Chau*. Hong Kong Lucida: A Thinking Street Photography Site. Retrieved from https://hongkonglucida.com/2016/01/26/cheung-chau/

Tay, Eddie (2016c, February). *Cheung Chau Yet Again*. Hong Kong Lucida: A Thinking Street Photography Site. Retrieved from https://hongkonglucida.com/2016/02/03/cheung-chau-yet-again/

Tay, Eddie (2018). *Anything You Can Get Away With: Creative Practices*. Singapore: Delere Press.

Tuan, Yi-Fu (1977). *Space and Place: The Perspectives of Experience*. Minneapolis, MN: University of Minnesota Press.

9 (Re)orienting borders with hybrid poetry in tertiary pedagogy

Pauline Felicia Baird

Introduction

The greatest challenge for any academic discipline is resisting the temptation to get comfortable—to be comfortably sure we have heard every story, opened every door, and listened to every speaker. Giving in to such a temptation kills curiosity, learning, and the transformative power of pedagogy. Instead, we must embrace our shortcomings, refuse to get comfortable, and listen for the whispers of the forgotten.

Dear Reader, my project is a love letter to honor the silenced voices of Caribbean village women told through their own words and stories.[1] I listened to the stories of Afrikan women from the village of Buxton, which is my hometown in Guyana. I listened to these stories in Guyana, New York, and the Bahamas to learn Afrikan-Guyanese[2] women's perspectives about their roles in the early village movement in the 19th century, post-emancipation (Baird 2016). I hear their stories as Caribbean rhetoric, which includes homegrown or vernacular practices, relationships, responsibilities, and the roles of women that link consciously or unconsciously to African ancestry (Browne 2013). Caribbean rhetoric positions itself in decolonial worldviews, which are crucial for framing my discourse on the role of hybrid poetry in change-making and in tertiary educational pedagogy. To borrow from Porter (2002), 'no tale is entirely personal, especially if an academic is telling it' (376). Narratives, including hybrid poetic ones, open the doors to other perspectives, dynamics, and insights of missing narratives and representations of Caribbean village women in postcolonial academic discourse—and thus challenge pedagogical practices in tertiary education.

I began (re)telling and sharing Caribbean women's stories in an Advanced Poetry class in Guam in 2016 following my PhD studies. The class included two faculty members and ten students; these third- and fourth-year undergraduates were drawn from the academic disciplines of business, journalism, art, and English. The demographics of the course, encompassing the faculty members as well, included Chamorro, Filipino, mixed Chamorro and Filipino, Caucasian American, and, to comprise myself, Afro-Guyanese.

As a scholar of rhetoric and composition, I situate my work in both Caribbean rhetorics and cultural rhetorics. In the practice of cultural rhetorics, my work is intercultural, making space for 'valu[ing] the efforts and practices used to make something, and to use that understanding to build a theoretical and methodological framework that reflects the cultural community a researcher works with' (Riley-Mukavetz 2014). Thus, I wrote hybrid poetry as a methodology, making sure that Caribbean women's rhetorics are voiced and visible. I gathered stories and created a remix of poetry drawn from a combination of autobiography and the lived experiences of women from Buxton.[3] My words and the women's words intertwine in some stories so that the women and I are in a co-author relationship. This relationship is indicative of how women can tell and theorize village stories.

Throughout my discourse, I will tell stories that deal with theory, saying, 'Listen to this story' or 'Listen' as a way of connecting *you, the reader* to the women, and the stories, and the methodologies, thus building on the cultural rhetorics principle that stories are theories (Maracle 1994; Powell 2012; Powell et al. 2014). In the section that follows, the terms hybrid poetry, Caribbean rhetoric, and decolonial options are defined to situate hybrid poetry as a change agent in tertiary pedagogy.

Hybrid poetry

Hybrid poetry is a rhetorical tool comprising form and content or verse and narrative. It can be long or short verse or fragments useful for communicating linguistic events. In 'Tips from Amy King VIDA' (2015), King described hybrid poetry as 'a mix of old and new, of traditional and experimental approaches to poetic form.' Hybridity involves a composer experimenting with mixing, blending, or creolizing (Hannerz 1997, 2010) by creatively putting together a collage of gathered unoriginal material (Ferguson 2015). Beyond art, hybrid poetry offers multiple options for situating stories.

Listen to this story, with common patterns in the direct speech of Caribbean women, that was created using the everyday words of these selfsame women.

> My mother used to *seh* [a common phrase]
> Are whispers in my ears
> teaching me how
> To reach back and carry mama
> into our oral histories

This short hybrid poem draws on village women's story-making practices. It intentionally disrupts the habit of complacency we tend to develop in terms of our engrained stories. All my life I have heard stories beginning with 'My mother used to seh.' Before I began to read Caribbean women's stories as rhetorical studies, I questioned the value of these women. I questioned the value of these women's stories to me, to the academy, and to society. Thus, as an impetus to intervene and create social justice, I inserted Caribbean women's rhetorics into the canon of women's rhetorics and breached the existing Eurocentric binaries in my PhD dissertation (Baird 2016). This enabled me—we—to *hear* women.

But how to listen to women who have not been 'heard from'? As an oral methodology for the gathering (of) stories, I speak their words aloud to hear the cadence of their voices, while simultaneously addressing their formal arrangement. I hear stories of motherhood, gender, home, land, and everyday living practices. By showing my class how the strands of our stories are pulled together to co-create on the one hand transforms and transports Caribbean women's oral histories across academic borders, and on the other disrupts halls of silence (Minh-ha 2009).

Poetry from story as rhetoric

Stories matter. Caribbean women's stories matter. As a reminder, Afrikan-Guyanese women are also Caribbean women. Their stories capture the multivalences of village women's oral performances. The fluidity of hybrid poetry is suited to epideixis or performance of oral delivery—our terms for creating change. As I will explain later in this chapter, I transcribed women's oral narratives to written prose (Baird 2016) and then arranged them in verse. I employed the practice of remixing as a tactic that makes available the spoken word, not unlike what rappers, poets, and other artists do to be heard (Palmeri 2012; Lessig 2008; Bachmann-Medick 2016).

The spoken words 'My mother used to seh [say]' preface a methodology of how Afrikan-Guyanese village women tell, propagate, and demonstrate ways of listening and learning from everyday experiences. The poem draws attention to the pedagogical practices exercised in the mother-child relationship. In a classroom, these words might resonate with students' personal experiences. As a result, students might explore how their cultural knowledge might allow them either to enter Caribbean women's stories or not to do so. Such engagement with oral histories through hybrid poetry opens conversations about ways of constructing frameworks that support the use of lived experiences, and multicultural stories in higher education. Multicultural stories of lived experiences can broaden transnational conversations about women's everyday rhetoric. We can explore how the relationships in the home, with each other, the school, and the wider community might align (Riley-Mukavetz 2014). Those rhetorics can foster openness to interdisciplinary communication in cultural and ethnic studies, linguistics, and anthropology, among many other disciplines.

Pedagogy's domain resides not only in the academy, but also in the village system among women rhetors. 'My mother used to seh'—the direct speech of Caribbean women—give voice to a homegrown methodology for listening to mundane interactions among women. In the short story "Girl" (1978), the Caribbean writer Jamaica Kincaid's narrator offers insight into how and where women and girls construct homegrown pedagogy. Her mantra 'this is how' (Charters 2003: 320) addresses issues including, but not limited to, gender, girlhood, and womanhood. In sum, hybrid poetry as a pedagogical methodology can be a vehicle for advancing civic and academic community engagement by examining everyday life.

Caribbean rhetoric

Here is another story, as told in an interview with Jennifer Lee, January 2015 (in Baird 2016: 26).

> My mother seh this
> About her mom.
> That when they were doing the roads
> women used to go and break bricks.
> 'Why the women break the bricks
> and not the men?'
> *I don't know*
> 'This world is not fair
> That women have to care
> for children and break the bricks,
> what were the men doing?'
> 'I don't hear [her say] anything.'

This story is an example of how Caribbean rhetoric sounds and looks. Caribbean rhetoric encompasses the homegrown or vernacular cultural performances of Caribbean people. Hence 'Caribbean' rhetorics disrupt the notions of mimicry and reification in Western culture (Browne 2013; Walcott 1974). These performances, whether the storytelling is shared in prose, poetry, dance, steel pan music, or carnival, are all recognized 'available means'—or rhetorics of living and surviving (Ritchie & Ronald 2001). Browne (2013) notes that Caribbean rhetoric, as a discipline, flies beneath the radar of the discipline of rhetoric and composition. Where curricula do not reflect Caribbean rhetorics, making hybrid poetry can unsettle the (complacent) status quo.

These stories bear witness to our culture, which is 'always and already rhetorical' (Powell et al. 2014). In a similar manner to how Indigenous scholars write to include their practices of using story to teach history and to preserve sovereignty, my goal is to write, contest, and broaden the discourses of who *can* speak, create, and tell stories (King et al. 2015). People who tell stories live and have lived. They are real. Thus, when I create hybrid poems, I am unveiling stories hewn from Caribbean women's lips. These lives can no longer exist solely in the shadows—of women's histories layered in oral traditions. They must exist in broader social spaces.

Through hybrid poetry, a methodology for understanding embodiment emerges. Women's bodies carry knowledge. The phrase 'My mother seh,' for instance, works as an instrument to nuance how to situate people in my village without 'denying or effacing the memories of others and of situating

... others' memories within the context of the collective—not just how I come to be, but how we come to be' (Condon 2012: 85). Minh-ha (1989) argues that stories are wedded to histories. Ergo, from mother to mother to daughter, embodied knowledge is negotiated in communication; it is not random. It is highly structured and embedded in masking (Browne 2013). Introducing the older people from villages to younger students supplies the latter with much to consider about the real relationships in their historical accounts of mundane activities.

Sometimes students have a tendency to think the academy is for telling stories other than their own; thus, 'they are silenced and alienated from self and context before even they generate their text(s)' (Asher 2009: 3). With the storytelling element as a methodology in hybrid poetry, we have a useful framework for breaking down interactions and complicating the straightforward reading of texts. Exploring village women's stories through the making of hybrid poetry facilitates critical reflection, critical awareness, and praxis in intercultural and cross-disciplinary contexts.

Decolonial option

Including hybrid poetry from marginalized peoples' narratives in tertiary spaces is an attempt to perform Mignolo's (2007) notion of the decolonial option.[4] Colonialism is the systemic control of a nation by another to influence the individual and/in society at every level. Colonial legacies in Eurocentric education privilege western histories in lieu of the (hi)stories of and from the people being educated (Asher 2009). Mignolo (2007) proposed a delinking from educational systems that divorce people from their own stories and geographies. Connecting Caribbean women to their stories 'contribut[es] to build[ing] a world in which many worlds coexist' (Powell 2012). Taking these stories to the tertiary classroom links the personal experiences to the places where students and teachers think, dwell, and envision possibilities for transformative stories. Adapting stories is just one example of transforming storytelling by a co-authoring with ordinary women in/from my culture.[5]

In sum, Caribbean women's scholarship remains integral to identity negotiations, personhood, and world citizenship, even though women's oral histories are not often formally studied as rhetoric. Caribbean women, however, need not hide their contributions to discourses on the human experience. As Gloria Anzaldúa (1999) professes, people take their practices from 'land' or home with them and negotiate their identities (16). Making space for students' and teachers' stories of home in tertiary curricula allows those participants to recognize and use hybrid knowledge to make new kinds of options for extending women's narratives into academic spaces and across borders. As a pedagogical methodology, hybrid poetry becomes a vehicle to 'facilitate an understanding of shifting textual and material borders that operate as a creative and political mode of destabilizing not only complex social locations, but also research frameworks'

(Fotopoulou 2012). Stories traverse borders, and each crossing loosens the tongues of the people waiting finally to be heard.

Situating hybrid poetry in cultural rhetorics

If we should continue to honor women's rhetorics in the academy—and beyond—using hybrid poetry, we have one more tactic for making more women from more villages visible. Tactics used for constructing the histories of people who do not appear in dominant academic spaces (Certeau 1988; Kimmerer 2013) extend to the commonplace—to village stories. Hence, scholars who practice cultural rhetorics may focus on everyday rhetorics with(in), across, and alongside communities. According to the Cultural Rhetorics Theory Lab (2012), cultural rhetorics involve a set of constellating methodological, theoretical, and pedagogical practices drawn from rhetoric and composition studies, various ethnic studies fields, postcolonial studies, decolonial studies, gender studies, performance studies, and cultural studies, among others. Practitioners of cultural rhetorics, for example, may strive to understand meaning-making in communities through their art forms, such as weaving baskets and other materials, combined with people's lived experiences.

Coming to multigenerational women's knowledge by way of mixed genres and vernacular practices is not uncommon. Emulating Miranda (2013), who made visible her ancestors, I created 'a space where voices can speak after long and often violently imposed silence' (xx) for Caribbean village women. Rhetorically, I listened to the women *for* their stories. Doing so, I enacted 'there-ness'—being present in storytelling (Riley-Mukavetz 2014: 119)— by articulating women's words aloud to be well heard. Again, my focus on the rhetorics of Caribbean women from villages is to intervene in Browne's (2013: 3) argument that Caribbean rhetorics must be 'seen and heard,' even by Caribbean educators (like me) working at the intersections of cultural rhetorics and Caribbean rhetorics. Poetry that engages with women's stories in higher education transports women and stories transnationally.[6] In the rest of this chapter, I make connections between story, land, and people, thereby taking responsibility for bringing women into the academy through hybrid poetry.

Hybrid poetry as a methodology

Many students bring mother and grandmother stories to the academy. The class of students predominantly from Asia and Micronesia is no different. Students exchanged stories in narrative-poetic forms, providing a space for the participants to enter discourses and explore their shared beliefs. Their poetry drawn from lived experiences complicates how learners' orient relationships with stories across the cultures represented in the classroom. For example, a knowledge of hybrid poetry-as-methodology in cross-cultural pedagogy might allow students to become accountable for their own stories, those of others, and to affirm (or not) their places as qualitative knowledge-makers in tertiary pedagogy.

Poetry—beginning with story

I began my own stories in class with historical references to my home:

> I come from here—
> Buxton Village. A small place
> African women and men molded
> 'One million tons of mud and water'
> by 'hand and shovel' moved
> cotton and sugar plantations—
> I come from there.

Buxton Village is a hybrid place; it's a place of legacies. The people created villages from plantations. Buxton Village in Guyana, South America, is a place where the canals of the sugar plantations rib the landscape, and there is no escaping the crossing of waterways to go to one's dwelling. Thus, hybrid poetry is a discourse on my 'awareness of the graftings, transitions, and translations through which we define our present and articulate an ethics equal to the way we live now' (Bhabha 1995: 116). To pull together hybrid poetry is to acknowledge a corollary of memory, words, negotiated activities, experiences, and spaces that authenticate existences both in the now and in the future.

Hybrid poetry and coming to praxis

I asked the teacher of the Advanced Poetry class, a colleague teaching in the English Department, for permission to join his class as a student. My colleague sought permission from the students for me to enter that classroom space. The students welcomed me. In this act, the class allowed me to cross internal institutional borders, and to break hierarchies. As a professor, I was a student in that class; thereby, ma(r)king it an unequal place.

I wrote a poem each day in the semester, using prompts from Kowit's (2017) book, *In the Palm of Your Hand*. He advises poets to write near rocks, waterways—or anywhere. I felt comfortable writing in a place that was my current residence. I had lived on a Pacific island for eight years, and throughout that time, I taught at the university. My presence in the poetry class nevertheless meant that I was crossing many divides, including age and power.

Exploring Caribbean village women's rhetorics in poetry generates critical reflection and awareness, along with praxis in intercultural and cross-disciplinary contexts. A pedagogical approach to hybrid poetry, when read as cultural rhetorics, adds another layer of classroom practice that scholars of cultural rhetorics might draw on to extend how they can exercise story as decolonial methodology. Teachers might share their poetry-making practices and invite students to do the same with a view to interrogating lived experiences. As I shared earlier, my methodology included listening to Caribbean women, writing their stories, speaking their words aloud, and creating poetry to share in class to provide visibility to, and discourse about, village women.

Hybrid poetry as a rhetoric of inclusion

Buxton Village is a place of hybrid peoples. I am descended from transplanted Africans whose descendants later became Guyanese or creole indigenous Afrikans (diaspora), owing to their kinship to land. As creole-indigenous citizens, they developed new post-emancipation citizenship from 1838. Buxtonians are primarily Africans who, immediately upon being 'freed,' purchased part of a plantation. By 1840–1841, the place had been converted into a village! These formerly enslaved laborers had become landowners!

Guyana's coastal plain is prone to flooding. Hence, as part of its characteristics, nature seeks to dominate. Nevertheless, the people continue the struggle over living with, and alongside, land and water in postcolonial times. After doing physical labor and being 'degraded' and 'held captive' for over three centuries (Rodney 1982; Nehusi 2018: 81), the people formed communities that still carried on the colonial traditions of conquering and taming the land.

Telling (my) stories invokes my consciousness about how I myself struggled to tame stories, to remix stories, to make stories logical. For example, in the class, students exchanged poems, and everyone made comments to affirm the message, encourage the writer, or to suggest changes. I regard such activities as the struggle to jostle fragments, stories, and verses into poetry as necessary elements in both decolonial writing and the pedagogy of inclusion. The land, water, and people are engaged in reciprocal relationships. The creation of hybrid poetry speaks to cultural rhetorics: the notion of stories dwelling alongside, across from, and with(in), other stories.

Hybrid poetry as stories of home

We all come from somewhere. We all have stories of home. Stories about home are repositories of knowledge. They encapsulate systems of knowledge-making that are essential for exploring community-based relationships, responsibilities, and reciprocities. Yet students and teachers may never talk of home in their classes. To begin telling stories, Verzemnieks (2018) strongly recommends that students start with *I come from here* stories.

At university, I introduce myself to the students and teachers by talking specifically about land—where I come from, my village, its people, and our practices. Talking about the land from whence I come helps me bear testimony to the embodied efforts of Africans who created an alternate society for themselves and left it for their descendants. But, how did we fare?

As a child, I grew up where the Atlantic Ocean meets Guyana's muddy coast, in the shadows of the majestic Komaka (or silk-cotton) trees. I ran, running carefree, playing barefoot in the dirt and freely climbing trees. I remember my Granma scooping up calabash bowls of rainwater from the catchment and drenching my feet. As she washed the dirt off my feet, she returned the DNA of our enslaved forebears from my little feet at the bottom of the stairs to her wooden bungalow, back into the ground.

Hybrid poetry as vehicle

Hybridity marks how I orient myself in the world and the classroom. The hybrid poetry I create includes a consciousness of Caribbean ancestral knowledge. It also integrates the telling of stories in other places, such as 'the Pacific' and 'the University.'[7] Such inclusion gives meaning to Mignolo's (2011) notion of decoloniality as an option for pedagogy—telling stories from the places where we think and dwell. Mignolo's (2011) critical consciousness and orientation to geographies constellate with Adam Banks's (in Aronson 2013) direct appeal for a change in pedagogical approaches to composition in higher education.

Banks is a former Chairperson of the Conference on College Composition and Communication (CCCC). When asked, 'How CCCC Can Help Re-vision Higher Education,' Banks noted that we need to employ the 'rhetorical techniques and traditions of marginalized groups' in order that:

> a black student, no matter where she comes from, whether that's the hills of Appalachia, or Chicago or Philly, should be able to hear her voice or the voice of people she comes from … or an indigenous young man, whether coming from a reservation community or from Any City, USA should see something in writing instruction that leaves him feeling that he and his people's traditions are being honored.
>
> (in Aronson 2013)

Clearly, higher education must embrace a variety of pedagogies. I regard hybrid poetry-making and sharing as ways to connect to Banks's (in Aronson 2013) and Mignolo's (2011) notion of a pedagogy of inclusion. My poetry aims to bring to bear a range of discourses among students from their geographic and linguistic backgrounds to make their educations relevant in/to the 21st century.

What can happen when we start writing down these stories and introducing them in academic settings? How can we impact other cultures with oral traditions, such as Indigenous and Pacific cultures? I suggest that writing down our oral histories and sharing them adds our stories' landscapes of knowing. Having multiple sites for sharing stories helps stem the loss of oral traditions currently happening across many cultures. Making our stories heard and told in the ways we want, and in places we decide, engages a decolonial option for change. In the hands of students at the tertiary level of education, poetry created from our various places of knowing can serve an activist agenda by unsettling classroom practices.

Properly executed hybrid poetry, in other words, can challenge the underlying assumptions of students and teachers, particularly concerning reorienting boundaries, power structures, knowledge practices, discourse, resistance, gender, ability/disability, curricula, and visibility, among other conditions. Bringing Caribbean women's rhetoric from villages into classrooms with diverse demographics shifts the focus of *what is* possible. It is possible to cultivate pedagogical practices that allow students to co-create stories and broaden their understandings of rhetorics in their own settings as well as in multiple other settings. Further, we can explore the possibilities presented by technology to preserve, animate, and disperse cultural products more discursively.

Hybrid poetry to interrogate what's at stake

The poetry teacher[8] of the class once asked me 'What's at stake?' after reading one of my poems. According to Kowit (2017), writing is practice in place and space. While comfort was a factor in writing a poem each day, I needed to consider what contributions my poetry has in the wider community and in the classroom. The history of many nations comes to mind. People celebrate women and their oral stories. Thus, my hybrid poetry found resonance in Asian Pacific classrooms. Using women's words to tell their stories, I deliver the women to the students. Doing so situates 'silent' village women alongside students' lived experiences with their grandmothers, mothers, aunts, and other females. Contending with these women's stories helps students contest nuanced notions of women being silent and invisible as a mark of their gender roles.

Here is yet another story I tell

In my home village, I found only one newspaper article (from 1946) written by a woman to, and about, women. In contrast, many books about women in my village have been authored by men. When their words are missing from academic spaces, women's voices remain sometimes unheard, rendering them invisible to readers. I told that story to situate the agency of translating women's oral stories into written texts, which disrupts the power dynamic. Further, having women's words read in class by polyglot university students often breaches pedagogical barriers. Indeed, women's discourse can teach students how to transform and transport women's oral narratives to new kinds of audiences, one brief story at a time.

Women's stories, written by women, can be vaulted into college pedagogy through feminist methodologies. Applying a feminist methodological principle of rhetorical listening with strategic contemplation, I critically reflect on what is left out of these stories of the African journey to social uplifting (Royster, Kirsch, & Bizzell: 2012). I looked beyond the archives to render women visible, audible. In a 2016 interview with 36-year-old Buxtonian Tamika Boatswain (who lives in the Bahamas), I gathered stories. I asked,

'How can we find the stories by our women?' She responded, 'You must go to the people who tell stories. They didn't write our stories. You must go and talk to people' (Baird 2016: 148). I imagine the Komaka Tree in our village overhearing our conversation. I offer this conversation in poetry thus. Listen.

> Komaka listens
> Listens on the breeze
> To two girls who left
> When One returns and asks
> Girl One: How can we find the stories by our women?
> Girl Two: *They didn't write our stories.*
>   *You must go to the people who tell stories.*
>   *You must go and talk to people.*[9]

The poem draws on the interview to enact new ways of performing social justice, identity, and interpersonal relationships. Boatswain contends that the colonials, 'They,' did not write the stories of ordinary people, but those stories are not missing; they are in the oral traditions (Baird 2016: 147). Tamika's model of storytelling is an embodied practice—we must go to people to get stories, not just the archives. In writing hybrid poetry, I am relearning how we get access to make and to tell stories. Scholars such as Shawn Wilson (2008) have been recording Indigenous peoples' practices and methodologies and sharing them with young children, future generations, and the world. Recording Caribbean women's stories follows that tradition.

Poetry as a vehicle for (re)turning to another home

My presence in the aforementioned poetry class just following my PhD studies meant that I was crossing many divides of belonging and ethnicity. Attending the poetry class also meant that I would experience transitions from being a graduate student to an assistant professor. I would also put into practice the 'story-as-methodology' I theorized as a graduate student towards a decolonial approach to Caribbean rhetorics. I was a returnee to the island of Guam and to university, three months after graduating with a PhD in rhetoric and writing from Bowling Green State University. I had returned from Ohio, USA, to the island—from big to small; from national politics to (inter)national local politics. The island holds the contentious status of an unincorporated territory of the United States. Many of the indigenous Chamorros contest the United States' presence on their land. It does not escape me that many of the Indigenous islanders are Americans as much as they are Chamorro—a hybrid status of a sort.

Regarding 'identity,' poetry about 'what home is' can provide an entry point to interrogate rhetorics of belonging and relationship building. As I read, listened to, and explored the students' poetry, I faced my concerns about: (i) situating Caribbean women's rhetoric alongside the rhetorics of the local people, (ii) the broader and urgent questions of their sovereign status, and (iii) my status as a foreigner in the Western Pacific community. I find that (hybrid) poetry can help students cultivate empathy and invite careful attention to other people's stories.

Poetry as maps

Poetry, like story, maps place and space. In my experience, both preserve places and communities, and both challenge the way we think of access to maps. I recall trying to show a student where I am from by using Google Maps. 'I am from HERE,' I indicated, pointing to the Guyana map online. Oops! Zoom, Zoom, Zoom! I looked at Google Maps to find my village, but I couldn't. The land must be there, but it did not show up in any way I recognized. If the search engines do not have it, does a place exist to others? How can I make women visible on landmasses that are themselves not always visible?

I panicked.

Then I wrote:

> Far from my Komaka
> land—Buxton Village
> I try to go home
> again by satellite
>
> No body no eyes
> Yet it sees my
> home from its
> virtual perch high
> in the sky
>
> A poverty of images
> Google Earth shows me
> Zooms in on
> rectangles white
> Some after-party rubbish
> Littering on the ground around
> Sprawling green
> branches?
>
> I Zoom for perspective
> Virtual angles
> Moving by mouse
> Walking streets and alleys
> Why do I see no
> house?
>
> I have been gone awhile
> Not touched the land
> Not with my feet
> ZoomInZoomOutPan

Trees and white
White and trees
Searching by index and thumb
What are these white rectangles
And trees?

Ah! Komaka
Trees and tombstones
Not one without the other.
Both are homes of the ancestors
And my cyber beacon—
another way to walk
home.

I had observed the land—
The trees on the island;
they were recognizable
in cyberspace.

Trees play vital roles in my village: they provide food, shelter, and spiritual benefits. Moreover, they are maps that can lead to our home. Using my knowledge of the trees, of the cemetery, with the Google search engine, I gained access to the village virtually. I had been used to situating a small place in the former British Guiana, in South America, with digital maps. However, the knowledge of how to locate my home exists within my village's cultural practices. In the village, we say home is where our navel-string is buried under the long-living trees. Yet, that the sites/sights of majestic Komaka Trees in Buxton Village can lead me home came as an unexpected outcome of writing poetry.

Pedagogy that explores ancestral knowledge is cultural rhetoric. By using that subconscious knowledge with, and alongside, search engines, we come to complex understandings of how we talk about home and have access to it. In my poem, I use the Komaka Tree as a motif for place and home. I believe this is when I exercise the decolonial option. For example, in my experience as a Caribbean woman living in another homeland, the search for my village via Google Maps was fruitful only because I could recognize the Komaka trees. The trees lead me to the cemetery where my ancestors are. Certeau (1988) calls this practice of using creative ways of knowing and doing 'tactics.' By them, I could map my entire village street by street without seeing the street names on the map. Google Maps is intended to give users guidance and access to land-based entities. The search engine, however, did not provide equal access to my village; not the same equal access, at least, as it did in a search for my graduate school, Bowling Green State University. Stories like these map topics of belonging, longing, and returning, to the village. They also shed light on how people are made invisible.

By invoking the Komaka Tree, I enacted a reflective methodology that is part of story-as-methodology. Through storytelling, this exchange of knowledge becomes the academic community's shared discourse. For instance, I explained to my classmates that the name Komaka is Amerindian, the Indigenous peoples in South America. In Amerindian cosmology, the tree is the residence of the spirits or/of ancestors. In African traditions, the Baobob and Kapok trees play significant roles in everyday life. Like the Amerindians, Afrikans in Buxton Village ascribe spiritual significance to trees such as the Komaka.

Here is how I tell this story:

> The Komaka tree watches
> watches and touches
> a young girl
> on her way home
> after school run
> among the wind-blown clouds
> of silk-cotton.
>
> jump up on tippy toes snatch
> snatch a tiny puff of white
> cradle it
> cradle it between
> thumb and index
> tear out
> a little black seed
> shake it
> shake it off her fingers
>
> broken winged
> broken winged silk-cotton
> floats then settles
>
> settles on the village dirt where it will live
> live perhaps 100 years?

When I tell this story of the village in class, I am acutely aware that I am a daughter of Africans with first-hand accounts. Though these accounts are missing from the written village history, they exist in the stories that their descendants tell while sitting under trees, in the farm, in the yard, and even in concrete apartments in New York City (Baird 2016). And I write them into poetry in the academic spaces. As in Buxton Village, Pacific island peoples circulate Indigenous stories about trees. The Komaka Tree acts as a witness in the poems which invokes Chamorro beliefs about the sacred Taotaomona trees native to the island.

LISTEN:

> The ones who live in the Komaka tree watch
>   watch over those under
>   the Komaka tree
> from their perch stories in the sky
> and when the pods break and silk cotton blankets

the village listen to the old women's murmur
>it's a sign
>dem spirit a-come [the spirits are coming]
come down to touch their land—the Village
>>by bird call
>>carrion crow flight
>>nine night
>>forty night
>>come-true
>>wake
>>in rum drinking
>>house building
>>n' drum beating

now that the tree
has fallen where
did the spirits go?
And while we're pondering, tell me,
when have you ever a
Komaka sapling seen?

And when a Komaka falls
>falls
>to flood
>or natural causes down
>from battered bark and bough,
where do the spirits go? Where?
To another tree?

Upon hearing about the Komaka Tree, my students in Guam invoked the sacred Taotaomona trees native to the island in this way:

STUDENT A: *Reminds me of the Chamorro legends of the Ifit tree and the flame tree*
STUDENT B: *If it is a creepy tree, expand on it more. I like it!*

Hybrid poetry, additionally, is a convenient rhetorical tool for student's entering cross-cultural and intercultural conversations about land and relationality. The island of Guam is another *home-land*. It is where I made a new home, and my stories connect with the culture. Listening to student feedback about the trees becomes a necessary part of a relational methodology to honor hidden stories. Consequently, students create a way to relate to the land on which the university is built—the land from where the Chamorro people come:

Student A scribbled on my manuscript: *Strong sense of the circle of life, relationships between nature and people (which is rarely seen nowadays) and the perpetualness of beloved ancestors. The detail is superb, almost dreamlike. Masterfully done!*

I felt that Student A connected with my story and understood: 'this is how' we can bear culture and the relationships we make with land. Overall, Student A's comments allow us to learn how others experience the stories we tell.

Conclusion: Poetry is an option

I sometimes worry about essentializing women and stories, even though I am conscious that no story is complete, linear, or singular. I am also inclined by training to seek an acceptable academic medium to tell their stories. I resist. I offer an alternative approach, or decolonial option, that involves writing Caribbean village women's storytelling practices into the rhetorical canon using hybridity as a political act.[10] The acts of reading and writing were historically detrimental to Afrikan-Guyanese village women. We can now unsettle colonial academic privileges with our stories. Caribbean women can tell their stories in one line, one verse, one statement, one fragment. Using those storymaking ways presents a challenge, however. It is a messy experience because of the struggle to tell women's stories within academic stories by way of fragments of remembered family stories—so much remains unsaid.

Listen to this story drawn from an interview with Cheryl Glen in preparation for my PhD dissertation (Baird 2016). Cheryl's grandmother bore many children and had problems recalling their names. After reading the poem, some students could hardly decide whether to feel pity or respect for the grandmother.

Listen.
    Grandmother and Granddaughter

    Komaka tree listens
    listens to grandmother and
    granddaughter
    Mavis
    Shirley
    Mildren
    Seifred
    Ada
    Ida
    James
    Cheryl
    Vincent
    Joan
    Umm—Carol, Buddy.
    'But Mudduh, yuh mean to tell me they didn't have abortion in yuh time?'
    Godfrey
    Carlton
    Hazel
    Huh…umm…umm…umm…

Pam
Sarah
Joseph.
'Mudduh? Why you mek all these many chi'ren fuh a man who didn't seem to care for you?'
Manny
Clement
Umm…umm…huh…
Junior
George
Andrew
Charles
Chile, I always thinking dat one a dem chi'ren gon do something to tek me outta poverty.

As student H has said: *I don't know whether I should feel pity for her or if I admire her strength and perseverance.*

I am encouraged to perform Caribbean women's rhetoric. I do so by responding to Royster, Kirsch, and Bizzell (2012), who asked: 'How can we render women visible who have not been studied before?' We can listen to women and co-create stories with them. As reciprocity and gratitude to women before me, I presented the everyday rhetorics of Caribbean women from villages. We can tell our stories. These stories are yours. When we tell stories, we (re)create avenues for us and others to look backward and forward, and to ensure the survival of our culture.

With a good heart, I thank you for listening to our stories.

Notes

1 Letter writing has been employed historically by women so as to be seen and heard (Donawerth 2011)
2 Afrikan-Guyanese include diasporic peoples who are descendants of formerly enslaved Africans.
3 Remix, here, entails a manipulation of artifacts to create new ones (Knobel & Lankshear 2008).
4 Appleton (2019) recommends that teachers reorient or shift their attentions to how they negotiate barriers. They should teach w'ith the intent to reshape curricula and systems. The end goal is to 'diversify tertiary education, digress from the canon, decenter knowledge production, devalue hierarchies, and disinvest in citational power structures.' These five options act as countermeasures against the current practice of teachers merely adding a few works from non-white scholars to curricula. This is not enough. Decolonial options, such as Appleton's, recommend challenging institutional spaces, such as 'a poetry class,' to provide students the space to make new kinds of spaces for culturally sensitive contributions to learning. I contend that a shift in focus of what we can do with women's stories in the classroom enacts a decolonial option with a view to connecting rather than merely breaking with/from. In so doing, we can reconfigure our positions about how to navigate institutional borders.

5 Adapting stories forms a part of ongoing discussions on cultural appropriation. Hybrid poetry is an appropriation in the sense that the stories are repurposed and reformed (as they did not exist as poetry originally in my Caribbean culture). But this does not carry the notion of cross-cultural borrowing for private ownership (see Young 2008).

6 I have personally done so in my research and teaching in Guyana, Trinidad and Tobago, Ohio, Guam, Palau, and Japan.

7 I highlight the Pacific and the university to demonstrate my own movements from my original village on the Atlantic to my present life and work circumstances in Guam and Japan.

8 *What Island* author P. K. Harmon.

9 The author of this chapter is Girl One; Tamika is Girl Two.

10 Historically, post-secondary education in the Anglophone Caribbean privileged traditional colonial ways of writing. Students write themselves out of the Caribbean language and culture to gain educational and economic advantage (Milson-Whyte et al. 2019).

References

Anzaldúa, G. (1999). *Borderlands: La frontera*. San Francisco: Aunt Lute Books.

Appleton. N. S. (2019, February 4). *Do not "Decolonize" … If you are not decolonizing: Progressive language and planning beyond a hollow academic rebranding. Critical Ethnic Studies.* University of Minnesota Press. Retrieved from http://www.criticalethnicstudiesjournal.org/blog/2019/1/21/do-not-decolonize-if-you-are-not-decolonizing-alternate-language-to-navigate-desires-for-progressive-academia-6y5sg

Asher, N. (2009). Writing home/decolonizing text(s). *Discourse: Studies in the Cultural Politics of Education*, 30(1), 1–13, doi:10.1080/01596300802643033

Aronson, D. (2013). Tectonic shifts, turbulence, and opportunities: Adam Banks on how CCCC can help re-vision higher education. *The Council Chronicle*, 23(2), 16–17.

Bachmann-Medick, D. (2016). *Cultural turns: New orientations in the study of culture*. Berlin: De Gruyter.

Baird, P. F. (2016). *Towards a cultural rhetorics approach to Caribbean rhetoric: African Guyanese women from the village of Buxton transforming oral history*. (Doctoral Dissertation). Retrieved from https://etd.ohiolink.edu/

Bhabha, H. (1995). Cultural diversity and cultural differences. In B. Ashcroft, G. Griffiths, & H. Tiffin (Eds.), *The post-colonial studies reader*. New York: Routledge.

Browne, K. A. (2013). *Tropic tendencies: Rhetoric, popular culture, and the Anglophone Caribbean*. Pittsburgh, PA: University of Pittsburgh Press.

Charters, A. (2003). *The story and its writer: An introduction to short fiction*. Boston: Bedford/St. Martin's.

Certeau, M. (1988). *The practice of everyday life*. Berkeley, CA: University of California Press.

Condon, F. (2012). *I hope I join the band: Narrative, affiliation, and antiracist rhetoric*. Logan: Utah State University Press.

Cultural Rhetorics Theory Lab. (2012). "What is cultural rhetorics?" *Brochure*. Retrieved from https://crtheorylab.wordpress.com/

Donawerth, J. (2011). *Conversational rhetoric: The rise and fall of a women's tradition, 1600–1900*. Carbondale, IL: Southern Illinois University Press.

Ferguson, K. (2015). *Everything is a remix remastered [video]*. Retrieved from https://vimeo.com/139094998

Fotopoulou, A. (2012). Intersectionality, queer studies, and hybridity: Methodological frameworks for social research. *Journal of International Women's Studies*, 13(2), 19–32.

Hannerz, U. (1997, January 1). The world in creolization. In K. Barber & C. Young (Eds). *Readings in African popular culture*. Bloomington, IN: Indiana University Press.

Hannerz, U. (2010, November 29). Diversity is our business. *American Anthropologist*, 112(4), 539–551. 10.1111/j.1548-1433.2010.01274.x

Knobel, M., & Lankshear, C. (2008). Remix: The art and craft of endless hybridization. *Journal of Adolescent and Adult Literacy*, 52(1), 22–33. doi:10.1598/Jaal.52.1.3

Kowit, S. (2017). *In the palm of your hand: The poet's portable workshop: A lively and illuminating guide for the practicing poet*. Thomaston, ME: Tilbury House.

Kincaid, J. (1978). Girl. *The New Yorker*. Retrieved from https://www.newyorker.com/magazine/1978/06/26/girl

King, L., Gubele, R., & Anderson, J. R. (2015). *Survivance, sovereignty, and story: Teaching American Indian rhetorics*. Logan, UT: Utah State University Press.

Kimmerer. R. W. (2013). *Braiding sweetgrass*. Minneapolis, MN: Milkweed Editions.

Lessig, L. (2008). *Remix, making art and culture thrive in the hybrid economy*. Creative Commons Version. London: Bloomsbury Academic.

Maracle, L. (1994). Oratory: Coming to theory. In Wendy Waring (Ed.), *By, for, & about: Feminist cultural politics*, 235–240. Toronto: Women's Press.

Mignolo, D. W. (2011). *The darker side of western modernity. Global futures. Decolonial Options*. Durham, NC: Duke University Press.

Mignolo, D. W. (2007). Delinking: The rhetoric of modernity, the logic of coloniality and the grammar of de-coloniality. *Cultural Studies*, 21(2), 449–514.

Milson-Whyte, V., Oenbring, R., & Jaquette, B. (2019). *Creole composition*. SC: Parlor Press.

Minh-ha, T. (1989). Grandma's story. *Woman, native, other: Writing postcoloniality and feminism*, 119–152. Bloomington, IN: Indiana University Press. Retrieved from http://www.jstor.org/stable/j.ctt16xwccc.7

Minh-ha. T. (2009). Poetry and anthropology. In Maria Damon and Ira Livingston. Eds. *Poetry and Cultural Studies*, 347–354. Champaign, IL: University of Illinois Press.

Miranda, D. A. (2013). *Bad Indians: A tribal memoir*. Berkeley, CA: Heyday.

Nehusi, S. K. (2018). *A people's political history of Guyana 1838–1964*. Hertford: Hansib Publications Limited.

Palmeri, J. (2012). *Remixing composition: A history of multimodal writing pedagogy*, Carbondale, IL: Southern Illinois University Press.

Porter, J. (2002). Why technology matters to writing: A cyberwriter's tale. *Computers and Composition*, 20, 375–394.

Powell, M. (2012). 2012 CCCC Chair's Address: Stories take place: A performance in one act. *College Composition and Communication*, 64(2), 383–406.

Powell, M., Levy, D., Riley-Mukavetz, A., Brooks-Gillies, M., Novotny, M., & Fisch-Ferguson, J. (2014). Our story begins here: Constellating cultural rhetorics. *Enculturation: A Journal of Rhetoric, Writing, and Culture*, 17(1). Retrieved from http://www.enculturation.net/our-story-begins-here

Riley-Mukavetz, A. (2014). Towards a cultural rhetorics methodology: Making research matter with multi-generational women from the Little Traverse Bay Band. *Rhetoric, Professional Communication and Globalization, 5*(1), 108–124.

Ritchie, J. S., & Ronald, K. (2001). *Available means: An anthology of women's rhetoric(s)*. Pittsburgh, PA: University of Pittsburgh Press.

Rodney, W. (1982). *A history of the Guyanese working people, 1881–1905*. Baltimore, MD: Johns Hopkins University Press.

Royster, J. J., Kirsch, G. E., & Bizzell, P. (2012). *Feminist rhetorical practices: New horizons for rhetoric, composition, and literacy studies*. Carbondale, IL: Southern Illinois University Press.

"Tips from Amy King VIDA." (2015, June). *Talking writing: A magazine for creative writers and readers*. Retrieved from http://talkingwriting.com/

Verzemnieks, I. (2018). *I come from here: Portraying place, community, and history*. Presidential Lecture at the University of Guam. New York: W.W. Norton & Company.

Walcott, D. (1974, February). Caribbean: Culture or mimicry? *Journal of Interamerican Studies and World Affairs, 16*(1), 3–13.

Wilson, S. (2008). *Research is ceremony: Indigenous research methods*. Black Point, Nova Scotia: Fernwood Publishing.

Young, J. O. (2008). *Cultural appropriation and the arts*. Malden, MA: Blackwell Publishing.

10 Edifying and frangible creative artforms

A working definition for interstitial poetry and its conceptual framework for virtual environments

Dean A. F. Gui

Circa 1950, pedagogical paradigm shifts in higher education started taking hold worldwide with the arrival of (i) Creative Writing as subject and discipline alongside (ii) distinctive developments in Poetry and Fiction. The impacts of these two critical events partly made it possible for me to become a Master of Arts in Creative Writing (1997), specializing in Poetry, and to write my first ekphrastic inquiry poem (2020)—the one that begins this chapter's Introduction.

The poem is also a trajectory of four timelines (personal and pedagogy, poetry, virtual environments, and theories and methods) that have been influential not only in shaping my identities today as a poet, a researcher of virtual environments, a university teacher, and a doctoral student in Hong Kong,[1] but also towards the conception and composition of this chapter (Figure 10.1).[2]

My reviewer, in 'urging' my foregrounding and frontloading of the proposed definition more strategically (which involved decisions about how to filter drafted content and cited literature I was first averse to parting with), dislodged the very personal stories and experiences that influenced my decision to undertake a study that defines interstitial poetry (IP) while also building a conceptual framework aligning IP with virtual environments (VEs). The content that the reader should observe in the poem is the result of eight edited original pages of a draft. This approach is an adaptation of Monica Prendergast's (2006) ekphrastic inquiry. It was a welcome methodology, one involving discoveries about how to envision integrating excess text (or new-document-cut-paste-save and 'deletion' methodologies) into my research while at once repurposing said excess for illustrative and practical uses. Through the genesis of the organic structure, I can now take the reader on a journey that interweaves the four trajectories in the exploration of interstitial poetry, virtual environments, narrative, and poetry that concludes with some personal remarks on the conception of this research, and insights into some related mixed genres of poetry.

(English) poetry exists as a unique, fluid, and multifarious text form, adapting across time and transcending space, in both literary and academic counterparts. Poetry is created in response to volatility, fatality, resistance,

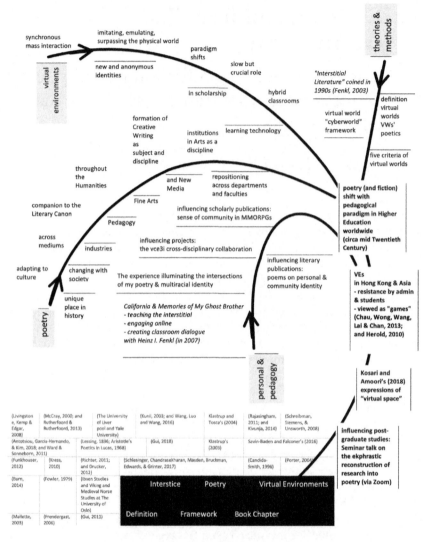

Figure 10.1 Example of an Ekphrastic Inquiry Poem.

and disparateness (Silliman et al. 1988; Muhammad & Gonzalez 2016); poetry represents all the hyphenated, fleeting and diasporic communities that have influenced it and been influenced by it (Longenbach 2009); and poetry exists because of humankind's eternal struggle to make sense of our lives and our deaths (Storck 1912; Awan & Khalida 2015). These important textual and multi-mediated archives contain our most intimate snippets of memory, unrealized ideas, cultural beginnings and ends, possible futures, *and* personal narratives.

It is odd, then, that the poetry of virtual space, so far, has not been granted the same attention as its textual archives. I am uncertain as to the extent that this delivery approach of mine convinces you, the reader, of my proposed definition—or of the level of impact the framework of attributes characterizing interstitial poetry in VEs might retain in its various applications. However, it is my intention to demonstrate through my sections 'The Definition,' 'The Framework,' 'The Case Study,' 'The Story,' and 'A Parting Poem' that this exploratory study not only addresses a missing entry in referencing materials (through the working definition), and contributes to pedagogy and scholarship already underway in the fields of Creative Writing, Fine Arts, and New Media (through the conceptual framework), but also, as Lisbeth Klastrup resounds, conveys 'a vocabulary with which to discuss' and debate, in public and academic communities.

The definition

In 2007, I taught the novel Memories of My Ghost Brother *(Fenkl 1996) at a community college in Oceanside, California. I had the fortune of becoming acquainted with the title's author Heinz Insu Fenkl through a series of email communications that led to an open dialogue between Fenkl, my students, and myself. This experience also marked the origin of intersections between my poetry and my multiracial identity, which would only surface again in transformative ways through virtual environments and scholarship a decade later. As Fenkl observed, 'What the Interstitial does, actually, is transform the reader's consciousness ... caus[ing] a reinterpretation of the reader's experience of the past ... though perhaps this begins with a re-examination and reinterpretation of other texts the reader has experienced.*[8]

Interstitial poetry, I propose, is:

> a multimedia poetic art-form and genre that is either transported to, developed for, created within, or born of 'the interstice'; it evolves as an edifying and frangible archive of intimate, cultural, and conceivable knowledge; it is nourished from the transactions of internal and external mediators; yet it is designed to endure within the interstice for preservation and survival.

If we refer to the tree poem and follow the trajectory for poetry (from the tip of the branch, towards the roots), we see that poetry finds itself in a unique, influential, but oftentimes unnoticed, place in academia, while virtual environments have been increasingly, but slowly, integrated into blended classrooms or technology-enhanced learning. Poetry tends to be created in response to the chaos and complications of humankind and nature, whereas virtual environments are compromised universes at the mercy of humankind and nature in a restless onslaught upon their stability, security, and survivability. And, notwithstanding the confrontation with this function and purpose paradox, poetry is still dispersed across multifarious virtual cyberscapes. Ergo, C.T. Funkhouser's (2012: 5) and Heinz Insu Fenkl's (2003) definitions, which guide the trajectory towards (i) representation and (ii) distinction from other interstitial-hyphenated terms and other contemporary hyphenated poetic forms that appear similar in concept but serve very different purposes (I address four of these terms later in this chapter).[4] I attempt to demonstrate the relevance of Funkhouser's and Fenkl's definitions to that of interstitial poetry (and to related terms) through the following comparison table (see Table 10.2).

The terms and corresponding definitions surround the middle column of replicated shared/similar features between all three multi-genre/forms of creative text. Near the top, the phrase 'multimedia artform' is displayed alone—it is the only term that appears verbatim between interstitial poetry (IP) and digital poetry (DP). The remaining truncated items, as reflected in the column headings, are related in connotative or illustrative ways, and are consequently not necessarily compatible either. It is not my intention to elaborate on the resulting shared/similar features derived from this section's investigation. The last row featured in Table 10.1, however, contains the divergent elements that, more significantly, bare the traits distinctive to interstitial poetry, and will therefore (hopefully) prove supportive of the conceptual framework that I will submit for readerly consideration. I do so shortly after I work to contextualize qualities unique to interstitial poetry.

These are the features I extract from the end of my Interstitial Literature (IL) column:

I   the difficult relationship between publishing, **categorizing**, and the consequential (mis)shelving of interstitial works;
II   **negating itself** should its identity become known.

While attributing 'categorization' to interstitial poetry does not necessarily prove germane to its defining characteristics, one feature of interstitial literature suggests an important parallel—namely, Fenkl's imagining of the 'DMZ between nations at war' (2003: 3). Envisage, pace Fenkl, interstitial poetry as the DMZ, with the virtual landscape of a nation at war with other nations, implicating governments, Internet servers, and, at times, even, the users/gamers of the physical/off-world(s). Fenkl furthermore emphasizes the need for interstitial literature to remain within the interstice in order to continue carrying meaning while deterring interference from mainstream publishing. If an interstitial text receives attention, thereby gaining in popularity and readership, it consequently risks 'self-negation,' as it no longer exists between spaces. I would not suggest that interstitial poetry is purposed in such a way that its progenitor would feel a need to actively eschew or defend against curious passersby and fanatical diaspora—that's just not the kind of setting interstitial poetry should find itself in (I'm quite sure). It would not be unwise, however, to remain cognizant of the unknown or unexpected disruptive agents that are drawn to the spaces where interstitial poetry finds itself; for, should the disruption prove excessively aggressive, 'deletion' might be the condition that results for both poetry and environment. A subsequent 'frangible' state would allow for a 'susceptibility to being broken without implying weakness or delicacy' (*Merriam-Webster*). This is the description

Table 10.1 Shared, Similar, and Contrary Features of Interstitial
Poetry, Interstitial Literature, and Digital Poetry

	Interstitial Poetry (IP) *A multimedia poetic art-form and genre that is either transported to,* *developed for, created within, or born of the interstice; it evolves as an edifying* *and frangible archive of intimate, cultural, and conceivable knowledge; it is* *nourished from the transactions of internal and external mediators; yet it is* *designed to endure within the interstice for preservation and survival.*	
Interstitial Literature (IL)	Shared or Similar Features between IL, DP, and IP	Digital Poetry (DP)
Theory towards an interstitial DMZ: Articulating the difficult relationship between publishing, categorizing, and the consequential (mis) shelving of interstitial works (the DMZ between nations at war); Due to the dichotomous view of the publishing and sales worlds; In contrast to the 'and's possibilities of the literary world; The interstitial work nevertheless could self-negate should its identity become known.	**Multimedia artform** poetic *the of the literary world* **distinct literary effects** transported to, developed for, created with, born of the interstice *interstitial work within the DMZ* **mediates through interaction within the WWW** edifying **inspirational connections** *'and's possibilities* frangible **fragmentary** *negating* archives of knowledge **exhibits authorship** *mis-shelved interstitial works* remain in the interstice to ensure preservation and survival **depends on network stability and capacity for agency** *risk of identity becoming known* **its readers** internal and external mediators *publishing and sales worlds*	Multimedia artform that: Mediates through interaction with text located within the World Wide Web (WWW); Depends on network stability and capacity for agency; Instigates the interlocution between sound, image, and language that ultimately establishes distinct literary effects while conceding tentative disconnection between media; Exhibits fragmentary authorship, while affording inspirational connections for its readers.
IL Features Contrary to IP		DP Features Contrary to IP
The difficult relationship between publishing, categorizing, and the consequential (mis)shelving of interstitial works **Negating itself should its identity become known**		**Mediates through interaction with text located within the World Wide Web (WWW)** **Fragmentary authorship affording inspirational connections for its readers**

(Legend: <u>Features belonging to IP</u>; *Features belonging to IL;* **Features belonging to DP**)

I offer for interstitial poetry, in place of self-negation, since it must remain within the interstice in order to ensure its preservation and survival.

These are the features I highlight from the end of my Digital Poetry (DP) column:

I   mediates through interaction with texts located **within the World Wide Web (WWW)**;
II   **fragmentary authorship** affording inspirational connections **for it readers**

Though DP and IP both are in agreement with a poetry that is multimedia art-form, the demarcation of the WWW for DP suggests that in order for a work to be considered digital poetry, the work itself must be produced in (or born in/from) a particular information system, called the World Wide Web (which is part of the system of interconnected computer networks, called the Internet). IP is not limited to this type of designation, as evidenced in Bernstein's (1998) seminal work investigating common structural patterns observed in hypertext (hypertext is not dependent on the WWW, and predates the latter), and Beyoncé's album *Lemonade*; the initial viewing of this video launched on the HBO television network (Rogers, Vernallis, & Perott 2016), the recording of which might not necessarily be contingent upon the Internet (although it certainly is contingent upon the use of electricity).

This type of fragmentary[5] authorship[6] offering 'connections for its readers' to me suggests that the enticing artifact offered by an imperfect creator must still be agreeable to, and actively received, by an intended audience. This contrasts acutely with IP, in that information is an exchange between the input received from various internal and external participants alongside the potential dissemination of educational and informative knowledge that includes an audience of *not only* readers.

In other words, the unique features of Interstitial Poetry integrate:

I   A tendency to be situated within spaces that are prone to internal and external disruptions, subjecting it to dependence on those spaces (to ensure preservation and survival); thus
II   Marking its susceptibility to deletion, but not necessarily originating in a susceptible state (frangible);
III   membership that extends beyond mediations or origins through the World Wide Web (in that IP can be transported to, developed for, created within, or born of the interstice); and
IV   its function (as an archive) to provide a mutual exchange of information input (by internal and external mediators) and information output (in the form of intimate, cultural, and conceivable knowledge).

The irony or paradox also noted here is that internal and external participants of information sharing can also duly function as internal and external disruptors to environmental spaces occupied by IP.

The framework

My first encounter with the digital/poetry combination transpired around a decade prior to my contact with H.I. Fenkl through Oikarinen's Internet Relay Chat (IRC)—the infinite hours I spent cyber-sexing with various encounters of bodiless text culminated in the published poem, 'Neuromancer,' a dedication to my limerence for what (I had convinced myself) was a hot leather Daddy named Joey (who, in retrospect, could have been a hot Mum or even a hot Extra-Terrestrial).

Virtual environments, by nature, are unstable, volatile spaces (Crang, Crang, & May 1999) continuously subjected to bandwidth limitations, platform conformity, connection stability, host company profitability, government restrictions, user interest and interaction, and (sometimes) as a result, irrecoverable fatalities and redundancies (Fairfield 2009). It is perhaps no wonder, then, that numerous, current works have purported VEs to be interstitial spaces, ones that are neither public nor private (Wallace & Schalliol 2015), ones that are relentlessly 'regulated and policed' (Leaver 2003: 119) just like our physical spaces—with various industries and professions dependent on the continued relationship between these two spaces (Wallace & Schalliol 2015). Yet VEs also provide the potential for numerous 'interstitial connections' (Hansen 2002: 361), serving as potential gateways to new identities (Macintosh & Bryson 2008), as well as perspectives and interactions between traditionally disparate or resistant groups (Moloney 2002).

My consideration of an existing framework for VEs included seeking for the conveyance of these qualified properties: (i) a set of criteria (or a framework of attributes), either 'in addition to' or 'rather than' a standard definition; (ii) a concentration clearly on virtual environments in the more general sense of being one system amongst others within the digital network, but a system that includes a distinct and diverse membership; so that (iii) it should be free from language that refers to a specific environment (or its attributes), such as 'avatar' or 'gaming.' I ended up tactfully adopting (and adapting) the definition of 'Virtual Environment' published by *EduTech Wiki* (Virtual Environment 2019), and its representative display of VEs and virtual technology.[7] It runs thus: 'Virtual environments are 'space' that contain people and interactive things, and convey a sense of presence.' This definition proves to be one of the few that is not only clear (although somewhat thin). Tellingly, this thin (so far) definition is directly followed by a multifarious range of representative products and services. Three sets of studies offer frameworks very much within the scope and focus of my own intended framework:

(1) Savin-Baden and Falconer's (2016) enlightening study on instances of learning within the in-between of virtual spaces suggests five criteria of virtual worlds; these seemed restricted, however, in extent and range of attributes, and were also clearly leveled at virtual worlds;

(2) Klastrup (2003) and Klastrup and Tosca's (2004) research affords exquisite detail in the innovative undertaking of defining virtual and transmedial worlds, while also respectively developing a virtual worlds poetics and framework for transmediality in cyberworlds. The authors' rigorous offering of a virtual world's framework, while attractive, does seem customized strictly for the 'cyberworld' of gaming; and

(3) Kosari and Amoori's (2018) unrelentingly detailed investigation into a reconceptualization of the Third Space as the in-between 'virtual-real' space, representing the volatile state of mind of an online gamer, and which gamers should learn to identity in order to psychically manage appropriately. From amidst a plethora of visuals and complex theoretical layering, the authors dedicate the section on virtual space to a list of nine research-informed descriptions of 'virtual space.' While one of the suggested characteristics does seem questionable—i.e. 'virtual space is relatively independent of the real space' (5)—the overall focus and comprehensiveness of these statements were comparable and adaptable, were fit and meet, to the objectives of my latitudinarian study.

The resulting framework (Figure 10.2) is an adaptation of Kosari and Amoori's (2018) expressions of 'virtual space' integrated with my interstitial poetry (IP) definition:

I too borrow from Kosari and Amoori the idea that language is the matrix not only through which (i) we communicate between (mental) spaces, but also through which (ii) we access *metaphor* for mapping between Virtual and Real spaces, thus enriching conceptual networks *and* actual realizations of 'poetic imaginations and the production of artworks' (Kosari & Amoori 2018: 172). In order to enrich the conceptual networks and productions of art in my study, I adapt 'virtual space' from the authors' list in order to exchange it for 'virtual environments.' I also reposition the pairs accordingly, for my framework. The relevant five VE characteristics paired with their respective IP attributes that result are explained here[8] (coding for VE and IP is also noted in the VE/IP column, and carried through to the Case Study, for convenient referencing):

Before illustrating my points with a case study, let me interrupt with a brief deconstruction of my evolving conceptual framework via each of my implemented 'rings.'

The Outer Ring (VE characteristics) (Figure 10.3)

The idea of incorporating a planetary system (as well as the representations of organic life throughout this chapter) serves to represent the various networks and interconnections I attempt to express in my study. It also reflects the 'dimensions of space ... the place and distance between natural things, artificial things and humans' noted throughout Kosari & Amoori (2018: 167–168). Finally, these figures are visual metaphors mapping (also noted earlier in Kosari & Amoori) the literature presented in this study and the ideas I work to convey.

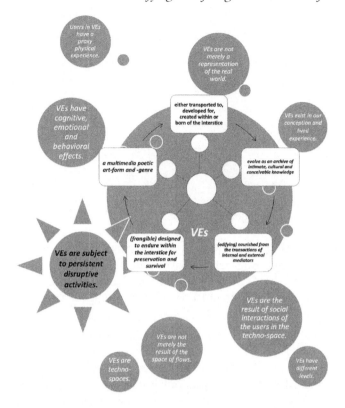

Figure 10.2 Conceptual Framework for the Interstitial Poetry of Virtual Environments.

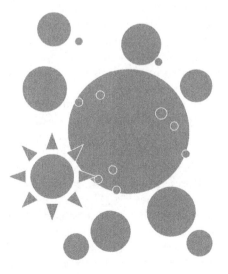

Figure 10.3 Framework: The Outer Ring.

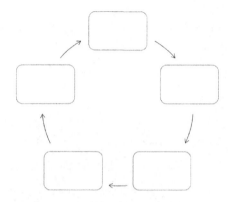

Figure 10.4 Framework: The Middle Ring.

The Middle Ring (IP attributes) (Figure 10.4)
The concept of this ring echoes Savin-Baden & Falconer, who envision 'in-betweenness' (2016: 3), a mediation for learning through the interstices of the virtual and the real, and their re-envisioning of virtual spaces that extend beyond the hybrid.

The Center Ring (VE + IP illustrated) (Figure 10.5)
Klastrup and Tosca (2004) demonstrate their transmedial worlds framework for 'cyberworlds' through *The Lord of the Rings: The Fellowship of the Ring* transmedial universe (the various instantiations of the original text). The authors suggest a correlation between transmediality and adaptation theory (briefly acknowledging Lessing's seminal examination of ekphrastic responses/adaptations between Poetry and Painting in 'Laocoon', 1836), noting their shared attribute of 'content' transference between media, but stressing meaning-making properties of media as a feature unique to adaptation theory. The center ring I propose represents the actual illustrative network used for examining specific examples of IP in their respective VEs.

My overall design attempts to illustrate (through a loose interpretation of planetary relationships) that interstitial poetry (likened to the organisms on earth), scattered across its virtual environments (earth), must orbit around the specific VE Characteristic and IP Attribute with the strongest pull (or closest common features) between them (sun),[9] and align accordingly with the various VE characteristics (system of terrestrial planets) before being able to identify the specific VE (the intimate communities), and confirm the specific IP (new/future lifeforms) to be studied. The conceptual framework I have developed and presented could be applied to other digital environments, and even non-digital ones.[10]

What I find exciting about the concept behind this framework (which is beyond the boundaries of this chapter) is the potential to develop additional frameworks for spaces where interstitial poetry can be found, and in using those frameworks to identify specific examples of interstitial poems—the process of understanding (and recording) all that makes up the frangible and edifying within those poems, can begin! However, applying the attributes

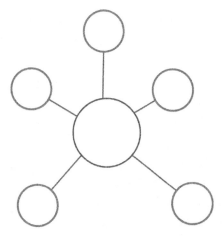

Figure 10.5 Framework: The Centre Ring.

of virtual environments to this interstitial poetry framework remains sound, given that these spaces are possibly where the opportunities for encountering poetry prove most abundant.[11] In the case study that follows, I work to demonstrate how my framework can be applied to a specific interstitial poem.

The case study

In 2012, after having moved back to Hong Kong, I lead my first University-funded project which is a cross-departmental collaboration with several key stakeholders from the original HKPolyU Virtual Campus (VC) (in Second Life) project, through the introduction of an 'extended' virtual campus (HKPolyU Evolution) that embodied an interdisciplinary ethos and pedagogy. Shortly after, my research on hybrid identity in Second Life, and sense of community in World of Warcraft *is published (see Gui 2013).*

I would like to offer, as a means to initially validate my framework, an illustration facilitated through 'Alicia's Poem,' a Quest located in the MMORPG, *World of Warcraft*, in two stages: *World of Warcraft* (*WoW*) as a Virtual Environment, and *WoW* Case Study: 'Alicia's Poem—An Alliance Quest.' See Figure 10.6,[12] in respect to *WoW* as a VE, specifically in its relationship to the VE/IP Framework presented in Figure 10.2.

In light of the five attributes of interstitial poetry (IP) from the VE/IP F (Table 10.2), within the WoW/VE relationship, and mediated through 'Alicia's Poem,'[13] see also Figure 10.7.

In summary, then, how an interstitial poem works within and in tandem with its virtual host environments is illustrated with the 'Alicia's Poem' (the Quest), and Alicia's poem (the poem to be delivered in the Quest). Quests constitute a significant portion of an MMORPG's objectives, and in this case, so I demonstrate, Alicia's poem is not only shaped through a series of transmediations and finally situated in its virtual destination. Alicia's poem also reverberates through multiple interventions by guild members memorializing Caylee Dak in-world, as well as community broadcasting of 'Alicia's

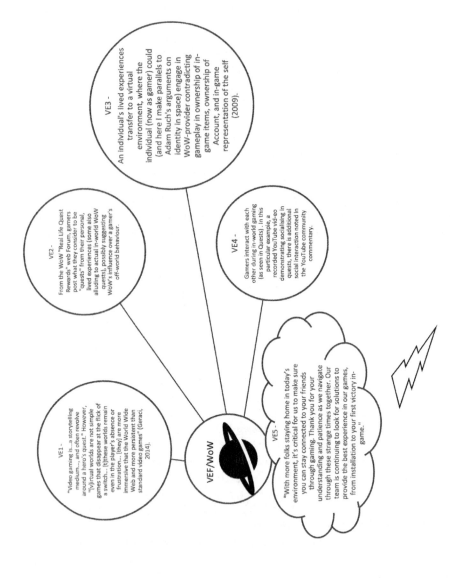

Figure 10.6. WoW as a Virtual Environment (VE).

Table 10.2. Relationships in the Adapted Virtual Environments/
Interstitial Poetry (VE/IP) Framework (F)

	VE/IP	Relationship Explanation
VE1	Similar to real space, virtual environments have cognitive, emotional, and behavioral effects.	The relationship between the virtual and the interstitial, in this case, is the extent to which the former affects its players in the composing of poetry both in-world and off-world; and the former taking credit as the sole proprietor of the virtual form that every poem inhabiting its spaces takes on as a layer of its multi-mediation.
IP1	*A multimedia poetic art-form and genre*	
VE2	Virtual environments are not merely a representation of the real world.	VEs do more than imitate our world; they are guardians, beneficiaries, mediators, and abiogenetors of creative writing and art; and they are collaborators with interstitial poetry and human users in affecting our world in transformative ways.
IP2	*That is either transported to, developed for, created within, or born of the interstice;*	
VE3	Virtual environments exist in our conception and lived experience.	The space of VEs is potentially much more than their digital locations, but this potential exists purely in our imaginations, which are contingent upon our conceptual and lived experiences (which rely on the conceptions leading to those lived experiences ... and so on, ad infinitum), and for some of us, those experiences take place during the solo, diasporic, or unintentional journeys across the virtual landscape, where interstitial poetry (if present) could evolve to also become, as witness and scribe, more than intended.
IP3	*To evolve as an archive of intimate, cultural and conceivable knowledge:*	
VE4	Virtual environments are the result of social interactions of the users in the techno-space.	Interactions in VEs are both diverse and complex, but it is this exchange between various in- and off-world agents and mediators that define the VE. IPs, in this instance, tentatively participate as both agents and mediators, disseminating the information archived as knowledge (further defining the VE or defining us).
IP4	*(Edifying) nourished from the transactions of internal and external mediators;*	

(Continued)

Table 10.2 (Continued) Relationships in the Adapted Virtual Environments/
Interstitial Poetry (VE/IP) Framework (F)

VE/IP		Relationship Explanation
VE5	**Virtual environments are relatively independent of the real space.**	I wish to submit an alternative to this characteristic, as possibly an unobserved perspective, by merging Savin-Baden and Falconer's (2016) first criteria of 'persistence'
IP5	*Yet (frangible) designed to endure within the interstice for preservation and survival.*	(changes that are made in world remain, and the world continues to develop and be active, whilst individuals are logged off the world (4)) and Bakioglu's (2009) discussion of 'disruptive cultural activities' (a disruptive cultural activity interfering with the daily life of [the virtual environment] which ultimately has social, cultural, and economic consequences (5)) to form a 'Persistent disruptive activities.' In full, it states:
		Virtual environments are subject to persistent, disruptive activities.
		It can be argued that no other online environment is subjected to the onslaught of aggressive, sudden, irrecoverable, and oftentimes terminal disruptions from the external world—namely, government policies, processor power and internet stability, host company profitability, and user interest and interaction—as intimately as the virtual environment. As in the case of host-company sustainability—when the mother company of a virtual environment 'goes belly up' (so to speak), such as There.com and Flagship Studios (Fairfield 2009), the virtual space is also, irrevocably and finitely, gone, as well.

Poem,' not to mention external community adaptations of Alicia's poem. The potential for learning and scholarship with interstitial poetry, when there is language and a framework to express it, proves tangible.

In order to conclude this section, I would like to leave the reader with some queries related to the last entry in the case study regarding the notion of interstitial poetry (and, not any less significantly, interstitial virtual environments) being *subject to persistent disruption/frangible*: What kind of impact would 'Alicia's Poem' have had if it had been rejected as a *WoW* Memorial Quest? Where else could the adapted poem have been published? Did the abrupt relocation of the Quest in 2014 to a different server affect the impact or influence of the poem in any way? The possible responses or scenarios to these questions could substantiate the edifying yet frangible state of poems in virtual environments (as in the case of Alicia's poem), and prove instructive insofar as setting up the task for players, participants, and learners to consider ways of avoiding or mitigating such tentative situations.[14]

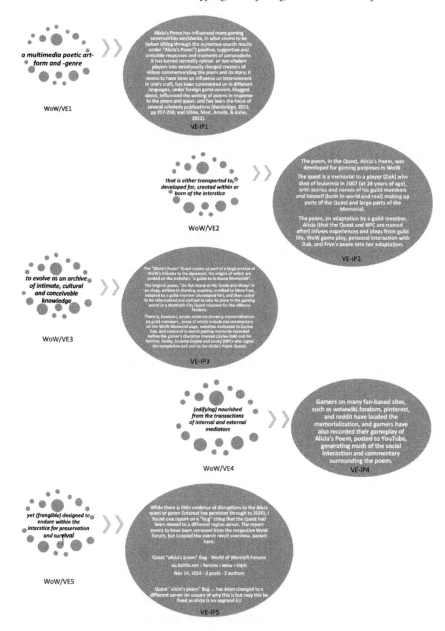

Figure 10.7 **WoW** Case Study Mediated through 'Alicia's Poem—An Alliance Quest,' with Attention to the Five Attributes of Interstitial Poetry (IP) from the VE/IP F, within the WoW/VE Relationship.

The story

In a (fairly) recent email communication with a colleague I had become newly acquainted with, I inquired into a matter relating to the definition of interstitial poetry. The brief reply became an illuminating and intoxicating vision for this chapter.

Throughout this chapter—its narrative strands, visual metaphors, and methodological interweaving—I have referred to a catalogue of contemporary practices and forms in poetry. But allow me to accentuate three in particular: (i) ekphrastic inquiry poetry (from the opening of this chapter), (ii) hybrid adaptations of poems (in Note 10, and as passing commentary on hybridity in the Framework and Case Study sections), and (iii) transmediated poetry (in the analysis of Alicia's poem). Accordingly, in Table 10.3 I present an intentional transitionary-commentary to acknowledge these three 'cousins' to interstitial poetry, highlighting where similarities emerge in their heritage, and where these kinships deviate:

Finally: interstitial poetry is not a resulting external 'Other' product (whether physical or ethereal) born 'from' opposing or conflicting cultures or spaces; it does not (subsequently) subscribe to the hybrid either/or, neither/nor thinking of the binary world (as noted in Fenkl 2003); it does not depend on the text-form of the poem as the referent for mediation (consider spoken-word performances in Second Life, for example); and it cannot exist outside of the interstice (while also being subjected to the lifespan of the interstice).

A parting poem

One day after the email exchange with my colleague on the issue of interstitial poetry, I deliver my inaugural Research Post-graduate Student Session on 'The transformation of leftover research into consumable poetry' via Zoom. Later that same evening, I start to outline a paper on edifying and frangible creative art forms which ultimately closes with:

By way of a conglomeration of literature, visual representations, and narrative snippets, I have guided my reader through the trajectories and processes that intersect through and meander around my defining of interstitial poetry. I have generated a framework for identifying interstitial poetry in virtual environments; I have applied the framework to a Quest poem situated in the MMORPG, *World of Warcraft*. I have too paused after distinguishing interstitial poetry from similar mixed genres and poetry formations. My presentation of a working definition of 'interstitial poetry,' complemented by my virtual environments framework, has, I trust, functioned as a sensible foundation on which scholars and academics in the fields of creative arts, language, literature, literary criticism, cultural studies, and interdisciplinary studies might increasingly integrate into research, pedagogy, and the scholarship of teaching and learning (SoTL). There are opportunities to learn; and there is a pressing need for further research centered on (sans intrusion) the individual, the diaspora, and the 'diasporic imaginary' (Axel 2002). We need a circumspect record of both the digital world and the natural one, a record that conscientiously

Table 10.3 Similarities and Deviations between Ekphrastic (Ek), Transmedial (Tm), Hybrid (Hy), and Interstitial Poetry (IP)

	Ekphrastic	Transmedial	Hybrid	Interstitial
Purpose	– Approach to writing that transforms a work of art into a story – Expresses the poet's mind (Heffernan, 2015: 35)	– Literary texts written, read, circulated and reworked across variety of media – The 'digital' medium to delivery and present texts (Schaefer 2015)	– Gateway to understanding the unfamiliar – Language deconstructing borders – Language of collectives across cultural boundaries (Yazdiha 2010)	– Archive – Receive user input – Offer (transformative) knowledge
Genre, Form, Both?	Mostly genre ('form' contingent upon purpose for ekphrastic engagement)	Both – Intertextual interface is a transfer protocol between mediums and processes (Schaefer 2015)	Both – New form that speaks and embodies (Yazdiha 2010)	Both – Remediation (one possible practice) – Visual, audio, spatial (forms)
Theories & Concepts	Fitzpatrick & Reilly (2019) – Review of works by creative researchers – 'Making as method' research practice in Indigenous ideas of crafting	Spinosa (2018) – Four criteria of zombie authorship – Develop new language to discuss contemporary literature and technology engagement – Authorial intention/implication with machine interaction (political and poetic) – Intervention of digital or machine not required to achieve goals	Bhabha (2013) 'hybridity' – Postcolonial & Cultural discourse – Two related entities – Fusing into one unique, separate identity	Fenkl (2003) – Interstitial literature Funkhouser (2012: 5) – Digital poetry

(*Continued*)

Table 10.3 (Continued) Similarities and Deviations between Ekphrastic (Ek), Transmedial (Tm), Hybrid (Hy), and Interstitial Poetry (IP)

	Ekphrastic	Transmedial	Hybrid	Interstitial
Illustrations	Reason (2012) – Creative writing (poetry and prose) – Audience as spectator-author – Responses to dance performance	Schaefer (2015: 170) – Observed in delivery and presentation of e. e. cummings's poem 'l[a]' – Alison Clifford's online artwork, 'The Sweet Old Etcetera' – *YouTube* videos	Kelen (2009) – *Hybrid talk in mongrel town* – Exploring Macao identity – Multicultural and cross-cultural poetry Poetry/Poet that is a hybridization – English muse – Resident and other decolonizing territories of British Empire (Yazdiha 2010)	'Alicia's Poem' – Quest in *WoW* – Shaped through – Transmediations – Interventions – Broadcasting
Sound Features	Also becomes creative source material – On audience research – For reader/researcher (Reason 2012)	Reworking across variety of media – Exemplifies phases – Adaptation – Intermedial transposition – Remediation (Schaefer 2015)		Similarities to Ek, Tm, & Hy – Concepts and praxes that are multifarious & diverse – Audience/participant – Media/mediums – Agents/actors/interlocutors
Disparate Features	Poetry as form of research dissemination (Reason 2012)	Interextual interaction between media and processes – They do not blend – Content transferred from one to the other (Schaefer 2015)	American politics and ideology – Dividing creative writing communities (Perloff 2004)	Differences with Ek, Tm, & Hy – IP is not bound to specific audiences or uses – IP also does not blend, but content becomes an extension of infrastructure, appearance, poetics – IP cannot be claimed by nations or used to divide/polarize communities – IP, still, is bound to its interstitial space – IP can arise/appear as Ek, Tm, or Hy, but IP form is a tentative, terminal state of a poem

Figure 10.8 Your Golden QRs (A Parting Poem).

integrates in-between spaces and the transformations occurring in these spaces—this, rigorously, before these environments disappear.

The potential to study the interstitial poetry of virtual worlds, MMORPGs, life simulation/sandbox games, virtual reality, augmented reality, and mixed reality, all through desktops, consoles, and mobile platforms, is certainly profuse. Albeit I also realize that affording myself of an original, interstitial poem with qualities of the virtual, for my readers' benefit, is improbable (considering the hardcopy print medium portal said readers need to use to access this chapter). Nevertheless, as I commenced, so shall I conclude. I thereby leave the reader with a parting poem (see Figure 10.8[15]), one that gives voice to some of the mixed medium poets, interstitial and virtual works, and relevant resources that the reader may find constructive and/or informative.

Interspersed between these nodes are segments of my somewhat loose interpretation of Fenkl's description of the interstitial as noted in my introduction. A continuation of said overview and methods are tucked into the final notation.[16] For the reader who prefers to abstain, I would ask you to consider the following: in what ways does this poem embody the interstitial? In what ways might the disruptions (or interruptions) affect a reader's perception of or interaction with the medium? What forms of technology have been integrated into this situation? Finally, how could this poem be adapted across and within disciplines for teaching and learning purposes?

Notes

1 This information is situated along the 'trunk' of my rendition of a tree in Figure 10.1.
2 The trajectories, specifically, outline the impact of (i) poetry and (ii) virtual environments (VEs) on tertiary education; (iii) the development of specific theoretical work within the research community; and (iv) my personal development as teacher, researcher, and poet. The citations appearing at the bottom of Figure 10.1 are meant to represent leaves that have fallen from the branches (of literature) and fruit (of the trajectories), and surround the roots of the tree (the pure black form which depicts this chapter).

3 Para 1, V. "Illuminating the Interstitial," http://interstitial.dreamhosters.com/ archive/why/the_interstitial_dmz_5.html
4 Other definitions examined include interstitial fiction (Jones 2008), interstitial writing (Bartoloni 2003), interstitial art (Sherman 2003), electronic literature (Hayles 2007), interstitial journalism, interstitial architecture, interstice (Nethersole 2001), and liminal (Leaver 2003).
5 Fragmentary, here, conveys remote from ever finding full transformation/ reformation.
6 Authorship in light of writing/creating.
7 Including (in the language mostly of specialists): shared spaces; the taxonomy of virtual environments; text-based virtual reality, such as MOOs and MUDs; some Multi-user chat (MUC) systems, e.g. those that add graphics and/or objects; Multi-user games with persistent storage features (mostly MMORPGs); Multi-user 2D interactive environments; Multi-user 3D interactive environments with persistent storage capabilities; a multi-user variant of desktop virtual reality; Immersive 3D environments, i.e. true immersive virtual reality environments; any other form of virtual habitats; Collaborative virtual environments (CVEs)—this includes habitats like MUDs and MMORPGs, as well as some CSCW systems; Virtual reality (immersive); Immersive virtual environments, i.e. a term that englobes various types of virtual and augmented realities; and Mixed reality, i.e. the combination of augmented reality with virtual reality or desktop virtual reality.
8 Here follow full descriptions of the *five* most germane characteristics. See Kosari and Amoori (2018: 178–179) for a description of all nine characteristics.

(i). *Virtual space is not merely a representation of the real world.* In some cases— such as cinema and television–one sees representations of the real world. This is also true about computer games, virtual reality (VR), and to some extent augmented reality (AR). However, representing the real world is not the only concern of virtual space. To say so reduces VR to the merely representational.
(ii). *Virtual space exists in our conception and lived experience.* The real space of an entity is not only mental. Space in the social sense exists only in our conception and lived experience. Therefore, space is more than place; it depends on our conceptions about, and lived experiences in, it.
(iii). *Virtual space is relatively independent of the real space.* The operations of the virtual space depend to a great extent on electricity. Without voltage, it disappears. But this disappearance is not real. Virtual space is more than an extension of the real space. Maurice Maeterlinck once asked where the flame goes when a candle is put out. Here we might wonder what happens to the virtual space when there is a blackout. Based on the previous statement, one could say that as long as the virtual space exists in our conception and lived experience it exists, thus constraining any talk about its destruction/disappearance.
(iv). *Similar to real space, virtual space has cognitive, emotional, and behavioral effects.* Sometimes these effects are in relation with the real space, and sometimes they are the result of the manufactured virtual space. These effects are there even when electricity dies and the virtual space appears absent.
(v). *The virtual space is the result of social interactions of the users in the techno-space.* Space is a social entity and comes into existence as a result of social interaction; it is connected to our conceptions and lived experiences. Interactions in virtual space are multifold (person–person; person–avatar; person–computer/ machine) and complicated.

9 Ideally, one identical commonality should be shared between VE and IP and serve as an anchor for subsequent investigative work.

10 I evoke, again, Bernstein's (1998) seminal investigation of common structural patterns observed in hypertext as a way of identifying these complex forms and offering a 'vocabulary' (21) for analyzing, describing, and designing them (as a potential Hypertext Framework). Let me also educe Rogers, Vernallis, & Perott's (2016) review of Beyoncé's album *Lemonade*, acknowledging the 'poetic interstitial' (2) interludes that make up the spaces of poetry, visual tableaux, and sound collage linking video clips in this evolution of contemporary music videos (towards a possible Social Media Framework).

11 Subsequently, the virtual environment is my haunting ground for research, and it is also where I tend to take my students to orientate them, during 'computer lab week.' The visitations, to Second Life specifically, are purposeful in that these are opportunities for students of mine whose assessment prompts are attached to developing digital documentaries—to 'to what extent do you agree' prompts in reference to ways for learning English, or audiovisual hybrid adaptations of poems, as means to find inspiration or even to learn innovative techniques for recording and developing (i.e. with Machinima technology).

12 Here's my list of indexed sources: VE1, https://us.forums.blizzard.com/en/wow/t/real-life-quest-rewards/304329; VE4, https://youtu.be/pef4LqB-dRCE; and VE5, from Blizzard Entertainment (creators of *WoW*) Support, in a Breaking News report on "Ongoing Slow Download Speeds" (date unknown) in relation to the COVID-19 pandemic, https://us.battle.net/support/en/article/breaking/23377993.

13 In response to a player's video development (based on the poem): 'Damn, dude. This is a step beyond your earlier works. I'm proud to see how far you've come as a creator and animation [*sic*]', https://youtu.be/Jj4-5dGCPtw. And from the *WoW* Memorial: 'Caylee Dak is in tribute to Dak James Krause. Dak was born in 1979 in California and died of leukemia on August 22, 2007, a year after he was diagnosed. He was a member of the guild Boulderfist Heroes on the Boulderfist server, and is remembered by his guildmates for his helpfulness, friendliness, and positive attitude despite his situation.' A few months before he was diagnosed with cancer, Dak introduced himself on the Boulderfist Heroes forum: https://www.wowhead.com/a-guide-to-in-game-memorials#caylee-dak-dak-krause. And, also, from the intro to *A Guide to In-Game Memorials*: 'Somewhere along your various journeys, you may have done a quest for a Tauren begging you to help him find his dog. Or perhaps you found a charming wishing well in the Jade Forest. Maybe some flowers by a tombstone in Hillsbrad Foothills caught your eye. If any of these sound familiar, then you've seen one of Blizzard's tributes to real people who have passed away. This guide will go over where these memorials are and to whom they pay tribute: https://www.wowhead.com/a-guide-to-in-game-memorials#outland-memorials.' Here's an assemblage of links and memories devoted to Dak: http://www.boulderfistheroes.com/forums/viewtopic.php?p=14683, as well as examples from *YouTube*: https://youtu.be/RvFnAguLU9I;   https://eu.forums.blizzard.com/en/wow/

14 Figures 10.5, and 10.6: Microsoft 365 Word for Mac, SmartArt & Icons (Used with permission from Microsoft); Figures 10.2, 10.3, 10.4, and 10.7: Microsoft 365 Word for Mac, SmartArt (Used with permission from Microsoft).

15 QR Code is a registered trademark of DENSO WAVE INCORPORATED (permission to use not required): https://www.qrcode.com/en/faq.html#patentH2Title
16 The reader will need mobile technology supporting a QR reader app; each QR code is linked either to an example of poetry (exemplifying the words and phrases interspersed across the spaces between the QR codes) or to an illustration of a virtual environment. The variation in QR code size should have some effect on the reader's interaction with the mobile QR code reader and positioning over the codes in order to access their electronic destinations.

References

Awan, A. G., & Khalida, Y. (2015). New trends in modern poetry. *Journal of Literature, Languages and Linguistics*, 13, 63–72.

Axel, B.K. (2002). The diasporic imaginary. *Public Culture*, 14(2), 411–428. https://www.muse.jhu.edu/article/26278

Bainbridge, W. S. (2013). *eGods: Faith versus Fantasy in Computer Gaming*. Oxford UP.

Bakioglu, B. S. (2009). Spectacular interventions of second life: Goon culture, griefing, and disruption in virtual spaces. *Journal for Virtual Worlds Research*, 1(3).

Bartoloni, P. (2003). *Interstitial Writing: Calvino, Caproni, Sereni and Svevo*. Troubador Publishing Ltd.

Bernstein, M. (1998, May). *Patterns of hypertext*. In *Proceedings of the Ninth ACM Conference on Hypertext and Hypermedia: Links, Objects, Time and Space—Structure in Hypermedia Systems: Links, Objects, Time and Space—Structure in Hypermedia Systems* (pp. 21–29). Pittsburgh, PA: ACM.

Bhabha, H. (2013). In between cultures. *New Perspectives Quarterly*, 30(4), 107–109.

Crang, M., Crang, P., & May, J. (Eds.). (1999). *Virtual Geographies: Bodies, Space and Relations*. Psychology Press.

Fairfield, J. A. (2009). The end of the (virtual) world. *West Virginia Law Review*, 112, 53.

Fenkl, H. I. (1996). *Memories of My Ghost Brother*. EP Dutton.

Fenkl, H. I. (2003). Towards a Theory of the Interstitial [Version 1.0]: The Interstitial DMZ. *Interstitial Arts: Artists Without Borders*. http://interstitial.dreamhosters.com/archive/why/the_interstitial_dmz_1.html

Fitzpatrick, E., & Reilly, R. C. (2019). Editorial for special issue: Making as method: Reimagining traditional and Indigenous notions of "craft" in research practice. *Art/Research International: A Transdisciplinary Journal*, 4(1), i–xvi.

Funkhouser, C. T. (2012). *New Directions in Digital Poetry* (Vol. 1). A&C Black.

Gibbs, M., Mori, J., Arnold, M., & Kohn, T. (2012). Tombstones, uncanny monuments and epic quests: Memorials in *World of Warcraft*. *Game Studies*, 12(1).

Gui, Dean A. F. (2013). Virtual hybridity: Multiracial identity in second life explored. In M. Childs & G. Withnail (Eds.), *Experiential Learning in Virtual Worlds* (pp. 171–192). InterDisciplinary Press.

Hansen, M. B. (2002). Wearable space. *Configurations*, 10(2), 321–370.

Hayles, N. K. (2007). Electronic literature: What is it? *Electronic Literature: New Horizons for the Literary*, 1. https://eliterature.org/pad/elp.html

Heffernan, J. A. (2015). Ekphrasis: Theory. In *Handbook of Intermediality. Literature–Image–Sound–Music*, 35–49.

Jones, T. (2008, 31 August). What is interstitial fiction? *Tim Jones: Books in the Trees* [blog]. http://timjonesbooks.blogspot.com/2008/08/what-is-interstitial-fiction.html

Kelen, C. (2009, November). Hybrid talk in mongrel town—questions of identity in the cross-cultural space of the new Macao poetry. *Transnational Literature*, 2(1). http://fhrc.flinders.edu.au/transnational/home.html

Klastrup, L. (2003). A poetics of virtual worlds. *Fine Arts Forum*, 17(8), 100–109.

Klastrup, L., & Tosca, S. (2004, November). *Transmedial worlds-rethinking cyberworld design*. In *2004 International Conference on Cyberworlds* (pp. 409–416). Tokyo: IEEE.

Kosari, M., & Amoori, A. (2018). Thirdspace: The trialectics of the real, virtual and blended spaces. *Journal of Cyberspace Studies*, 2(2), 163–185.

Leaver, T. (2003). Interstitial spaces and multiple histories in William Gibson's Virtual Light, Idoru and All Tomorrow's Parties. *Limina: A Journal of Historical and Cultural Studies*, 9, 118–130.

Lessing, G. E. (1836). *Laocoon; or the Limits of Poetry and Painting*. J. Ridgway & Sons.

Longenbach, J. (2009). *The Resistance to Poetry*. University of Chicago Press.

Macintosh, L., & Bryson, M. (2008). Youth, MySpace, and the interstitial spaces of becoming and belonging. *Journal of LGBT Youth*, 5(1), 133–142.

Moloney, J. (2002, September). *String CVE Collaborative Virtual Environment software developed from a game engine*. In *Connecting the Real and the Virtual—Design Education [20th Conference Proceedings]* (pp. 522–525). Warsaw, Poland: eCAADe. ISBN 0-9541183-0-8.

Muhammad, G. G., & Gonzalez, L. (2016). Slam poetry: An artistic resistance toward identity, agency, and activism. *Equity & Excellence in Education*, 49(4), 440–453.

Nethersole, R. (2001). The priceless interval: theory in the global interstice. *Diacritics*, 31(3), 30–56.

Paris, A. (2014). From English poetry to American song: Remediating William Blake into the psychedelic musical beat of the '60s. *University of Bucharest Review, Literary and Cultural Studies Series*, 4(1), 88–96.

Perloff, M. (2004). *Differentials: Poetry, Poetics, Pedagogy*. University of Alabama Press.

Prendergast, M. (2006). Found poetry as literature review: Research poems on audience and performance. *Qualitative Inquiry*, 12(2), 369–388.

Reason, M. (2012). Writing the embodied experience: Ekphrastic and creative writing as audience research. *Critical Stages*, 7.

Rogers, H., Vernallis, C., & Perott, L. (2016). Beyoncé's *Lemonade*: She dreams in both worlds. *Film International*.

Savin-Baden, M., & Falconer, L. (2016). Learning at the interstices; locating practical philosophies for understanding physical/virtual inter-spaces. *Interactive Learning Environments*, 24(5), 991–1003.

Schaefer, H. (2015). Poetry in transmedial perspective: Rethinking intermedial literary studies in the digital age. *Acta Universitatis Sapientiae, Film and Media Studies*, 10(1), 169–182.

Sherman, Delia. (2003). An Introduction to Interstitial Arts: Life on the Border. *Interstitial Arts*, www.endicott-studio.com/IA/IA-intro.html [accessed March 5 2020].

Silliman, R., Harryman, C., Hejinian, L., Benson, S., Perelman, B., & Watten, B. (1988). Aesthetic tendency and the politics of poetry: A manifesto. *Social Text*, 19/20, 261–275.

Spinosa, D. (2018). Vulva zombies: Authorship in Erín Moure's pillage laud. *Mosaic*, 51(2), 123–138.

Storck, W. F. (1912). Aspects of death in English art and poetry—I. *The Burlington Magazine for Connoisseurs*, 21(113), 249–256.

Virtual Environment. (2019, July 5). *EduTech Wiki, A Resource Kit for Educational Technology Teaching, Practice and Research.* http://edutechwiki.unige.ch/mediawiki/index.php?title=Virtual_environment&oldid=72470 [accessed June 23 2020 from]

Wallace, D., & Schalliol, D. (2015). Testing the temporal nature of social disorder through abandoned buildings and interstitial spaces. *Social Science Research*, 54, 177–194.

Yazdiha, H. (2010). *Conceptualizing hybridity: Deconstructing boundaries through the hybrid.*

11 Intersectional poetry and techno-cultural mobility

Reconstructing creativity, space, and pedagogy as global practice

Jason E. H. Lee

Poetry in the time of COVID

I'm hosting a live poetry reading online with friends, acquaintances, and other literati across two time zones between Hong Kong and London. Though the former has seen a second wave of coronavirus infections pass by remarkably well (the same cannot be said of the latter, which is still some way off its peak), current social distancing conditions require that we gather not in some convivial bar or café but on the virtual stage. After warming up with the usual small-talk and exchanging mutual condolences over everyone's disrupted schedules, proceedings turn towards the act of sharing, the roster is announced and everyone settles into the flow of the evening. Midway through my reading, however, I'm interrupted by one of the inevitable and prolonged Internet lags, with the audio poetry digitally remixing as the camera images of my face and that of another on-screen poet blur and pixelate into one another. At that precise moment, just as the visuals are suspended between space and time, it is hard to tell how this virtual performance is being registered, how this haphazard entity has been created, or indeed, whose utterance is now being transmitted and heard over the video stream in this wholly unintended act of intermediality.

Sitting in my tiny Mongkok hotel room within earshot of yet another gathering protest against the local government (which is being played out live on local TV), what felt at first like a 'consensual hallucination' between participants, mediated by my dodgy iPhone connection, quickly became a kind of 'eversion,' leading to that impression that the digital world is turning itself out and flowing into the physical world. As Steven Jones (2016) remarks in his timely re-introduction of/to the digital humanities, 'There is no cyberspace out there, because the network is down here, all around us' (4). In terms of the affordances of technology in this current day, remote video sharing places ever greater demands on our cognitive bandwidth—we must now mediate a range of diverse synchronous activities, from still-emerging habits and modalities of online conversation, to toggling between multiple sidebar conversations, to manually assigning discussion and tutorial activities, polls, breakout rooms, and so on (Blum 2020). What also contributes to this outward eversion or mixed-reality that we inhabit is the conflation of previously separated spheres of activity—staring into our own and others' living rooms and bedrooms as our home and work lives become hopelessly decompartmentalized. It is no wonder, then, that for all the potential good these tools engender, they can still lead the digital initiate into a state of anxiety and exhaustion.

In drawing together the controversies and opportunities presented in the chapters of this *Poetry in Pedagogy* volume, I couldn't help but see how they are all connected to these frenetic virtual moments that I, along with millions of other poets, instructors, and creative arts practitioners, are currently experiencing. As the world wakes up to the global impact of COVID-19, people and communities everywhere are turning towards video sharing platforms like Zoom, Google Meet, Microsoft Teams, and Skype to participate in massive, sequestered social interaction, *and* utilizing the arts and poetry in particular as a medium to make sense of the bewildering state of the planet in order to connect to family and loved ones.[1] Unsurprisingly, these physical limitations and social distancing measures necessitate even more cross-collaboration across cyberspace—led as much by individuals thirsty for meaningful human contact as organizations looking to recoup the lost labor of absent employees. These individual and corporate concerns also underpin wider motivations from communities using myriad poetic forms to seek redress in an increasingly volatile and polarized world, as the appearance of sound-bite poems and excerpted lines in support of social and political causes ranging from various international civil rights movements to the ongoing human rights protests in Hong Kong can all attest.

This mobilization of poetic voices across global space gives us an opportunity to interrogate the standard model of university teaching and research, and steer these ensuing discussions in more positive directions, despite the prospect of yet more academic job cuts, abrupt shifts to online modes of instruction, and the fear and loathing that the globalization of distance learning inevitably brings. Already, as this conclusion makes its way into print, we are seeing the consequences of the accelerated international marketization of higher education, as universities begin to see their financial bottom lines crash. As one recent *Financial Times* survey article on the impact of the coronavirus on higher education illustrates, international students had up until now shouldered between a quarter to one-third of all tuition costs in elite institutions across the US, the UK, Australia, and Canada; in the UK alone, tuition fees and education contracts outstrip all other income streams, to the tune of 20 billion pounds (or almost 25 billion USD) for 2018–2019, leaving universities with the problem of absorbing a potential shortfall of 7 billion pounds as students decide to stay at home (Jack & Smyth 2020).

Amid these doom-and-gloom forecasts, institutions are beginning to resort to dual modes of instruction, combining traditional face-to-face classes with online teaching, and, it would be safe to assume, some of these modes of delivery will be offered through Massive Open Online Courses (MOOCs) to help bridge the shortfall of already-available online courses and mitigate the lack of expertise among faculty. However, it's worth pointing out that these online systems have evolved from the original vision of the MOOC set up by George Siemen and Stephen Downes in 2008. Rather than operate on principles of open-ended connectivity and decentralized collaboration, these neoliberal for-profit MOOCs tend towards duplication, albeit at a lower cost and to significantly reduced completion rates and learning outputs. Commenting on the efficacy of these MOOCs, Siemen (2014) himself reflected that 'To date, higher education has largely failed to learn the lessons of participatory culture, distributed and fragmented value systems and networked learning' (n.p.). More recently, and much to the detriment of greater social inclusion and student equity (Lambert 2020), MOOCs have also been criticized for failing to live up to their utopian goal of widening global education participation. Though the deployment of online systems has come a long way since Siemen's lament, with a far greater range and capacity for interactive peer learning across multiple platforms now possible, there remains a sense that e-pedagogy continues to lag behind the technology, and that involving/connecting various stakeholders across the world's digital frontiers remains the next big step for higher education globally.

It is at this curious 'intersection' of precarity and opportunity in technology education that intersectional poetry enters. Given hybrid poetry's (i) positioning across multiple curricula within and beyond the humanities, its (ii) compositional flexibility between material, digital, and analog forms, its (iii) de-centering of writerly/readerly processes, and its (iv) networked rhizomatic formations, this seems an opportune moment for a hybrid poetry to leave its mark on our brave new uncertain world. For instance, Mary Jacob and Stephen Chapman (in this volume) offer video poetry in distance-learning biotechnology modules to foster greater interaction between students across STEM disciplines. We might yet see further possibilities for shifting from transmissive learning styles to more transactional and transformative ones, by using digital narrative-led expositions to both personalize and actualize students' own learning achievements and to frame scientific content in an accessible manner for a wider general public via intermedial word-image combinations.

As my Zoom poetry reading experience implies, recent developments in video-technology insist more and more on a new ontological reality for both viewer and participant. No longer are we gushing out of some preconceived center (as I and many of the collaborators in this volume have shown with their invocations of Gilles Deleuze and Felix Guattari's [1987] rhizome)—now, even our own material center can no longer hold, and neither can the insistence that there exists a fixed point or singular textual origin where the creative process takes root and remains. In particular, programmable media forms seem to herald an event horizon for digital poetics, as free-flowing textual signifiers enter the virtual domain and become stripped of their own original contextual meaning. These multiple pathways for interpreting the intersectional poem necessarily evoke Roland Barthes's (1974) ideas in *S/Z* of the 'plural text,' a text that proves multidirectional, where 'networks are many and interact, without any of them being able to surpass the rest ... we gain access to it by several entrances, none of which can be authoritatively declared to be the main one' (5). This format, which Barthes calls the writerly text, encompasses different avenues for meaning-making on the reader, but also becomes firmly intertwined with how we inhabit our fractured reality, and how we negotiate it through creative praxis.

As the volume's chapters proceed through a variety of diverging swirls, from Asia, to the Atlantic, to the Pacific, to the nominally global, from the material to the virtual world, and from critical practice to open-ended creative play, it is worth reflecting on how we might constructively align these new creative processes, and worth considering what future pedagogical initiatives might arise from them. As I demonstrate in the rest of this conclusion, all contributors to this book have an investment in expanding participatory culture by invoking poetry's ability to negotiate the slippage between different media processes by crisscrossing cultural and aesthetic norms. In so doing, each contributor activates a practice I have come to call techno-cultural mobility. The genesis for this term stems not merely from a convenient amalgam signaling a free-flowing exchange between 'technology' and 'culture,' but from my own pedagogical experiments in teaching Shakespeare in Asia (Lee 2018) and, in particular, my following of Stephen Greenblatt through the deconstructive tendencies of New Historicism.

Techno-cultural mobility and the hybrid poem

Having successfully challenged traditional Shakespeare(an) scholarship throughout his career by insisting on a 'dialectic of cultural persistence and change,' Greenblatt (2010) offers the idea of cultural mobility as a funnel that continually destabilizes any 'rooted sense of cultural legitimacy' (2). Cultural mobility here encompasses a broader coverage than mere cultural transfer or appropriation (itself now a loaded term in our current culture wars) and goes well beyond simple ideas of transmission and reception, as it serves to highlight ongoing and relational cultural processes through variously shifting technologically mediated contact zones. In one sense, Greenblatt saw in this turn to mobility studies an opportunity to foreground the 'restless process through which texts, images, artifacts, and ideas are moved, disguised, translated, transformed, adapted, and reimagined in the ceaseless, resourceful work of culture' (3). Not only has his shared manifesto supported multiple interpretations of Shakespeare's texts, legitimizing the Bard's contemporary afterlives in fields as diverse as performance studies, comics, cinema, digital media, and video games, but also in terms of pedagogy—a cultural mobility paradigm offers new opportunities for teachers to measure the full range of diverse student engagement using creative, immersive, and multimodal assessment frameworks.

Where intersectional poetry is concerned, these transactions are perhaps even more intuitively linked, so I exemplify with examples from Shirley Geoklin Lim's chapter. Looking historically at ways to make the new 'new,' Lim notes how non-Western poetic forms (haiku, ghazal, pantum) have helped to re-energize older Aristotelian typologies of poetry. Moving into the new millennium, she reports how contemporary media platforms habitually give rise to new 'cultural forms' through e-poetry, thereby revitalizing older genres of poetry through code-switching, multilingual stylistics, and multiple registers, *and* rewarding rather than penalizing non-standard English usage. E-poetry examples, which can easily be uploaded to YouTube, can be both visual and kinetic, drawing upon text-image couplings in a networked exchange, but also allowing for important and necessary deviances from traditional poetic forms (as Lim demonstrates in the case of her student's villanelle). The resulting semiotic flow and breaking of boundaries creates both a liberation of/from form and a triumphant mishmash of different media without diminishing the importance of poetic language. Instead, using visuals makes practitioners more aware of their audiences' reception, as they incorporate other material—audio, music, kinetics, mixed collage—into their creative work, which in turn creates new, associative patterns of meaning.

Similarly, by referencing Brian Kim Stefan's examples of generative poetry, Lim helps us to understand the valences of e-poetry and the two-way mediation process between digital media and material artifacts. This reciprocity between the two naturally leads to born-digital poetry, as well as liminal, interactive, and kinetic forms that reflect the growth of what Dean A. F. Gui in this volume terms 'interstitial poetry.' These forms are differentiated from other digital ones by virtue of being 'transported to, developed for, created within or born of the interstice' and which later 'evolve as an edifying and frangible archive of intimate, cultural and conceivable knowledge.' The fragility of interstitial poetry lies in its being, pace Gui, 'situated within spaces that are prone to internal and external disruptions.' The instability of virtual environments notwithstanding, these spaces become sites for cultural contestation as well as transmedial negotiation, neither giving way to one or the other format, and forever locked in exchange between the material world of lived reality and the immaterial worlds (i.e. Second Life, *World of Warcraft*) that they co-inhabit.

If the 'materiality' of e-poetry seems to be overriding traditional print-bound formats, it has also irrevocably changed the way we try to map our own behavioral and cognitive responses to these technological processes. This co-evolved state we are now experiencing recalls N. Katherine Hayles's idea of intermediation in electronic literature, whereby 'Humans engineer computers and computers re-engineer humans in systems bound together by recursive feedback and feedforward loops, with emergent complexities catalyzed by leaps between different media substrates and levels of complexity' (2007: 102). The digital heterarchy between digital and human is 'evoked when the text performs actions that appear to bind together author and program, player and computer, into a complex system characterized by intermediating dynamics' (Hayles 2007: 105). This is further explained by Hayles, who observes that 'When a programmer/writer creates an executable file, the process reengineers the writer's perceptual and cognitive system as she works with the medium's possibilities' (Ibid). Given how interlinked our minds are with digital media in the creation of new work, evaluating the adaptive process through which we write, edit, curate, translate, and interpret requires a certain measure of discipline, a quality which instructors can instill in their students through the setting of preconfigured writing tasks.

As individual chapters by Shirley Geok-lin Lim, James Shea, and myself illustrate, opportunities abound for students and instructors to use purer hybrid poetic forms to engage in constraint-bound writing exercises through digital and non-digital means, using accessible platforms like YouTube and Instagram to disseminate their work. Shea offers a hybrid pedagogy for bilingual students combining traditional and unconventional forms that follow the tenet of 'freedom through discipline'; Shea's defamiliarizing of poetic forms and artifices via the Oulipo tradition, which has had an outsized influence on later computational writings by Stefans and others, helps to automatize textual production (and so can be seen as a kind of techno-text, albeit in material form) for non-native English students of Hong Kong. Similarly, in my own chapter example, I refer back to Marjorie Perloff's 'unoriginal genius,' and the value-added potential of using constraint-bound exercises in wider community-based writing projects via ethnographic and performance-based pedagogies. On the one hand, as objects of wonder and amazement, the car vanity plates and other image-poems I assign originate from the material world, yet become imbricated in digital form by virtue of students' use of smartphone technology. On the other hand, the street and found poems serve as critical interventions, in that they help the student to focalize 'the mundane, everyday object, defamiliarizing them, deconstructing them, and consequently, memorializing them as artifacts.' The mobility encompassing this community-minded, technologically mediated practice has a dual purpose: to (i) concretize the experience of mixed-reality using a variety of different perceptual tools, and to (ii) reassemble fragments of the local culture as they are made available to the poet.

Poetic intersections at the third space

It's worth returning here to Homi K. Bhabha's original designation 'Third Space,' which refers to the interstices between colliding *cultural sites,* liminal spaces where 'the process of *cultural* hybridity *gives rise to something different, something new and unrecognizable, a new area of negotiation of meaning and representation*' (Bhabha 1990: 211). The sense of a mutable third space—or of third space*s*—remains fundamental to the pedagogical framing of many of these volume's chapters. By theorizing an in-between space that sits apposite rather than in pure opposition to different spheres of cultural activity, these third spaces help to deconstruct the binaries of physical and mental space, which the noted geographer and urban theorist Edward Soja (1996) used to develop his own critical spatial practice that radically expands upon our own awareness of socially produced spaces (just like academe). Moving into educational praxis, Kris D. Gutiérrez (2008) looked towards mediating a collective third space via a zone of proximal development—that is, a 'transformative space where the potential for an expanded form of learning and the development of new knowledge is heightened' (152). Besides opening up a number of horizontal learning components (construed here more or less as experiential or service-learning activities), Gutiérrez posits a 'sociocultural literacy' to draw 'attention to contradictions in and between texts lived and studied, institutions (e.g., the classroom, the academy), and sociocultural practices, locally experienced and historically influenced' (149). Using forms like the syncretic *testimonio*, as well as regular personal narratives to compare and contrast, as well as persuasive rhetoric, she bounds poor immigrant youths within their existing repertoires of practice, allowing nondominant groups to retain a stake in these curricular spaces.

In a similar gesture towards sociocultural literacy, Jason S. Polley works to decouple the artificial boundary between creative and critical writing by putting English literary creation on a par with everyday forms of conversation so as to debunk the 'elitist myth about an unadulterated proper or standard form of English.' Framing his assessment practice as 'low-stakes writing'—as nominally opposed to the 'high-stakes' writing measured in the end-of-term essay—Polley deconstructs the institutional prerogatives of 'testing' through traditional metrics that bypass creative or cultural content; he aims to at first engage his student-participants intuitively. Similarly, Pauline Felicia Baird positions her own cultural rhetorics methodology via Walter Mignolo's (2007) decolonial strategy to delink, if not bypass, Western standards of knowledge creation, which have historically dispossessed 'other' people of their stories and geographies. Through epideictic or performance-based oral storytelling forms, Baird announces her own community's 'terms to create change,' recreating a documentary of Caribbean village women's everyday life to ensure their poetic voices are seen and heard transnationally and to permit other non-Western students to engage in meaningful community-sharing practices. In retelling her own as well as others' stories through personal testimony, she recalls how the struggle to order fragments into a storytelling narrative is one of the 'necessary elements in decolonial writing and the pedagogy of inclusion' which 'speaks to the cultural rhetorics notion of stories dwelling alongside, across from, and with(in), other stories.' Reinterpreted through a mobility paradigm, Baird's ethno-poetic study also aligns with the border thinking mentality of many third-space theorists in her continual revisiting and questioning of the ideologies, hierarchical structures, and pedagogical forms that hold sway in the institutional spaces of the academy.

Taking Gutiérrez's sociocultural literacy in a different direction, Stephanie Laine Hamilton presents a different kind of techno-cultural mobility between intersectional poetry, one that allows for a greater focalizing between historical and literary forms—if not *between its spatial networks*, then *through its temporal linkages*. Comparing Late Antique and mid-twentieth-century poetry forms, Hamilton cross-examines some of the more transgressive, comedic elements of Later Imperial literature and culture, drawing parallels between these and the dynamic experiential poems that have become more ubiquitous today. Significantly, she finds that while 'Cento and cut-up disrupted understood literary systems in their respective periods; today re-defined hybrid historical praxes can function to represent dynamic and active voices from both the past and the present, resulting in hybrid, heritage-forward experiential forms.' In outlining the history and practice of the cento form, Hamilton reviews the differences between cento and the William Burroughs & Brion Gysin 'cut-up' method, with the former attempting to fuse a conceptual and stylistic unity out of disparate parts and the latter reveling in the abrupt shifts between them. The orality of the former versus the very text-based cutting procedure of the latter also recreates a culture of parallel authorship, albeit one that operates in a defamatory or iconoclastic fashion. Taking marginalized perspectives and streaming them back towards their respective dominant literary centers—often by using the very language signs and implicit discursive power and control systems against them—Hamilton's examples also recall many contemporary poets' attempts to subvert official narratives through erasure poems, which have themselves gone through a process of combined textual and digital mediation, as manuscripts are printed or transcribed, words manually erased from them, and then digitally re-uploaded as the finished product.

If Hamilton's period study of classical formulas of cut-up writing can teach us something about transposing cultural values of poetics across not only space, but also time, it can also help us to understand how these movements can better reconcile our own human sensibilities to the natural world. As W. Brian Whalley shows through his appreciation of elliptical poems by Ted Hughes, Simon Armitage, and others, Anthropocene poetry complements multimodal forms with its planetary focus and attempts to map out the earth's vast timescales and glacial actions through deep time. Evoking the geomorphological as well as cultural heritage of landscapes via 'place attachment,' Whalley draws on connections between the earth sciences as a cognitive-interpretative process and the humanities' reliance on affective process of human responses and feelings. When combined, these dual modes of 'thinking' as well as 'feeling' can better connect non-expert readers and audiences to the scientific discourse of the Anthropocene, with the intended goal of changing how we interact with the world in order to galvanize ourselves and others around us in response to the risks of catastrophic climate change.

Closing thoughts

All of which leads me back to that big question about the role of the digital humanities, as more than just a tactical term to 'penetrate layers of administrative strata to get funds allocated, initiatives under way, and plans set in motion' (Kirchenbaum 2012: 417). If a post-COVID future for higher education will come to rely ever more on digital learning, then we must be prepared to shake up traditional T&L practices by using poetry as a transmedial device that can connect the overlapping fields of new media, creative writing, the visual arts, ethnography, and literary form(s). As we have come to see, there are some poems that are born digital, some that become digitized, and yet still more that may one day have digitalization thrust upon them. It is important to think about how the poetic medium is wrapped within its technological membrane, and how these emerging intersecting forms can be connected to pedagogies that can better serve their multiple constituents across the disciplinary divide. 'When literature leaps from one medium to another,' Hayles reminds us, 'it does not leave behind the accumulated knowledge embedded in genres, poetic conventions, narrative structures, figurative tropes, and so forth. Rather, this knowledge is carried forward into the new medium, typically by trying to replicate the earlier medium's effects within the new media's specificities' (Hayles 2007: 106). The extent to which these new pedagogical initiatives can replicate our awareness of cross-genre codes remains unanswered for now, but in the case of the intersectional poem, some of the volume's contributors seem to reflect upon Loss Pequeño Glazier's (2002) idea of 'the digital poem as the process of thinking through this new medium, [of] thinking through *making*' (6).

As we continue to map this ongoing shift from virtuality to mixed-reality, the intersectional/multiform (to borrow from Gui's introduction to this volume) continues to animate our own anxieties regarding our own subjectivities, let alone our own creative potentials. What will the future hold for the poetic medium, we might ask ourselves? We are likely to see more kinematic as well as text-image poetic forms proliferate across cyberspace with continual advancements in augmented reality, given that 'institutional and disciplinary changes are part of a larger cultural shift, a rapid cycle of emergence and convergence in technology and culture' (Jones 2016: 8). So too will the print medium continue to lose its already tenuous status as our primary source of textual production, as poetry becomes conceptualized, co-created, and then consumed online. Perhaps the greatest change we may see will come from within ourselves, as we no longer come to draw from the wellspring of our imagination to compose poetry—perhaps it will be in this final stage that we will realize just how far we have lost ourselves in this intersection between the material and the digital world.

Note

1 Various news organizations, like CNN and the BBC, started inviting poets to read and share their creative experiences on COVID-19 as a way of expressing hope and solidarity to their public viewers. See, for instance, video-poems by Tomos Roberts (2020) and Hussain Manawer (BBC Breakfast 2020).

References

Barthes, R. (1974) *S/Z*. (R. Miller, Trans.). New York, NY: Hill and Wang.
BBC Breakfast (2020, June 2). Hussain Manawer's Poem in Tribute to Coronavirus Victims [Video]. *BBC*. Retrieved from https://www.bbc.com/news/av/uk-52883230/hussain-manawer-s-poem-in-tribute-to-coronavirus-victims

Bhabha, H. (1990). The Third Space: Interview with Homi Bhabha. In J. Rutherford (ed). *Identity Community, Culture, Difference* (pp. 207–221). London: Lawrence & Wishart.

Blum, S. D. (2020, April 22). Why We're Exhausted by Zoom. *Inside Higher Ed*. Retrieved from https://www.insidehighered.com/advice/2020/04/22/professor-explores-why-zoom-classes-deplete-her-energy-opinion

Deleuze, G. & Guattari, F. (1987). *A Thousand Plateaus: Capitalism and Schizophrenia*. London, UK: Bloomsbury Academic.

Glazier, L. P. (2002). *Digital Poetics: The Making of E-Poetries*. Tuscaloosa, AL: University of Alabama Press.

Greenblatt, S. (2010). Cultural Mobility: An Introduction. In S. Greenblatt et al. (eds.). *Cultural Mobility: A Manifesto* (pp. 1–23). Cambridge: Cambridge University Press.

Gutiérrez, K. D. (2008). Developing a Sociocritical Literacy in the Third Space. *Reading Research Quarterly* 43: 148–164.

Hayles, N. K. (2007). Intermediation: The Pursuit of a Vision. *New Literary History* 38(1): 99–125.

Jack, A., and Smyth, J. (2020, April 21). Coronavirus: Universities Face a Harsh Lesson. *Financial Times*. Retrieved from https://www.ft.com/content/0ae1c300-7fee-11ea-82f6-150830b3b99a

Jones, S. E. (2016). The Emergence of the Digital Humanities (as the Network is Everting). In M. K. Gold & L. F. Klein (eds.). *Debates in the Digital Humanities 2016* (pp. 3–15). Minneapolis, MN: University of Minnesota Press.

Kirchenbaum, M. G. (2012). Digital Humanities As/Is a Tactical Term. In M. K. Gold (ed.). *Debates in the Digital Humanities* (pp. 415–428). Minneapolis, MN: University of Minnesota Press.

Lambert, S. R. (2020). Do MOOCs Contribute to Student Equity and Social Inclusion? A Systematic Review 2014–18. *Computers & Education* 145 (103693). Retrieved from https://doi.org/10.1016/j.compedu.2019.103693

Lee, J. E. H. (2018, May). *Shakespeare and Techno-Cultural Mobility, or, What My Low-Tech Hand-Held Device Taught Me About Shakespeare*. Paper presented at the 3rd Biennial Asian Shakespeare Association Conference, Manila.

Mignolo, W. D. (2007). Delinking: The Rhetoric of Modernity, the Logic of Coloniality and the Grammar of De-coloniality. *Cultural Studies* 21(2), 449–514.

Roberts, T. [Probably Tomfoolery] (2020, April 29). The Great Realisation [Video]. *YouTube*. Retrieved from https://www.youtube.com/watch?v=Nw5KQMXDiM4

Siemens, G. (2014, Jan 31). The Attack on Our Higher Education System, and Why We Should Welcome It. *Ideas.ted.com*. Retrieved from https://ideas.ted.com/the-attack-on-our-higher-education-system-and-why-we-should-welcome-it/

Soja, E. W. (1996). *Thirdspace*. Malden, MA: Blackwell.

Index

Page numbers in *italic* indicate figures. Page numbers in **bold** indicate tables.

Printed in Great Britain
by Amazon

39142463R00137